Entertaining at Home

Rachel Allen

Entertaining at Home

Collins

First published in 2010 by Collins

HarperCollins Publishers
77–85 Fulham Palace Road
London W6 8JB

www.harpercollins.co.uk

14 13 12 11 10
9 8 7 6 5 4 3 2 1

Text © Rachel Allen, 2010
Photographs © Kate Whitaker, 2010

Rachel Allen asserts her moral right to be
identified as the author of this work.

A catalogue record for this book is available
from the British Library.

ISBN: 978-0-00-788238-0

This edition produced for The Book People Ltd,
Hall Wood Avenue, Haydock WA11 9UL

Design: Smith & Gilmour, London
Colour reproduction by Dot Gradations
Printed and bound in Germany by Mohn Media

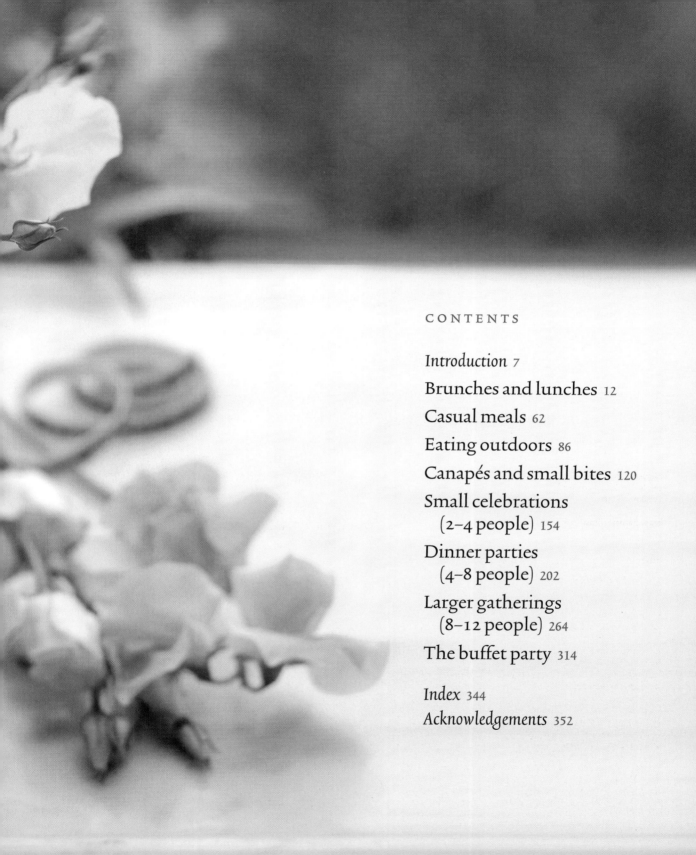

CONTENTS

Introduction

Friends, family, good food, good times – this is what entertaining is all about. It can be as relaxed as flopping down on the sofa with a few friends to share nibbles and drinks, or as formal as getting out your best china and ironing your tablecloth for a three-course meal. How you choose to share your time and your cooking creations with your loved ones is entirely up to you. What each kind of gathering has in common, however, is a happy, welcoming atmosphere, and the main ingredient for that is you.

The kind of entertaining my family tends to do at home is most often spontaneous and casual. Maybe there's a big pot of cassoulet bubbling away gently in the oven and we'll realise there's enough to share, so after a phone call or two we find ourselves with several hungry friends arriving at the door with bottles in hand. But there are also times when we'll have a larger gathering or a particularly special evening when we want to push the boat out and make more of an effort with both the food and the table decorations.

In this book I hope to give you the inspiration and tools you will need to entertain for any gathering, whether relaxed and intimate or a great big bash, while actually getting to enjoy yourself as well. It doesn't matter if you're a seasoned cook or a complete novice in the kitchen; I've tried to give you achievable recipes that take the mystery and complication out of cooking for a special occasion. And you'll find many of the recipes easy enough to cook to make *any* meal a special occasion.

Your guests

Whatever sort of entertaining you are doing, do let your friends know what kind of party it is, whether a casual plate-in-your-hand-type supper, a stand-around evening of cocktails and canapés, or a more chi-chi dressy affair. There's nothing worse than turning up in jeans only to find that everyone else is in a little black number.

Be sure to always ask about food allergies or other dietary requirements. It's often easier to make the same food for everyone, so don't plan your food until you know what your limitations are. Of course, if your plans are to have a barbecue or a big roast, you may need to prepare something special for your vegetarian guests, but for the most part, simple allergies shouldn't be such a problem that everyone has to have a limited menu. There are so many options – it's not as scary as you think.

If you're planning a very special occasion where you're either cooking a more elaborate meal or you have a large crowd, you may wish to send out proper invitations with an RSVP so that you know exactly how many you're cooking for before you do your shopping.

On the day of your party, think about having nibbles such as nuts or canapés ready to tide everyone over until all your guests have arrived – or to keep them fed if things are running late in the kitchen!

Your home

If you are doing more grown up, or 'formal' entertaining, take the time to think about atmosphere and how to create a welcoming setting so your guests feel you've made a little extra effort to make them feel special and relaxed. Little touches such as candles or fairy lights rather than harsh lighting from above can really help set the scene. Besides, who (or indeed what room) doesn't look better in the soft glow of candlelight?

Flowers make any home look more dressed up, but that doesn't necessarily mean investing in bouquets from the florist. Even just some little vases or jars of hand-picked flowers from your garden add a thoughtful touch. And you don't need to limit them to the table – put them in the kitchen, living room, even the bathroom.

Your table

If you're having a larger group of people and are feeling creative (and have the time), you may even wish to make table decorations and/or place settings for each of your guests. It also means you can control who sits next to who! It's great fun to make name tags and people love taking them home. Be as creative as you wish. Below are some of my favourite table-decorating ideas:

✳ Everyone loves place cards! Try old-fashioned packing labels with the guest's name written on and tied around a napkin or the base of a wine glass, or even pierced through onto a satay stick. Or if you're feeling ambitious, make cookies or biscuits for each guest with their name written in icing or chocolate.

✳ If you don't have napkin rings, just tie a pretty piece of ribbon around your napkins, perhaps in different colours for each napkin. To jazz it up further, you can tie on fresh rosemary and/or bread sticks.

✳ For a really special event, place mini wrapped presents on each place, tied up with twine or ribbon and with a name tag.

✳ For a seaside theme try candles in oyster or scallop shells or sand in the bottom of glass candle holders or pretty glass jars with tea lights; pebbles, slate or driftwood pieces with guest's names in chalk; shells on the table.

✳ For a holiday splash, place Christmas baubles in little glasses or shallow tumblers around the table; spray some holly lightly with glitter, place small branches in a flower vase with baubles hanging off (place sand in the bottom to keep the branches in place). You can write guests' names on bay, holly or ivy leaves with gold or silver pen.

✳ At Easter, you can try a similar trick – from small branches hang painted eggs. You can also spray the branches silver or gold. You could even do a mini version with quail's eggs! Place mini pastel-coloured Easter eggs or little chicks around the table.

✳ In autumn, place pumpkins and squashes in groups on the table and/or outside the front door.

✳ For national holidays, place little flags at each setting or down the centre of the table.

✳ For your floral arrangements, try not to have one enormous bouquet in the middle of your table. Instead, make smaller arrangements in lots of small glass holders of different sizes so your guests can see over them. Or try small terracotta pots of herbs or little flowering plants, or put miniature bulbs, such as bluebells or narcissus, in a pot or glass vase for a temporary display. Avoid overly scented flowers, which may overpower your food.

SETTING THE TABLE

Not everyone has an extensive range of cutlery to set a formal place setting, so don't panic about

doing this 'properly'. But I often do get asked, 'Where should the water glass go?' or 'Where should I put a side plate?', so if you want to set a fancy table, here is the general thinking on how your place setting should look:

Dessert fork and spoon   Water   Red wine   White wine

Bread plate   Starter fork   Main course fork   Plate and napkin   Main course knife   Starter knife   Soup spoon

What to serve?

Choosing your menu is the first important step to a good party. More often than not in planning what you serve, seasonality is the key. But menu planning is also about choosing dishes that will both complement each other and be enjoyable to eat together. So avoid a repetition of ingredients from course to course, as well as ensuring you have different colours and textures of food throughout. Ensure, too, that each of the elements when added up are not too heavy.

As before, be sure to get any dietary restrictions from your guests well in advance of your planning. Don't feel you need to plan three big fancy dishes – one show stopper will be enough to create a memorable meal if you are time-starved but still want to impress. Your other courses (should you choose to serve them) can then be less complicated. You also don't need to serve fancy dishes just because you're having guests – simple food beautifully presented in your warm loving home can have just as much of an impact, if not more so.

At the end of each chapter I have grouped together my favourite recipe combinations or advice for preparation to make well-balanced menus in order to help simplify your planning.

PREPARING AHEAD

Do remember that entertaining should be about you having a good time too, so the more prepared you are, the easier and more fun it will be. Much to my husband's complete puzzlement, I find list-making and even an 'order of work' (writing out in what order and when things should be prepared and cooked) a great help.

For stress-free entertaining, choose your menu well in advance rather than on the day or the day before. Shopping ahead is always going to make things easier! Be sure to include some recipes that can be prepared in advance so you can get ahead and not be stuck at the stove while your friends are all having a great time without you. If you are making something quite ambitious for a main course, then make sure your starter or dessert is easier to prepare. I have included lots of recipes for the time-poor, sweet-toothed among you.

It sounds so obvious, but write down exactly what you need, including any suggested cookware sizes, then check it very carefully so you can be certain you have everything you need once you get to the till.

On the day itself, set plenty of time aside to get yourself ready. Even if you're still putting things in the oven when your guests arrive, you want to feel ready to entertain. Easier said than done sometimes, but this is where working out the timings in advance will come in handy.

Also don't forget to place the basics on the table ahead of your guests arriving, like bread and butter or olive oil, salt and pepper, or any sauces you may need. You don't want to have to keep jumping up and running to the kitchen.

One very important point to make is that entertaining does not have to be costly. Clever, seasonal shopping, and even a bit of foraging if you have the time and the resource (even if just for flowers), can lead to a great get-together. Why not invite your friends over for a relaxed casserole, or ask them to each bring a dish? Either tell people what you would like them to bring (a salad, a dessert) or let them bring what they want for a 'pot-luck' party – though this may not be everyone's idea of a balanced meal! You can give them a general idea of what you want them to bring (a starter or a main, for example), so you don't end up with ten desserts and no dinner…

If you want to have a more formal meal on a budget, think about simple but delicious stews, pasta or vegetarian dishes. Entertaining doesn't have to be fancy – but just a little thought, such as laying the table beforehand, can make it feel special. If you're having a special celebration but don't want to splurge on Champagne, try less expensive, but still delicious, Prosecco or Cava. Or make it go further by making Champagne cocktails such as buck's fizz or Bellinis.

You also needn't feel pressure to serve a lavish three-course meal – one lovely main and a dessert is just as special.

Drinks

Not everyone is a wine expert. In fact, most people can feel a little intimidated when it comes to serving the 'right' wine with their meals. The easiest way to get around the stress of what to serve is to go to a good wine merchant and ask them to suggest not only what to serve with your meal, but how much to serve per person – which is, of course, entirely subjective, but the experts will take this into account! If you're planning a large party, wine merchants also often offer discounts on multiple bottles, so don't be afraid to ask what deals they have going for bulk purchases. For bigger parties, they may also supply returnable wine or champagne glasses free of charge. Just ask!

If you choose to serve cocktails, try to limit these to one or two, unless you really enjoy acting as bartender and/or have a big budget.

Be sure to have soft options for those who don't drink alcohol. Even if you just posh-up a big jug of ice water by adding lemon or lime, or mint – or even coriander.

Keeping calm …

Don't be afraid to ask for help! Nobody expects you to be a superhero, so if you need help chopping, recruit a friend or family member. If you're having a big party, enlist a few people to be on standby to pass things around and pick things up as the evening progresses. You don't have to do it all single-handedly.

One handy but easily forgotten tip when preparing is to clean as you go along so that your guests don't arrive to a mess and so you have an easier clean-up afterwards. Chuck out packaging, put things in the dishwasher and wash-up bowls or utensils. It'll also help keep your head clear if your space is as clutter-free as possible.

Try to remember that part of the fun of entertaining is the preparation itself. So crank up the music, pour yourself a glass, and go for it! Remember, everyone will appreciate your hard work and probably only you will notice if something isn't quite as you expected. It doesn't have to be perfect, it's all about the having fun and sharing great times with those you love. Be prepared to have a few mishaps and you'll have a much better time!

I hope this book helps you create many memorable meals. Above all, enjoy!

BRUNCH

Baked eggs with creamy kale
Wild mushrooms on toast with chive hollandaise
Citrus honeyed fruit
Sweetcorn fritters with mango and avocado salsa
Hot buttered oysters on toast
Lazy weekend Bloody Mary
Isaac's frittata

LUNCH

Spinach soup with rosemary oil
Skirt steak with spicy potatoes
Oven-baked courgette tortilla
Stir-fried tofu with noodles
Celeriac soup with roasted hazelnuts
Tuscan beans on toast
Creamy fish pie with mushrooms, cucumber and leeks
Tagliatelle with smoked salmon and avocado
Clams marinara
Crab bisque
Salade Niçoise
Chicken and cabbage salad
Thai noodle broth
Pork rillettes
Game terrine with celeriac remoulade
Penne with asparagus and Parma ham
Venison sausages with celeriac purée
Stocks

DESSERTS

Polenta, orange and almond cake
Almond meringue with apricot purée
Orange meringue roulade
Apple snow with shortbread biscuits
Mango and raspberry Bellinis
Apple and blackberry bread and butter pudding

BRUNCHES AND LUNCHES

Getting together with friends and family doesn't always mean
'dinner'. You can have just as special a meal before the sun goes down.
Birthdays, Mother's Day, or just getting together with the girls are reason
enough to plan a nice meal together. Brunch is one of my favourite meals –
it allows you to put a little extra something into what is essentially a late
breakfast, and it means you can have a sneaky glass of something fizzy
or a Bloody Mary before noon! Here you'll find many ideas for easy
and special daytime meals.

Baked eggs with creamy kale

VEGETARIAN
25g (1oz) butter
900g (2lb) kale with stalks
    removed before weighing
Salt and ground black pepper
350ml (12fl oz) single or
    regular cream
Pinch of freshly grated
    nutmeg
6 eggs
350g (12oz) Glebe Brethan
    or Gruyère cheese, grated

Six 100ml (3½fl oz) ramekins
    or ovenproof dishes

This is delicious for brunch. If you can't get kale, use spinach. I love to use the Irish farmhouse cheese Glebe Brethan for its delicious flavour and melting texture, but you can use Gruyère instead.

1 Preheat the oven to 180°C (350°F), Gas mark 4.

2 Add the butter to a large wide frying pan and place over a medium heat. Add the kale and season with salt and pepper. As soon as the kale wilts and becomes tender, add the cream and nutmeg, then allow to bubble for 3–5 minutes until thickened.

3 Divide the kale between the ramekins or dishes, placing it around the inside of each dish and leaving a small well in the centre.

4 Break one egg into each dish and sprinkle the grated cheese over the top. Bake in the oven for 8–10 minutes or until golden on top and bubbling around the edges. Scatter over a little pepper and serve immediately with a little toast on the side.

Wild mushrooms on toast with chive hollandaise

....

3 generous handful of
    wild mushrooms
50g (2oz) butter, plus
    extra for spreading
6 slices of bread
100ml (3½fl oz) chive
    hollandaise (see below)

For the chive hollandaise
2 egg yolks
100g (4oz) butter, diced
Squeeze of lemon juice
1–2 tbsp chopped chives
Salt and ground black pepper

I like to use chanterelles or oyster mushrooms for this recipe. Chanterelles are one of my favourite mushrooms. They have a huge amount of flavour and their colour is like liquid gold. Here they transform what is essentially just mushrooms on toast into a luxurious breakfast treat.

1 First make the hollandaise sauce following the instructions on page 159, stirring the chopped chives into the cooked sauce just before seasoning,

2 Next carefully clean the mushrooms. The best way to do this is to brush off any soil or debris with a pastry brush. Avoid washing them as this will make them soggy during cooking.

3 Place a large frying pan on a high heat and allow it to get quite hot. Add the butter and when it has melted and starts to foam, tip in the mushrooms. Season with salt and pepper and cook for 3–5 minutes, tossing regularly.

4 Meanwhile, toast the bread and spread with butter.

5 When the mushrooms are cooked, taste for seasoning then arrange on top of the hot buttered toast, drizzle with the chive hollandaise and serve immediately.

Citrus honeyed fruit

....

SERVES 6
VEGETARIAN
Juice of 1–2 limes
1–2 tbsp runny honey
2–3 tsp chopped mint
    (optional)
750g (1lb 10oz) mixed fruit,
    such as melon, bananas,
    raspberries, pineapple

The sweet-sour combination of lime juice and honey is a lovely way to enhance the flavours of some fruit. I like to add chopped mint for a fresh taste. This is ideal for serving at breakfast.

1 In a large bowl, mix together the lime juice, honey and mint (if using). Peel any of the larger fruit (if necessary) and cut into bite-sized pieces. Add all the fruit to the bowl and stir to cover.

2 Leave to macerate for 10–15 minutes before serving.

Sweetcorn fritters with mango and avocado salsa

....

MAKES 15-20 FRITTERS
SERVES 4-6
VEGETARIAN

2 eggs, separated
3 tbsp milk
50g (2oz) plain flour
1 tsp baking powder
½ tsp salt
200g (7oz) tinned or frozen
   and defrosted sweetcorn
   (drained weight)
4–6 tbsp olive oil

For the mango and avocado salsa
1 avocado
1 small or ½ medium–large
   mango
2 spring onions
1 tbsp extra-virgin olive oil
2 tbsp roughly chopped
   coriander
Squeeze of lemon juice
Salt and ground black pepper

These gorgeous light fritters make a delicious brunch when eaten with the avocado and mango salsa, but they can be served on their own as a starter. You'll need a good ripe avocado and mango for the salsa, which shouldn't be made more than half an hour to an hour in advance or the avocado will discolour.

1 First make the salsa. Peel the avocado and mango, remove their stones and cut the flesh into 1cm (½in cubes). Trim and finely slice the spring onions.

2 Put all the salsa ingredients into a large bowl, gently mix together and season to taste with salt and pepper, then set aside.

3 Place the egg yolks in another bowl and mix together with the milk. Sift in the flour, baking powder and salt. Mix together until smooth then stir in the sweetcorn.

4 In a separate bowl, whisk together the egg whites until they form stiff peaks, then carefully fold into the corn mixture.

5 Place a frying pan on a medium heat and add 3 tablespoons of olive oil. (If using a large frying pan, you may need to add more oil – it should completely cover the base of the pan.) When the oil is quite hot, add tablespoon-sized blobs of the mixture, very lightly flattening these with the back of the spoon if they are too lumpy. Cook for 30 seconds–1 minute or until golden and crusty underneath, then, using a fish slice or palette knife, gently turn over and cook for a further minute or so on the other side. They are cooked when they are golden in colour and have a light spring to the touch in the centre.

6 Remove from the pan and drain on kitchen paper. Repeat with the rest of the mixture. (You can do several at once, but be careful not to overload the pan or they will stick together. You will need to add more oil for each new batch.) Serve as soon as possible; kept warm in a baking tray in a low oven where they can sit for about 30 minutes, though they are best eaten straight from the pan!

Hot buttered oysters on toast

SERVES 6
18 oysters (3 per person)
50g (2oz) butter, plus extra
    for spreading
6 slices of bread
1 tbsp lemon juice
Salt (optional) and ground
    black pepper

For a little bit of decadence these make a fabulous starter or a light meal.

1 Open the oysters one by one. Place an oyster on a tea towel, flat side up. Wrap your non-cutting hand in another cloth so you won't get cut if the knife slips. Take an oyster knife, look for a chink in the shell at the narrow, hinged end, then insert the blade and, applying quite a bit of force, press, turn and lever upwards.

2 Put the opened oysters into a sieve set over a bowl and cut away the flesh from the shells. Discard the shells or wash them and use as salt and pepper holders. Tip the juices into a heavy-based frying pan, then, on a high heat, bring the juices to the boil. When they are boiling, whisk in the butter.

3 Add the oysters and, still on a high heat, toss for 1 minute or until the oysters are warmed through and have firmed up slightly and the sauce slightly reduced.

4 Meanwhile, toast the bread and butter it, and place on plates.

5 Just before serving, add the lemon juice and taste – it probably won't need any salt. Place the oysters on the buttered toast, pour over the juices, add a grinding of black pepper and serve.

Lazy weekend Bloody Mary

SERVES 10
50ml (2fl oz) Worcestershire
    sauce
1 tsp Tabasco sauce
1 tsp celery salt (optional)
5 tbsp lemon juice
1 tsp grated horseradish
1 tsp peeled and finely chopped
    shallot
1.8 litres (3 pints) tomato juice
2 tbsp dry sherry
300ml (½ pint) vodka
10 small sticks of celery, to serve

This refreshing tipple is strictly for Sunday mornings. Celery salt isn't essential, but it goes to perfection, so do get hold some if you can.

1 Whiz all the ingredients in a blender, then strain the mixture through a fine sieve. Serve in glasses over ice with a stick of celery.

Isaac's frittata

....

SERVES 4-6
VEGETARIAN
(with non-vegetarian variations)
8 eggs
50ml (2fl oz) milk
Salt and ground black pepper
2 tbsp chopped chives or
    parsley
110g (4oz) Gruyère cheese,
    grated
25g (1oz) butter

25cm (10in) diameter
    ovenproof frying pan

A frittata is a thick and almost endlessly versatile Italian omelette. It can be flavoured with just herbs and cheese or almost a whole fried breakfast!

1 Preheat the grill on a medium setting.

2 Break the eggs into a bowl and whisk together with the milk, seasoning with salt and pepper. Next gently mix in the herbs and grated cheese.

3 Place a large non-stick frying pan on a low–medium heat. Add the butter and when it has melted and starts to foam, add the egg mixture to the warm pan. Using a wooden spoon, scrape the cooked mixture from the bottom, from the outside in, filling its space with liquid egg by gently tilting the pan. Do this 5–6 times, then allow the mixture to cook for a further 2–3 minutes or until the bottom of the frittata is golden – you can tell this by lifting it slightly up at the edge using a palette knife or fish slice.

4 Take the pan off the heat and place under the grill, making sure that you leave a gap of a few centimetres between the frittata and the grill element. Continue cooking for a few minutes until the mixture has fluffed up nicely and is beginning to turn golden brown on top, by which stage the frittata will have cooked through to the centre.

5 Using a palette knife or fish slice, loosen the edges and slide onto a plate. Serve immediately or allow to cool to room temperature.

VARIATIONS
Make the recipe as above, adding the following to the basic egg mixture just before cooking:

Breakfast frittata: 150g (5oz) sliced mushrooms, fried in a little butter and seasoned with salt and pepper, and 10 rashers of streaky bacon, cut into 1cm (½in) pieces and fried until crispy.

Frittata ranchera: 150g (5oz) peeled and chopped onion, sweated in a little sunflower oil or butter, 4 small tomatoes cut into 5mm (¼in) dice, 1 tablespoon of finely chopped and deseeded red chilli (or more to taste) and 2 tablespoons of chopped coriander.

Spinach soup with rosemary oil

....

For the rosemary oil
1 sprig of rosemary,
    broken in half
50ml (2fl oz) olive oil

For the spinach soup
15g (½oz) butter
110g (4oz) peeled and
    chopped onions
150g (5oz) peeled and
    chopped potatoes
Salt and freshly ground
    black pepper
600ml (1 pint) vegetable stock
    (see page 50)
600ml (1 pint) milk
275g (10oz) spinach (any
    large stalks removed before
    weighing), chopped

The aromatic flavour of rosemary, drizzled as an oil over this soup, works to perfection with spinach. Instead of making the rosemary oil, you could add 1 tablespoon of chopped rosemary leaves to the soup just before blending, or a pinch of freshly ground nutmeg.

1 Put the rosemary in a small saucepan with the olive oil and heat gently on a low heat until tepid. Remove the pan from the heat and let the rosemary infuse for 10 minutes. Strain the oil through a sieve into a jug.

2 For the soup, melt the butter in a large saucepan, add the onions and potatoes, season with salt and pepper, cover with a lid and cook on a very low heat for 10 minutes, stirring every now and again.

3 Meanwhile, pour the stock and milk into another saucepan, bring to the boil and add to the vegetables. Bring the mixture back up to the boil, then tip in the spinach and cook, uncovered, over a high heat for 1–2 minutes or until the spinach is just cooked.

4 To preserve the fresh flavour, blend the soup straight away, in a blender or using a hand-held blender. Serve in individual bowls with a drizzle of rosemary oil over the top.

Skirt steak with spicy potatoes

....

SERVES 6

750g (1lb 10oz) potatoes
(unpeeled if small), cut into
1–2cm (½–¾in) dice
Salt and ground black pepper
75ml (3fl oz) olive oil
4 cloves of garlic, peeled and
crushed or finely grated
1–2 red chillies, deseeded and
finely diced
2 tbsp cumin seeds, toasted
and ground (see tip below)
6 generous tbsp chopped
coriander or parsley
6 thin skirt steaks (each
weighing about 110g/4oz)

A lunchtime steak is not for the faint hearted, so this is one to save for the weekend. Skirt steak is wonderfully tender and has a great flavour, though it needs to be cooked very quickly or it can overcook and toughen.

1 Place a saucepan of water on a high heat, add 1 teaspoon of salt and bring to the boil. Add the potatoes and cook for 3–5 minutes or until they have slightly softened, then drain thoroughly before tipping onto kitchen paper to dry completely.

2 Set a large frying pan on a high heat, pour in 50ml (2fl oz) of the olive oil and, when hot, add the potatoes and cook, tossing frequently, for 3 minutes. Add the garlic, chillies and cumin and cook for a further 3–5 minutes or until the potatoes are golden and crispy, then tip in the chopped herbs.

3 While the potatoes are cooking, fry the steaks. Place a separate frying pan (cast iron if possible) on a high heat and allow it to get very hot. Season the steaks on both sides with salt and pepper, add the remaining oil to the pan and cook the steaks for about 1 minute on each side. (If you overcook them, they will toughen.)

4 Remove the steaks from the pan and serve straight away (they can be kept warm in a low oven for 5–10 minutes, if needed) with the sautéed potatoes on the side.

RACHEL'S TIP

To toast and grind nuts or seeds, place the nuts or seeds in a frying pan on a high heat and cook, tossing frequently, for about 1 minute or until the nuts/seeds are browned. They toast very quickly, so take care not to burn them. To grind them into a powder, use a pestle and mortar, a coffee grinder dedicated to the purpose, or place the nuts or seeds in a plastic bag and use a rolling pin to crush them.

Oven-baked courgette tortilla

SERVES 6
VEGETARIAN
150g (5oz) new potatoes
Salt and ground black pepper
300g (11oz) courgettes
2 tbsp olive oil
8 eggs
2 tbsp single or regular cream
2 tbsp chopped mint
150g (5oz) feta cheese,
 roughly crumbled

25cm (10in) diameter
 ovenproof frying pan

In Spain, a 'tortilla' describes a large omelette that usually contains fried potatoes. Add to it practically anything you like, within reason, depending on what is in season. Here there are nuggets of softened feta and moist courgette with the cooling refreshment of mint.

1 Preheat the oven to 200°C (400°F), Gas mark 6.

2 Place the potatoes in a saucepan and cover with water. Add a good pinch of salt and bring to the boil, then cook for 20 minutes or until tender. Drain, then peel and cut into 2cm (¾in) chunks and set aside.

3 Halve the courgettes lengthways and slice into 1cm (½in) pieces. Pour the oil into a large ovenproof frying pan on a medium heat, add the courgettes, season with salt and pepper and cook for 5–7 minutes or until softened, tossing occasionally.

4 Meanwhile, in a large bowl whisk the eggs together with the cream and mint and season with salt and pepper.

5 Add the potatoes and feta to the courgettes in the frying pan and lightly mix together. Pour in the whisked eggs and cook for 5 minutes or until golden underneath, then cook in the oven for 10–15 minutes or until just set in the centre. Serve immediately with a fresh green salad.

Stir-fried tofu with noodles

....

SERVES 3
VEGETARIAN

2 tbsp toasted sesame oil

1 tbsp peeled (see tip below) and finely chopped root ginger

4 cloves of garlic, peeled and finely chopped

½ red chilli, deseeded and finely chopped

4 spring onions, trimmed and finely sliced

400g (14oz) firm tofu, cut into 1.5cm (⅝in) cubes

2 small pak choi, shredded into 1cm (½in) slices

250g (9oz) thin rice noodles or soba noodles

4 tbsp light soy sauce

1 tbsp Chinese rice wine or dry sherry

1 tbsp sesame seeds

2 tbsp chopped coriander

Tofu is a social butterfly, at its happiest when surrounded by lots of flavourful friends, literally soaking up anything you want to pair it with. This is an extremely quick and easy dish to make, as well as being very healthy and nutritious.

1 Set a wok or large, non-stick frying pan on a high heat and pour in the sesame oil. When it is very hot, add the ginger, garlic, chilli and spring onions and stir-fry quickly for 30 seconds or until the garlic begins to turn golden.

2 Add the tofu cubes and stir-fry for a further 4–5 minutes or until they begin to brown around the edges, then add the pak choi and stir-fry for a further 2–3 minutes or until the pak choi is wilted.

3 Meanwhile, cook the rice or soba noodles following the instructions on the packet.

4 Add the soy sauce, rice wine or dry sherry to the tofu mixture, along with half the sesame seeds and half the coriander. Cook for a further 2 minutes. Divide the cooked noodles between individual bowls, spoon over the tofu mixture and sprinkle with the remaining coriander and sesame seeds.

RACHEL'S TIP

To peel root ginger, try using the tip of a teaspoon rather than a peeler; this is not only easier, but you also remove less of the ginger flesh in the process.

Celeriac soup with roasted hazelnuts

SERVES 6
VEGETARIAN
25g (1oz) butter
1 onion, peeled and chopped
1 potato, peeled and chopped
1 celeriac, peeled and chopped
Salt and ground black pepper
About 900ml (1 pint 12fl oz)
   vegetable stock (see page 50)
75ml (3fl oz) single or
   regular cream
Handful of chopped mixed
   herbs

To serve
Handful of roasted, peeled
   (see Rachel's tip below) and
   roughly chopped hazelnuts
2–3 tbsp chopped parsley

Celeriac has a surprisingly subtle celery-like flavour considering its aggressively gnarled appearance. The hazelnuts in this soup provide a gorgeous crunchy contrast to the smooth creamy finish.

1 Melt the butter in a large saucepan on a low–medium heat, add the chopped onion, potato and celeriac and season with salt and pepper. Place a butter wrapper or piece of greaseproof paper on top, cover with a lid, reduce the heat to low and cook for 7–8 minutes, stirring regularly.

2 Pour in the stock, bring to the boil, then reduce the heat and simmer for a further 10 minutes or until the vegetables are completely soft. Add the cream and the chopped herbs and blend the soup in a blender or using a hand-held blender until it is smooth and velvety. Taste for seasoning.

3 To serve, ladle into warmed bowls and sprinkle with the roasted hazelnuts and parsley.

RACHEL'S TIP
To roast and peel hazelnuts, preheat the oven to 200°C (400°F), Gas mark 6. Place the hazelnuts on a baking tray and cook for about 10 minutes or until their skins have darkened, then remove from the oven. To remove the skins, wrap the nuts in a clean tea towel while they are still warm (I find this tends to slightly stain the tea towel, so don't use your favourite!) and rub together. The skins should come off easily.

Tuscan beans on toast

SERVES 6
VEGETARIAN

400g (14oz) dried haricot or
   cannellini beans
1 bay leaf
8 large cloves of garlic, peeled
6 slices of bread
Butter, for spreading
6 tbsp chopped parsley
2 tbsp lemon juice
4 tbsp olive oil, plus extra
   for drizzling
Salt and ground black pepper
Lemon wedges, to serve

This is the best ever beans on toast that you can imagine. But there's no tomato sauce here, just lots of delicious sweet pungent garlic, fresh lemon juice and lashings of chopped parsley. Serve on your favourite kind of toast.

1 Soak the beans overnight in enough cold water to cover by several centimetres. Drain the beans and place in a large saucepan filled with fresh cold water. Add the bay leaf and garlic and bring to the boil. Reduce the heat, cover with a lid and simmer for 1–2 hours or until very soft, skimming off any foam that rises to the surface.

2 Just as the beans have finished cooking, toast the bread, spread with butter and place on individual plates.

3 Meanwhile, drain most of the liquid from the beans, leaving a few tablespoons with the beans in the pan. Take out one-third of the beans and the garlic and mash together to form a rough paste.

4 Discard the bay leaf and stir the paste into the cooked beans, along with the parsley, lemon juice and olive oil. Season with salt and pepper and serve on the slices of hot buttered toast with some extra oil drizzled over and lemon wedges.

RACHEL'S TIP

If you are being spontaneous and want to make this immediately, instead of the dried beans you could use 3 x 400g tins of cooked haricot or cannellini beans. Drain and rinse the beans, then place in the saucepan with the bay leaf and garlic, peeled and crushed, and simmer on a low–medium heat for about 5–10 minutes (or until the beans are soft enough to mash), then proceed as above.

Creamy fish pie with mushrooms, cucumber and leeks

....

8 potatoes (about 1.2kg/2lb 10oz) potatoes, unpeeled
Salt and ground black pepper
50g (2oz) butter
500g (1lb 2oz) button mushrooms, sliced
600g (1lb 5oz) round white fish, such as haddock, pollack, cod or hake, cut into 6 portions
½ cucumber (about 200g/7oz), peeled (optional) and cut into 1cm (½in) cubes
250g (9oz) trimmed and finely sliced leeks
275ml (9½fl oz) single or regular cream
250g (9oz) Gruyère cheese, grated

30 x 20cm (12 x 8in) pie dish or 6 individual dishes about 10cm (4in) in diameter

This fish pie is so easy to make. You don't need to mash the potatoes and pipe them over the top as they are layered into the pie. Leeks and mushrooms are a classic combination, but the fairly unusual inclusion of cucumber gives this pie a lovely set of textures.

1 Preheat the oven to 180°C (350°F), Gas mark 4.

2 Fill a large saucepan with enough water to cover the potatoes, add 1 teaspoon of salt and bring to the boil. Add the potatoes and cook for about 10 minutes or until half cooked (but not soft all the way through). Drain and allow to cool, then peel and cut into slices 5mm (¼in) thick.

3 Meanwhile, set a large frying pan on a high heat and add the butter. When it melts and starts to foam, add the sliced mushrooms, season with salt and pepper and cook, stirring frequently, for 3–4 minutes or until lightly golden.

4 Place half of the potatoes in a layer in the single pie dish or individual dishes, followed by a layer of the sautéed mushrooms then the fish (one portion per dish if using individual dishes). Add the cucumber and leeks, season with salt and pepper, then top with a final layer of potato slices, and season again with salt and pepper.

5 Divide the cream between each dish, or if making a large pie then pour all the cream in the one dish – it should come about halfway up the layered ingredients. Finally, sprinkle each dish (or the single large dish) with the grated cheese.

6 Bake in the oven for 15–20 minutes for individual pies or 20–30 minutes for a single large one, until the top is golden and bubbling, by which point the fish should be cooked all the way through. Serve hot and bubbling.

Tagliatelle with smoked salmon and avocado

....

SERVES 6

600g (1lb 5oz) dried tagliatelle
25g (1oz) butter
50ml (2fl oz) olive oil
2 cloves of garlic, peeled and
   crushed or finely grated
3 tbsp chopped herbs, such
   as chives, tarragon or basil
300g (11oz) smoked salmon,
   cut into 1cm (½in) pieces
Salt and ground black pepper
1 tbsp cream cheese
2 ripe avocados, peeled, stones
   removed and flesh diced
Juice of ½ lemon

Rich and velvety, this simple dish is easy to throw together, yet with the avocado and smoked salmon it retains a degree of luxury. It should be served immediately as the avocado will quickly brown.

1 Cook the tagliatelle following the instructions on the packet.

2 While the pasta is cooking, place a saucepan on a medium heat and add the butter and olive oil. When the butter has melted, add the garlic and cook for 2 minutes, then add the herbs and smoked salmon, season with salt and pepper and cook for a further minute.

3 Remove from the heat and stir in the cream cheese, followed by the diced avocado. Drain the pasta and toss with the smoked salmon mixture, squeeze over the lemon juice, taste for seasoning and serve immediately.

Clams marinara

....

SERVES AT LEAST 6

1.5kg (3lb 5oz) fresh clams
Salt
5 tbsp olive oil
1 onion, peeled and chopped
4 cloves of garlic, peeled and
     finely chopped
2 tbsp plain flour
2 tsp sweet smoked paprika
250ml (9fl oz) dry white wine
3 tbsp chopped parsley
     (optional)
Squeeze of lemon juice
     (optional)

This clam dish is great rustic Spanish food for casual entertaining. Serve it as a tapa or in a big bowl in the centre of the table, letting your guests help themselves. Make sure you have lots of crusty white bread to mop up all the delicious juices. You can make this with paprika (sweet or hot) or you can use chopped parsley instead. I like to use sweet smoked paprika.

1 First wash the clams by placing them in a bowl of cold water with a good pinch of salt and leaving them for 10 minutes, so that they release any remaining sand. Drain in a colander or sieve and sort through them, discarding any shells that are open and which don't close when tapped on a worktop.

2 Pour the olive oil into a large, heavy-based saucepan on a medium heat, add the onion and garlic and cook for 6–7 minutes or until nearly soft and slightly golden.

3 Add the flour and the paprika and stir for 30 seconds, mixing them in with the oil. Pour in the wine, stirring to remove any lumps from the flour, then tip in the clams, cover with a lid and cook for 3–4 minutes over a medium heat or until they have opened (discarding any that don't).

4 Stir in half the parsley (if using) and taste the sauce for seasoning, adding a little lemon juice if necessary. Serve in a big wide bowl with the remaining parsley over the top and some good crusty white bread to mop up all the delicious juices.

Crab bisque

....

SERVES AT LEAST 6
50g (2oz) butter
1 onion (about 200g/7oz),
    peeled and chopped
Salt and ground black pepper
400g (14oz) cooked crab meat
    from 2 medium–large crabs
    (white and brown meat
    if possible)
100ml (3½fl oz) dry white
    wine
2 tsp peeled (see page 27) and
    finely chopped root ginger
600ml (1 pint) Crab or Prawn/
    Shrimp Stock (see opposite)
    or fish stock
200g (7oz) chopped fresh
    or tinned tomatoes
100ml (3½fl oz) single or
    regular cream

A bisque is a gorgeous rich creamy soup made using fish, shellfish or meat. This crab bisque is fab – the sweetness of the crab meat is lightened ever so slightly by the tomatoes and ginger. You can either buy cooked crab meat or to cook your own (see below). Serve the soup as a starter or for lunch with crusty bread.

1 Melt the butter in a large saucepan on a medium heat, then add the onion with some salt and pepper and cook for 6–8 minutes or until the onion is softened but not browned.

2 Add all the remaining ingredients apart from the cream and simmer gently for 15–20 minutes or until the tomatoes are completely soft.

3 Remove the saucepan from the heat and whiz the soup in a blender. Reheat gently if necessary and stir in the cream, season to taste and serve immediately with some crusty bread.

COOKING A CRAB

1 First place the crab in the freezer for a couple of hours so that it is unconscious before boiling. To cook it, place in a large saucepan, cover with water, add 1 tablespoon of salt for every 1.2 litres (2 pints) of water and bring to the boil.

2 Simmer on a medium heat for 20 minutes per 450g (1lb) and then pour off about two-thirds of the water, cover with a lid and continue to cook for a further 6 minutes. To check to see if the crab is cooked, gently shake it quite close to your ear and you shouldn't hear liquid splashing around. Remove the crab and allow to cool.

3 Once the crab has cooled, remove the large claws and crack these (using a heavy weight or nut crackers), then extract every bit of meat using the handle of a teaspoon. Retain the shell if making

dressed crab or stock, otherwise discard all of the shell. Turn the body of the crab upside down and pull out the centre portion.

4 Discard the gills, known as 'dead man's fingers', each about 4cm (1½in) long. Scoop out all the lovely brown meat and add it to the white meat from the claws. The meat can be used immediately or frozen for future use.

N O T E : 450g (1lb) of cooked crab in the shell yields approximately 175–225g (6–8oz) crab meat.

MAKES ABOUT 1.2 LITRES (2 PINTS)

1 litre (1¾ pints) crab, prawn or shrimp shells
1 glass of dry white wine
1 large onion, peeled and roughly chopped
1 stick of celery, trimmed and roughly chopped
1 carrot, peeled and roughly chopped
2 tbsp tomato paste
A few sprigs of parsley
1 small bay leaf
6 whole black peppercorns
1 tsp salt

Crab or prawn/shrimp stock

If you have any shells left over after preparing and eating shellfish such as crabs, prawns or shrimps, then use them to make this shellfish stock. It can be used for the Crab Bisque (opposite) as well as the Ballycotton Prawn Soup (see page 204). Stock can easily be frozen in small portions to be used whenever you need.

1 Place the shells in a saucepan, cover with 1 litre (1¾ pints) of water and bring to the boil.

2 Add the remaining ingredients, bring back up to the boil, then reduce the heat and simmer (but do not boil) for 30 minutes, skimming off any foam that appears on the surface. If you are making crab stock, it is necessary to simmer the shells in a pan covered with a lid for 20 minutes.

3 Pour through a fine sieve or through muslin and use immediately or either keep in the fridge for up to 48 hours or freeze for up to 1 month.

RACHEL'S TIP
If you are using large crab shells, first break them up slightly by placing them in a thick plastic bag and bashing them with a rolling pin or even a hammer.

Salade Niçoise

....

This is, of course, a classic, and when made with freshly seared tuna and delicious seasonal vegetables, lovely free-range eggs and really good olive oil, it is a perfect, fresh daytime dish.

18 small new potatoes, unpeeled

Salt and ground black pepper

18 French beans

3 handfuls of rocket leaves

3 chunky tuna steaks, seared (see page 171)

6 eggs, hard-boiled (see tip below), peeled and cut into quarters

2 tbsp chopped parsley

2 tbsp sliced or torn basil

6 very ripe tomatoes, cut into wedges

24 black olives with the stones in, or pitted if you prefer (see tip below)

2 tbsp capers, drained and rinsed

9 spring onions, trimmed and cut into 1cm (½in) chunks

18 tinned anchovies, drained and rinsed

Handful of chopped mixed herbs

For the dressing

3 tbsp extra-virgin olive oil

1 tbsp red wine vinegar

1 tsp runny honey

2 cloves of garlic, peeled and crushed

1 Place the potatoes in a saucepan and cover with water. Add a good pinch of salt and bring to the boil, then cook for 20 minutes or until tender. Drain the potatoes and cut into 2cm (¾in) chunks and set aside.

2 Meanwhile, bring another saucepan of water to the boil, add a good pinch of salt and cook the French beans for 3–4 minutes or until just cooked but still a little 'squeaky' when bitten, then drain and set aside.

3 Next make the dressing by placing all the ingredients in a clean screw-top jam jar. Season with a little salt and pepper, then place the lid on the jar and shake vigorously. Set aside.

4 Place the rocket leaves in a serving dish, then arrange the cooked potatoes and beans randomly on top, along with the remaining ingredients. Season with salt and pepper, pour over the dressing and sprinkle with the herbs. Toss the salad so all the ingredients are evenly coated in the dressing and serve immediately.

RACHEL'S TIPS

Boiling the eggs for 8–9 minutes will leave the whites completely cooked but the yolks still ever so slightly soft, which is ideal for this dish.

Try to resist buying olives that come ready-pitted in jars as they have much less flavour. To pit them, just give them a bash with the flat side of a chopping-knife blade and remove the stones.

Chicken and cabbage salad

SERVES 6-8

4 large cooked chicken breasts
  or thighs, shredded
1 tsp chopped tarragon
3 tbsp extra-virgin olive oil
1 tbsp balsamic vinegar
200g (7oz) streaky bacon
  rashers
½ green leafy cabbage, such
  as Savoy
2 green eating apples, grated
3 large carrots, peeled and
  grated
2 tbsp mayonnaise
  (see page 317)
Salt and ground black pepper

This is a wonderful, great big salad to serve as a centrepiece for a lunch with friends. Like any good salad, this one has a lovely balance of flavours and textures.

1 In a large bowl, mix together the chicken with the tarragon, 2 tablespoons of olive oil and the vinegar.

2 Cut the bacon rashers into 2cm (¾in) pieces. Quarter the cabbage lenthways, remove the core and finely slice the leaves.

3 Place a frying pan on a medium–high heat and pour in the remaining olive oil. Add the bacon and cook, stirring frequently, for 3–4 minutes or until the bacon is golden and crispy. Remove from the pan and drain on kitchen paper.

4 When the bacon is cooked, add it to the bowl with the chicken, followed by all the remaining ingredients. Season to taste with salt and pepper, then toss together and serve.

Thai noodle broth

SERVES 3-4
75g (3oz) egg or rice noodles
  (optional)
1 x 400ml tin of coconut milk
450ml (16fl oz) chicken stock
  (see page 51)
250g (9fl oz) peeled raw
  tiger prawns

For the paste
1 bunch of coriander
1 lemongrass stalk (outer layer
  removed), roughly chopped
3 cloves of garlic, peeled
2 tbsp light soy sauce
1 tbsp fish sauce (nam pla)
2 tbsp caster sugar
½ red chilli, deseeded

To serve
½ red chilli, deseeded
  and sliced
Juice of 1 lime
A few splashes of fish sauce
  (nam pla)

The Thai tradition of making a specially flavoured paste as a base for soups is a great way of dispersing flavours, but it's also such a convenient method for entertaining, as the paste can be made beforehand and will keep for a week or two. I've used tiger prawns here, but you could use any prawns or chicken.

1 Cook the egg or rice noodles (if using) following the instructions on the packet, then drain and rinse through with cold water. Drain again.

2 For the paste, remove the leaves from the coriander and chop 4 tablespoons of the leaves to serve. Set aside and put the stalks, together with the rest of the paste ingredients and 2 tablespoons of water, in a food processor. Whiz for 1–2 minutes or until smooth.

3 Pour into a large saucepan and cook for 1 minute on a medium heat, then add the coconut milk and stock and gently warm through for 5 minutes. Add the prawns and noodles (if using) and cook for a further 2 minutes.

4 To serve, stir in the chilli, chopped coriander leaves, lime juice and fish sauce, and pour into warmed bowls.

VARIATION
Thai chicken soup: Make the recipe as above, replacing the prawns with thin slices of raw chicken, adding the chicken 2 minutes before the noodles.

Pork rillettes

....

MAKES 1 LITRE
(1¾ PINTS)

500g (1lb 2oz) pork belly

500g (1lb 2oz) pork shoulder

200ml (7fl oz) dry white wine

6 cloves of garlic, peeled and roughly chopped

½ tsp freshly grated nutmeg

½ tsp ground black pepper, plus extra if needed

2 tsp sea salt, plus extra if needed

2 bay leaves

1 tbsp chopped thyme or rosemary leaves

Medium-sized casserole dish or ovenproof saucepan

This has to be one of my very favourite things to eat! It's a sort of rough pâté. Traditionally made just with pork, rillettes is now prepared with other types of meat and even fish, but the original is the best in my opinion. I usually pot it and serve it as a starter or for lunch with delicious breads from the market and some cornichons on the side. It will keep for a few months if left completely covered in the fat in a sealed jar.

1 Preheat the oven to 150°C (300°F), Gas mark 2.

2 Remove the rind and fat from the top of the pork and cut the flesh into 1–2cm (½–¾in) cubes. Also cut the pork shoulder into 1–2cm (½–¾in) cubes. Set the shoulder and flesh aside. Roughly chop the pork belly rind and fat into a few pieces and place in a roasting tin. Cook in the oven for ½–1 hour to render the fat, then pour the liquid into a bowl and discard (or eat!) the cooked rind. Set aside until later.

3 To make the rillettes, place all the remaining ingredients in a casserole dish or ovenproof saucepan with the meat. Place on a medium heat, stirring to mix everything together. Bring to simmering point, then cover with a lid and transfer to the oven. The rillettes need to cook for about 5 hours; all the fat on the meat should be rendered into liquid and the meat should be flaky and not at all chewy. You can break the meat up a little if you wish.

4 Taste for seasoning, then transfer to one or more sterilised preserving jars (see tip below), packing the meat down tightly and pouring over the rendered fat to just cover the meat. Allow to cool to room temperature so the fat has solidified before serving.

RACHEL'S TIP

To sterilise jars and bottles, put them through a dishwasher cycle, boil in a large saucepan filled with water for 5 minutes or place in a preheated oven (150°C/300°F/Gas mark 2) for 10 minutes.

Game terrine with celeriac remoulade

....

SERVES AT LEAST 6
25g (1oz) butter, plus extra
   for greasing
1 large onion, peeled and
   very finely chopped
Salt and ground black pepper
300g (11oz) boneless mixed
   game bird meat, minced or
   pulsed in a food processor
200g (7oz) minced pork (at
   least 20% fat)
50g (2oz) streaky bacon,
   minced or pulsed in a food
   processor
Large pinch of freshly grated
   nutmeg
3 juniper berries, crushed
2 tsp chopped thyme leaves
8–10 rashers of streaky bacon,
   rind removed
25g (1oz) shelled pistachios
2 boneless game breasts
   (about 200g/7oz in total),
   such as pheasant, pigeon,
   partridge or woodcock,
   cut into strips
Bay leaves and juniper berries,
   to decorate

For the celeriac remoulade
½ celeriac
250ml (9fl oz) mayonnaise
   (see page 317)
Juice of ½ lemon
2 tsp wholegrain or
   Dijon mustard

13 x 23cm (5 x 9in) loaf tin
   or casserole dish

I adore this kind of food for casual entertaining: thick slabs of a wonderful rustic winter terrine sitting on slices of crusty white or sourdough bread and some tangy celeriac remoulade on the side. This is great to serve for lunch when having friends staying over for the weekend. If you have a mincer, the texture will be better, however, you can mince meat in a food processor by pulsing a few times to get very small pieces.

1 Melt the butter in a saucepan and add the chopped onion with some salt and pepper, then cover with a lid and cook on a low heat for about 8–10 minutes or until the onion is softened and slightly golden. Set aside to cool.

2 Meanwhile, in a large bowl, mix together the minced meats with the nutmeg, juniper berries and the chopped thyme and season with salt and pepper. Add the cooked onions, then fry a little bit of this mixture in a hot pan and taste for seasoning.

3 Preheat the oven to 180°C (350°F), Gas mark 4, and butter the loaf tin.

4 Place the bacon rashers between two sheets of cling film and roll out with a rolling pin to make the bacon slices thinner and longer. Peel away the cling film from the bacon and line a loaf tin or small casserole by placing the rashers slices side by side along its width, making sure that each piece hangs over each side as it will be folded back over the top of the terrine.

5 Spread one-third of the minced meat mixture over the bacon on the bottom of the tin, then scatter with half the pistachios and arrange half the pieces of game on top to cover the surface. Spread out a second third of the minced meat mixture, followed by another layer of the pistachios and game fillets. Fill with the remaining minced meat mixture, level out with the back of a

(continued overleaf)

spoon, then fold the overlapping bacon back over the top to cover.

6 Cover with foil, place in a bain-marie (a roasting tin filled to a depth of a few centimetres with boiling water) and bake in the oven for about 1½ hours or until cooked through or firm to the touch in the centre. (To check that it's cooked, insert a metal skewer into the centre of the terrine and leave for 10 seconds; the skewer, once removed, will then feel too hot to hold against the inside of your wrist.) Remove the foil after the first 45 minutes.

7 Let the terrine sit in the loaf tin for about 20 minutes before turning out onto a plate and allowing to cool to room temperature. Decorate with some bay leaves and juniper berries.

8 Meanwhile, make the remoulade. Peel and finely slice the celeriac into matchstick-sized pieces or grate using the roughest part of the grater or in a food processor. Then mix with the remaining ingredients in a bowl, seasoning to taste.

9 Cut the terrine into slices and serve with crusty white or sourdough bread and the celeriac remoulade.

RACHEL'S TIP
If you are using your own game meat, use it from the legs, thighs, kidneys, livers and hearts. If you or someone you know has shot a pheasant, pigeon or partridge, you could use up the whole bird in this dish: I tend to use two pheasants or one pheasant and one pigeon, but you could otherwise use a pack of mixed game from the butcher or a supermarket.

Penne with asparagus and Parma ham

SERVES 6

600g (1lb 5oz) dried penne
18 asparagus spears
Table salt, sea salt and ground black pepper
25g (1oz) butter
6 tbsp créme fraîche
8 large slices of Parma or Serrano ham, roughly cut into strips
A few shavings of Parmesan cheese per portion (shaved with a peeler)

Parma ham is one of the world's great foods, with an incredible complexity to its flavour. This is a simple lunch dish that is all about letting great ingredients speak for themselves.

1 Cook the penne following the instructions on the packet, then drain, reserving a few tablespoons of the cooking liquid, and return to the warm pan (off the heat).

2 While the pasta is cooking, snap off the tough woody part at the bottom of each asparagus spear and discard. Fill a large saucepan to a depth of 4–6cm (1½ –2½in) with water, add some table salt and bring to the boil. Tip in the asparagus and cook in the boiling water for 4–8 minutes or until just cooked.

3 Drain the asparagus immediately, then cut each spear at an angle into 3–4 shorter lengths. Place in a bowl, add the butter and season with sea salt and pepper.

4 Add the crème fraîche to the drained pasta in the pan and toss to coat, then tip in the asparagus and Parma ham and season to taste with sea salt and pepper. Serve in warmed bowls with a few shavings of Parmesan on top of each portion.

Venison sausages
with celeriac purée

·····················

These skinless sausages make a substantial, comforting meal – a great winter lunch. Celeriac is quite an ugly-looking vegetable – those gnarled roots look positively ancient. When peeling it, you'll find the skin goes quite deep in places. But beneath that knobbly armour is flesh that, when cooked, has a subtle flavour with just a hint of celery.

SERVES 4–6
MAKES 12 SAUSAGES
25g (1oz) butter
1 onion, peeled and diced
300g (11oz) venison, minced
    or pulsed in a food
    processor
200g (7oz) minced pork
    (at least 20% fat)
50g (2oz) fresh white
    breadcrumbs
1 egg, beaten
2 cloves of garlic, peeled and
    crushed or finely grated
1 tbsp chopped rosemary
    leaves
1 tbsp wholegrain mustard
Salt and ground black pepper
1–2 tbsp olive oil

For the celeriac purée
1 celeriac, peeled and chopped
    into 1–2cm (½–¾in) dice
2 floury potatoes, peeled and
    cut into 1–2cm (½–¾in)
    dice
400ml (14fl oz) milk
2 tbsp single or regular cream
15g (½oz) butter

1 To make the sausages, melt the butter in a large frying pan on a medium–high heat, then add the onion and fry, stirring occasionally, for 8–10 minutes until slightly golden. Set aside.

2 Meanwhile, mix all the other ingredients except the seasoning and oil in a large bowl. Season with salt and pepper, then add the cooled onions to the mixture. If the mixture is very wet, add a few more breadcrumbs.

3 Preheat the oven to 200°C (400°F), Gas mark 6. Place a little bit of the mixture in the frying pan and cook for 1–2 minutes to check for seasoning. Shape the sausage mixture into about 12 sausages. Pour the olive oil into the frying pan and, on a medium heat, brown the sausages on every side. Then place on a baking tray and bake in the oven for 10 minutes or until cooked through.

4 For the purée, place the celeriac and potatoes in a large saucepan, then pour over the milk to just cover, simmer on a medium–low heat for about 15 minutes, then drain and mash very well. Season with salt and pepper, then add the cream and the butter. Unless serving immediately, place in a covered, ovenproof dish and keep warm in the oven after the heat has been switched off.

5 Serve the sausages with a spoonful of celeriac purée and a drizzle of cranberry sauce (see tip below).

RACHEL'S TIP
To make cranberry sauce, put 150g (5oz) cranberries in a saucepan with 50ml (2fl oz) water. Bring to the boil, then reduce the heat and simmer gently for 6–8 minutes until the cranberries have burst and are softened. Stir in 75g (3oz) caster sugar until dissolved.

Stocks

Many of the recipes in this book require stocks and nothing can compare to a homemade broth of boiled bones, vegetables and herbs. Stocks can be made in advance, stored in small containers and kept in the freezer for handy access. The recipes here are just a guideline but try not to add too much of any one vegetable or the flavour may dominate the stock. Livers are unwelcome as they will make the stock bitter, but necks, hearts and wing tips are perfect. Also avoid starchy vegetables, such as potatoes or parsnips, as they will turn the stock cloudy. Don't use salt when making a stock as if you eventually reduce it, the salt will remain and the liquid could be too salty. If you wish to concentrate the flavour, place the stock on a high heat and boil, uncovered, to reduce the liquid. To make your own frozen stock cubes, reduce the liquid to about a quarter of its original volume. Allow to cool and then pour into ice cube trays and freeze. Stocks can be refrigerated for three days or frozen for two months.

Vegetable stock

MAKES ABOUT 2 LITRES (3½ PINTS)
2 onions, peeled and roughly chopped
2 leeks, trimmed and roughly chopped
3 sticks of celery, trimmed and roughly chopped
3 carrots, peeled and roughly chopped
½ fennel bulb, roughly chopped
Bunch of parsley stalks
1 small sprig of rosemary
1 sprig of thyme

1 Place all the ingredients into a large saucepan or casserole dish. Add enough cold water to cover the ingredients by about 10cm (4in) and bring to a simmer.

2 Let the stock continue to simmer for an hour, then strain the liquid and discard the vegetables.

Beef stock

MAKES 3–4 LITRES (5–6¾ PINTS)

2kg (4lb 4oz) beef bones, preferably
   with a little meat still on
2 onions, peeled and cut in half
2 carrots, peeled and cut in half
2 sticks of celery, trimmed and
   roughly chopped
Bunch of parsley stalks
1 tbsp tomato paste
1 sprig of thyme
1 bay leaf

1 Preheat the oven to 230°C (450°F), Gas mark 8. Place the bones on a roasting tray and roast in the oven for about 30 minutes until browned.

2 Transfer them to a large saucepan and deglaze the roasting tray by placing it on a medium heat on the hob. Pour a little cold water into the tray (enough to cover the bottom) and bring to the boil, scraping the bottom with a whisk to dissolve the caramelised juices that are stuck to the tray. Then pour on top of the bones in the saucepan with the rest of the ingredients. Top up with enough cold water to cover everything by a good 10cm (4in) and bring to the boil. Reduce the heat and bring the stock to a simmer.

3 Leave the saucepan to simmer gently for 5–6 hours, skimming the foam off the top from time to time.

4 Strain the stock, discarding the bones and vegetables. Allow to cool so the fat will rise to the top where it is easy to skim off.

Chicken stock

MAKES 1–2 LITRES (1¾–3½ PINTS)

1 chicken carcass, cooked or raw
1–2 carrots, peeled and
   roughly chopped
1 onion or 4 spring onions,
   peeled and cut in half
1 leek or even just the green part,
   trimmed and roughly chopped
1 sticks of celery, trimmed and
   roughly chopped
Bunch of parsley stalks
1 sprig of thyme
1 small bay leaf

1 Place all the ingredients in a large saucepan or casserole dish. Add enough cold water to cover everything by about 8cm (3in) and bring to the boil. Reduce the heat and bring the stock to a gentle simmer and then leave for about 2 hours. For the best flavour, skim the foam off the surface from time to time, though it's not completely necessary.

2 Strain the stock so you are left with just liquid and discard the vegetables and carcasses. Chill, then lift the fat off the top and discard.

Polenta, orange and almond cake

....

SERVES 6-8
VEGETARIAN
375g (13oz) butter, softened,
    plus extra for greasing
200g (7oz) medium or coarse
    polenta, plus 1 tbsp extra
    for dusting
375g (13oz) caster sugar
5 eggs
Finely grated zest of 2 oranges
Juice of 1 orange
300g (11oz) ground almonds
1 tsp baking powder
4 tbsp chopped pistachio
    nuts, to serve

For the syrup
Juice and finely grated zest
    of 1 orange
50g (2oz) caster sugar

23cm (9in) diameter spring-
    form/loose-bottomed tin
    with 5cm (2in) sides

This flourless cake is made with a mixture of ground almonds and polenta, which gives a texture that is dense yet soft. The hot syrup poured over at the end makes it incredibly moist.

1 Preheat the oven to 170°C (325°F), Gas mark 3. Butter the cake tin, place a disc of greaseproof paper in the bottom and dust the tin with 1 tablespoon of polenta.

2 Cream the butter in a large bowl or in an electric food mixer until soft. Add the sugar and beat until the mixture is light and fluffy. Beat in the eggs, one at a time, then add the orange zest and juice. Fold in the remaining ingredients and spoon the mixture into the prepared tin. Place in the oven and cook for 80–90 minutes or until a skewer inserted into the centre of the cake comes out clean.

3 Remove the cake from the oven and allow it to cool in the tin for about 20 minutes before transferring to a serving plate. Using a skewer, make about eight holes, each around 2.5cm (1in) deep, across the surface of the cake.

4 To make the syrup, mix together the orange zest and juice with the caster sugar in a small saucepan. Bring to the boil and keep boiling for 2 minutes, then remove from the heat and immediately drizzle all over the polenta cake. Serve warm or at room temperature with a scattering of pistachio nuts and a dollop of crème fraîche.

RACHEL'S TIP
Depending on the oven, I sometimes quickly open it to place a piece of foil on top of the cake after 45 minutes, to prevent it from getting too brown.

Almond meringue
with apricot purée

....

SERVES 6-8
VEGETARIAN

3 egg whites
175g (6oz) caster sugar
100g (3½oz) nibbed or
   chopped almonds
200ml (7fl oz) double or
   regular cream
Icing sugar, for dusting

For the purée
2 tbsp lemon juice
100g (3½oz) caster sugar
225g (8oz) ready-to-eat
   dried apricots

The apricot purée is also divine served with natural yoghurt as a quick snack or for breakfast. It can be stored in the fridge in an airtight container and will keep for up to a week.

1 Preheat the oven to 150°C (300°F), Gas mark 2. Line two baking sheets with baking parchment.

2 Place the egg whites in a spotlessly clean dry bowl and whisk until the mixture is fairly stiff. Add a quarter of the sugar and continue to whisk until the mixture holds its shape. Gently fold in the remainder of the sugar, followed by the nibbed almonds.

3 Spoon half the meringue mixture onto each of the lined baking sheets and gently spread the meringue on each sheet to form a round 20–22cm (8–9in) in diameter. If you can fit both meringues on one tray, it's easier if you're not cooking in a fan oven.

4 Bake in the oven together for 25–30 minutes or until crisp on the outside and cream coloured. (If cooked, the meringue will lift easily off the paper.) Once the meringue is cooked, if possible leave it inside the oven for 1 hour to allow it to cool down slowly and lessen the risk of it cracking. Alternatively, remove it from the oven but don't put it anywhere too cold as soon as you take it out.

5 To make the purée, fill a large saucepan with 850ml (1½ pints) of water, add the lemon juice and sugar and bring to the boil. Add the apricots, return to the boil then reduce the heat and simmer, uncovered, for about 20 minutes or until the apricots are softened. Remove from the heat and allow to cool, then place in a blender or food processor and whiz to form a purée.

6 Place a meringue round onto a serving plate or cake stand. Whip the cream and spread onto the meringue round, pour over some apricot purée, then gently place the other round on top, saving the best-looking one for this. Dust with icing sugar and cut into slices to serve, with the remaining purée on the side.

Orange meringue roulade

SERVES 8–10
VEGETARIAN

Vegetable or sunflower oil,
  for oiling
4 egg whites
225g (8oz) caster sugar
Icing sugar, for dusting
200ml (7fl oz) orange curd
  (see page 56)
500ml (18fl oz) whipped
  cream

For the orange curd
2 eggs
1 egg yolk
100g (3½oz) butter
175g (6oz) caster sugar
Juice and finely grated
  zest of 3 oranges

20 x 30cm (8 x 12in) Swiss
  roll tin

Here is a light dessert with a lovely citrus zing. The orange curd is delicious and the quantity given here makes twice the amount you will need for the roulade filling. Either just make half the quantity given (using 1 whole egg and 1 yolk) or make the full amount and try it served on pancakes, toast or even ice cream. The curd can be stored in an airtight plastic container in the fridge for up to a week or in a sealed jam jar for two weeks.

1 First make the orange curd. Whisk together the egg and egg yolk. Then melt the butter in a saucepan on a low–medium heat. Add the sugar and orange juice and zest, and pour in the eggs.

2 Stir constantly with a wooden spoon, still over a low heat (if it is too high, the egg will scramble), for 10–15 minutes or until the mixture is fairly thick. If you find the egg does start to scramble, dip the bottom of the pan in very cold water and then sieve the mixture. The curd is ready when the mixture is thick enough to coat the back of the wooden spoon and leave a definite mark when you draw a line in it with your finger. It will thicken further once cool.

3 Remove the curd from the heat, pour into a bowl and allow to cool. If you wish to keep this for two weeks, store the orange curd in sterilised jars (see page 42).

4 To make the roulade, reheat the oven to 180°C (350°F), Gas mark 4. Line the Swiss roll tin with foil, then brush with a little vegetable or sunflower oil.

(continued overleaf)

5 Place the egg whites and sugar in the bowl of an electric mixer and whisk for about 10 minutes until the mixture forms stiff peaks.

6 Spoon the mixture into the tin and spread it out evenly. Place in the oven and cook for 15–20 minutes or until it looks marshmallowy and lightly springy to the touch in the centre.

7 Remove from the oven and turn the meringue out onto a sheet of baking parchment or foil that has been liberally dusted with icing sugar. Peel off the foil from the base and allow to cool.

8 To assemble the roulade, first spread the orange curd evenly to cover the meringue, then spread the whipped cream over the orange curd. Gently roll up the roulade starting at one of the long edges and rolling away from you, to form a log shape. Transfer to a long serving plate, making sure the 'join' is facing down, and dust with icing sugar. Cut into slices to serve.

Apple snow with shortbread biscuits

....

SERVES 6
VEGETARIAN
450g (1lb) cooking apples,
   such as Bramley, peeled,
   cored and cut into chunks
175g (6oz) caster sugar
2 egg whites
Shortbread biscuits
   (see below), to serve

This fantastically light meringue dessert is very quick to prepare, especially if you make the purée in advance and then just fold it into the whisked egg whites at the last minute. Eat on its own or with the shortbread biscuits. Once made, you can store these in a tin – if there are any left over! This recipe contains raw eggs, which should be avoided by pregnant women, the very young and the very old.

1 Place the apple chunks and sugar in a large saucepan with 100ml (3½ fl oz) water, cover with a lid and simmer on a low heat for 10 minutes or until the apples are quite soft. Remove the lid and continue to simmer for another 3–4 minutes or until the apples are quite mushy and all the liquid has evaporated.

2 Remove from the heat, allow to cool a little, then whiz in a blender or food processor for a few minutes to make into a purée. Taste the purée to make sure it is sweet enough, adding a little more sugar if needed. It should be slightly sweeter than you want it to be eventually as its flavour will be diluted by the egg whites. Transfer to a large bowl and allow to cool.

3 When you are ready to serve, whisk the egg whites in a spotlessly clean bowl until they form stiff peaks. Gently fold the egg whites into the apple purée. Serve in glass bowls or glasses with the shortbread biscuits on the side.

Shortbread biscuits

MAKES ABOUT
25 BISCUITS
VEGETARIAN
150g (5oz) plain flour, plus
   extra for dusting
50g (2oz) caster sugar
100g (3½oz) butter, softened
Icing sugar, for dusting
   (optional)

1 Preheat the oven to 180°C (350°F), Gas mark 4.

2 Place the flour and sugar in a large bowl, rub in the butter then bring the mixture together to form a stiff dough, or just whiz all the ingredients together briefly in a food processor until almost combined.

3 Pat out the dough into a round about 2cm (¾in) thick, then cover with greaseproof paper or cling film and chill in the fridge

for about 20 minutes. On a work surface lightly dusted with flour, roll out the dough to about 5mm (¼in) thick and cut into shapes – round, square, rectangular, heart-shaped, whatever takes your fancy. Place carefully on 2 baking sheets (no need to grease or line) and cook in the oven for 6–10 minutes or until pale golden.

4 Take out of the oven and allow to sit on the baking sheets for a few seconds to firm up slightly (don't leave them any longer or they will stick). Transfer to a wire rack to cool, then dust with icing sugar if eating with the Apple Snow.

Mango and raspberry Bellinis

SERVES 6
VEGETARIAN
1 x 750ml bottle of sparkling wine, such as Prosecco or Cava

For the fruit purée
1 mango, peeled, stone removed and flesh chopped
100g (3½oz) fresh or frozen and defrosted raspberries
3 tbsp lemon juice
4 tbsp caster sugar

6 champagne flutes

The classic Bellini cocktail – a divine combination of sparkling wine (normally Prosecco) and fresh peach juice – was invented in the 1940s by Giuseppe Cipriani, founder of the celebrated Harry's Bar in Venice. The cocktail's particular shade of pink supposedly reminded Cipriani of the colour of the toga worn by a saint in a painting by Renaissance artist Giovanni Bellini – hence the name.

1 Place all the ingredients for the fruit purée in a food processor and whiz for 1–2 minutes, then push through a sieve.

2 Mix in a jug or fill glasses with one-third purée and two-thirds sparkling wine, stirring gently to combine. Serve chilled.

VARIATIONS
Mango Bellinis: Purée the flesh of 1 large mango with 3 tablespoons of lime juice and 3 tablespoons of caster sugar, then mix with the sparkling wine, as above.

Raspberry Bellinis: Purée 250g (9oz) fresh or frozen and defrosted raspberries with 5 tablespoons of caster sugar and 5 tablespoons of lemon juice, then mix with the sparkling wine.

Apple and blackberry bread and butter pudding

....

VEGETARIAN

Butter, for spreading
12 slices of white bread, crusts
    removed
200g (7oz) cooking apples,
    such as Bramley
150g (5oz) blackberries
450ml (16fl oz) single or
    regular cream
225ml (8fl oz) milk
4 eggs
150g (5oz) caster sugar
1 tbsp granulated sugar
Pinch of ground cinnamon
    (optional)

20 x 25cm (8 x 10in) square,
    round or oval ovenproof
    dish

This is a really comforting, autumnal dessert, delicious with a dollop of whipped cream. It's also a great excuse to get the family out picking blackberries. These can be substituted with raisins, however, if you prefer.

1 Preheat the oven to 180°C (350°F), Gas mark 4.

2 Butter the bread, cut into smaller pieces and arrange 6 in the ovenproof dish, butter side down. Peel and core the cooking apples and cut into 2cm (¾in) chunks. Place the pieces and blackberries in a layer on top of the bread. Then arrange the remaining bread, again butter side down and overlapping if necessary, to cover the fruit.

3 Pour the cream and milk into a saucepan, bring to just under the boil and remove from the heat.

4 While the milk and cream are heating up, whisk together the eggs and caster sugar in a large bowl. Add the hot cream and milk and whisk to combine, then pour this custard over the bread and leave to soak for 10 minutes. Sprinkle the granulated sugar over the top and the cinnamon (if using).

5 Put the dish in a bain-marie (a roasting tin filled with just enough boiled water to come halfway up the side of the dish). Place in the oven and bake for about 1 hour until the top is golden and the centre set.

RACHEL'S TIP
This can be prepared in advance and left in the fridge overnight, uncooked. If making it this way, don't heat up the milk and cream but add them cold to the whisked eggs and sugar.

MENU IDEAS FOR BRUNCHES AND LUNCHES

MAIN COURSES

Chilli sin carne
Sweet potato and chickpea tagine
Roasted vegetable coconut curry
Bean burritos with refried beans, guacamole and tomato salsa
Fish tacos with pepper and spring onion salsa
Fusilli with beans, smoked salmon and olives
Chicken and olive tagine
Chicken, pork and prawn paella
Beef and red wine stew
Chinese-style ribs with coleslaw
Mild lamb curry
Slow-roast ginger and citrus shoulder of pork

DESSERTS

Spiced poached pears
Ginger and treacle pudding
Apricot crumble
Cherry custard pudding

CASUAL MEALS

Sometimes you just want to get together with your friends
for no reason in particular. It might be a spontaneous thought,
and next thing you know you're on the phone to all your friends
asking if they can come over. Poker night? Movie night? Just because
it's Friday? There are so many reasons just to get a big pot of something
on the go. Here you'll find great ideas for simple but delicious meals
that you can serve at any time and to just about anyone – including
many which kids love. You won't find starters here because this
is 'tuck-in' food. Instead you'll find plenty of hearty and
comforting mains and desserts!

Chilli sin carne

....

4 tbsp olive oil

1 large onion, peeled and finely chopped

8 cloves of garlic, peeled and finely chopped

4 carrots, peeled and finely chopped

4 sticks of celery, trimmed and finely chopped

Salt and ground black pepper

2 large red chillies, deseeded and finely diced

2 tsp coriander seeds, ground (see page 25)

2 tsp cumin seeds, ground

200g (7oz) soya mince or TVP (textured vegetable protein), covered in cold water and soaked for 45 minutes

2 x 400g tins of red kidney or pinto beans, drained and rinsed, or 125g (4½oz) dried beans, soaked and cooked (see right)

2 x 400g tins of chopped tomatoes

200ml (7fl oz) vegetable stock (see page 50)

150ml (5fl oz) red wine

3 tbsp chopped coriander, to serve

Large casserole dish or saucepan

This vegetarian chilli is so bursting with flavours that even the most ardent meat lover will be impressed. Make sure to serve it with all the traditional chilli accompaniments, rice, guacamole and tomato salsa (see page 69), sour cream and tortilla chips.

1 Pour the olive oil into a large saucepan or casserole dish on a medium–low heat and add the onion, garlic, carrots and celery. Season with salt and pepper and cook, stirring occasionally, for about 20 minutes or until the vegetables are softened and golden. Stir in the chillies and spices and cook for a further 5 minutes.

2 Add all the remaining ingredients and taste for seasoning. Increase the heat to medium and cook, uncovered, for about 30 minutes or until thickened. Scatter with the chopped coriander and serve.

RACHEL'S TIP

To cook dried beans and pulses, soak them overnight in plenty of cold water, enough to cover the beans by a few centimetres, then drain and cook in fresh water until soft. It is best not to add salt to the cooking water as this toughens the beans.

Cooking time varies according to the type of bean and also how old they are:

Chickpeas = 45–75 minutes

Haricot or cannellini beans = 40–60 minutes

Pinto or kidney beans = 45–60 minutes

Note: 1 x 400g tin = 250g (9oz) drained, cooked beans or 125g (4½oz) dried beans.

Sweet potato and chickpea tagine

....

SERVES 4-6

VEGETARIAN

2 sweet potatoes (about 650g/1lb 7oz)
5 tbsp olive oil
Salt and ground black pepper
1 red pepper
1 yellow pepper
3 tbsp olive oil
1 large (300g/11oz) onion, peeled and thinly sliced
3 cloves of garlic, peeled and thinly sliced
3 tsp peeled (see page 27) and finely chopped root ginger
2 tsp cumin seeds, toasted and ground (see page 25)
2 tsp coriander seeds, toasted and ground
2 tsp paprika
1 x 400g tin of chickpeas, drained, or 125g (4½oz) dried chickpeas, soaked and cooked (see tip opposite)
100ml (3½fl oz) vegetable stock (see page 50)
1 tbsp honey
3 tbsp chopped coriander
75g (3oz) blanched almonds, toasted (see page 25) and roughly chopped

I absolutely adore this vegetarian tagine recipe; it has a spicy, sweet complexity that might be bullied out of the way were any meat added. Chickpeas are better friends with the canning process than any other pulse, though they are also delicious cooked from dry (see tip opposite).

1 Preheat the oven to 230°C (450°F), Gas mark 8.

2 Peel and cut the sweet potatoes into 2cm (¾in) cubes. Put them in a bowl, mix with 2 tablespoons of olive oil and season with salt and pepper. Spread the potato pieces out in a large roasting tin, place the whole peppers at one end, on the same tin, and roast in the oven for about 20 minutes or until the sweet potato is tender. When cooked, transfer the sweet potatoes to a bowl and set aside.

3 The peppers will need an additional 10–20 minutes to roast, depending on their size. They are ready when the skin has slightly blackened and the flesh feels soft underneath. When cooked, remove and place in a bowl covered with cling film – this makes the skins easier to remove. When the peppers are cool enough, peel off the skin. Cut the peppers in half and remove all the seeds, then chop the flesh into roughly 2cm (¾in) pieces.

4 While the sweet potatoes and peppers are cooking, pour the remaining olive oil into a casserole dish or large saucepan and place on a medium heat. Add the onion, garlic, ginger, ground cumin and coriander and the paprika, and season with salt and pepper. Cook for 10–12 minutes or until the onions are soft and beginning to brown.

5 Add the drained chickpeas with the vegetable stock, bring to the boil, then reduce the heat and simmer for 5 minutes. Next add the cooked sweet potatoes, roasted peppers, honey and half the chopped coriander, stir gently to combine and taste for seasoning.

6 Transfer to a warmed serving bowl, scatter over the remaining coriander and toasted almonds and serve with couscous.

Roasted vegetable coconut curry

2 x 400ml tins of coconut milk

600ml (1 pint) vegetable stock (see page 50)

4 large carrots

6 parsnips

700g (1½lb) sweet potatoes

4 onions

150g (5oz) spinach (any large stalks removed before weighing)

400ml (14fl oz) natural yoghurt

For the paste

1 tbsp coriander seeds

2 tsp cumin seeds

2 tsp chana masala

50g (2oz) root ginger, peeled (see page 27) and chopped

12 cloves of garlic, peeled

4 red chillies, deseeded

200g (7oz) onions, peeled and quartered

50ml (2fl oz) vegetable oil

1 tbsp ground turmeric

2 tsp caster sugar

2 tsp salt

To serve

Bunch of coriander, chopped

100g (3½oz) cashew nuts, toasted (see page 25) and chopped

200ml (7fl oz) natural yoghurt or crème fraîche

Large casserole dish or saucepan

The creamy coconut milk and myriad spices grant these vegetables both elegance and luxury. Roasting the vegetables in the paste really brings out their sweetness. Making your own curry paste only takes a few minutes and the complex depth of flavour means it's always worth doing.

1 Preheat the oven to 170°C (325°F), Gas mark 3.

2 First make the paste. Place a small frying pan on a medium heat and add the coriander, cumin and chana masala. Cook, tossing frequently, for about 1 minute or until they start to pop, then crush (see page 25).

3 Place the ginger, garlic, chillies, onions and vegetable oil in a food processor and whiz for 2–3 minutes or until smooth. Pour into a large saucepan or casserole dish and stir in the ground spices, along with the turmeric, sugar and salt. Place on a medium–low heat and cook, stirring occasionally, for about 5 minutes or until the mixture has reduced slightly.

4 Remove the mixture from the heat and pour half into a large bowl. Pour the coconut milk and stock into the remaining half in the saucepan or casserole dish, stirring to combine. Leave to simmer for 15 minutes to reduce.

5 Meanwhile, prepare the vegetables. Peel the carrots, parsnips and sweet potatoes and cut into 2cm (¾in) cubes. Peel the onions and cut into eighths and chop the spinach.

6 Stir the yoghurt into the spice paste in the bowl, then add the vegetables and onions and stir to coat. Tip into 1–2 roasting tins and cook in the oven for about 1 hour or until lightly browned.

7 Remove the vegetables from the oven and add to the saucepan or casserole dish. Place on a medium heat for a few minutes to warm through, then stir in the spinach and spoon into bowls with a sprinkling of fresh coriander, a scattering of the toasted nuts and a spoonful of yoghurt or crème fraîche.

Bean burritos with refried beans, guacamole and tomato salsa

....

SERVES 8
VEGETARIAN

1 quantity of guacamole
  (see opposite)
1 quantity of tomato salsa
  (see opposite)
1 x 200g jar of jalapeño
  peppers (optional)
250g (9oz) Cheddar or
  Gruyère cheese, grated
250g (9oz) crème fraîche
16 tortillas
1 quantity of refried beans
  (see opposite)

These burritos are great for a casual crowd. Children will especially love creating their own at the table, choosing from a variety of fillings for the tortillas. I love to see everyone passing around various bowls and plates. This is what communal food is all about.

1 Preheat the oven to 150°C (300°F), Gas mark 2.

2 Place the guacamole, salsa, peppers (if using), grated cheese and crème fraîche in separate serving bowls on the table.

3 Put the tortillas in a roasting tin, cover with foil or an upturned bowl and place in the oven for 5–10 minutes or until warmed through, then divide between plates. Reheat the beans, pour into a serving dish and place on the table with the other bowls. People can help themselves and assemble their own burritos by spooning each of the fillings in a line on their tortilla, then rolling up and eating!

Refried beans

....

SERVES 8 AS A SIDE DISH
VEGETARIAN
25g (1oz) butter
1 onion, peeled and finely chopped
4 cloves of garlic, peeled and finely chopped
½–1 red chilli, deseeded and finely chopped
2 x 400g tins of pinto or kidney beans, drained
   and rinsed, or 250g (9oz) of dried beans,
   soaked and cooked (see page 64)
100ml (3½fl oz) beef or chicken stock
   (see page 51)
1 tsp ground cumin
1 tsp ground coriander
Salt and ground black pepper

1 Melt the butter in a large frying pan on
a medium heat, add the onion, garlic and
chilli and cook for about 8–10 minutes or
until softened and a little golden around
the edges.

2 Add the beans, stock, cumin and coriander
and season with salt and pepper. Cook,
stirring occasionally and mashing the beans
every so often using a potato masher, for a
further 7–8 minutes or until the sauce has
reduced slightly, then remove from the
heat and allow to cool.

Guacamole

....

SERVES 8 AS A SIDE DISH
VEGETARIAN
2 ripe avocados, peeled and stones removed
2 cloves of garlic, peeled and crushed
   or finely grated
2 tbsp extra-virgin olive oil
2 tbsp chopped coriander
Salt and ground black pepper
Juice of ½ lime or lemon

1 Place the avocado flesh in a large bowl,
add the garlic, olive oil and coriander and
mash together, seasoning to taste with salt,
pepper and lime juice.

2 Cover the bowl with cling film to stop
the mixture going brown and set aside
until it is needed.

Tomato salsa

....

SERVES 8 AS A SIDE DISH
VEGETARIAN
4 ripe tomatoes, cut into 1cm (½in) cubes
1 tbsp chopped red onion
1 clove of garlic, peeled and crushed
   or finely grated
½–1 red chilli, deseeded and finely chopped
2 tbsp chopped coriander
Juice of ½ lime
Salt and ground black pepper
Pinch of sugar

1 Mix all the ingredients together, seasoning
with salt, pepper and a pinch of sugar.

Fish tacos with pepper and spring onion salsa

SERVES 8
750g (1lb 10oz) filleted round
    white fish, such as haddock,
    whiting, hake or cod, in
    small fillets or one big piece
2 tbsp olive oil
Salt and ground black pepper

To serve
16 taco shells
1 quantity of guacamole
    (see page 69)
1 quantity of pepper and
    spring onion salsa
    (see below)
250g (9oz) crème fraîche

The first bite into a fish taco immediately transports me to the white sands of Puerto Escondido in Mexico. The flavours here are all so evocative: crunchy taco shells enveloping a crisp, refreshing salsa, a smooth and creamy guacamole (see page 69) and delicate flakes of fish. I can practically smell the sea!

1 Preheat the oven to 180°C (350°F), Gas mark 4.

2 Put the fish in a roasting tin, drizzle with the olive oil and season with salt and pepper. Place in the oven and cook for 10–20 minutes, depending on the size of the fish piece or pieces, until the flesh is opaque all the way through.

3 A few minutes before the fish are cooked, place the tacos in the oven to warm through, then bring to the table with bowls of the guacamole, salsa and crème fraîche. Cut or break up the fish into bite-sized chunks and place in a warmed serving bowl on the table. People can help themselves: just spoon a little from each bowl to fill the tacos, and eat!

Pepper and spring onion salsa

SERVES 8 AS A SIDE DISH
VEGETARIAN
2 yellow peppers (or 1 red and
    1 yellow), very finely sliced
8 spring onions, trimmed
    and sliced
8 radishes or ⅓ cucumber,
    left unpeeled and cut into
    thin strips
½–1 red chilli, deseeded
    and finely diced
Juice of 2 limes
2 tbsp extra-virgin olive oil
2 ripe tomatoes, finely diced
2 tbsp chopped coriander
Salt and ground black pepper

1 Mix all the ingredients together in another bowl and season to taste with salt and pepper.

Fusilli with beans, smoked salmon and olives

....

SERVES 8-10
300g (11oz) smoked salmon
500g (1lb 2oz) dried fusilli
4 tbsp olive oil
Salt and ground black pepper
1 red pepper, deseeded and
   finely sliced
1 x 400g tin of kidney beans,
   drained and rinsed
½ red onion, peeled and
   sliced
Handful of chopped mint
Handful of chopped coriander
Juice of 2 limes or 1 lemon
16 olives, pitted (see page 38)
   and roughly chopped
125ml (4½fl oz) crème fraîche

This dish is perfect for any form of casual entertaining. If made in advance, it can be chilled and brought back up to room temperature.

1 Preheat the oven to 200°C (400°F), Gas mark 6. Place the smoked salmon on a baking sheet in the oven and roast for about 10 minutes or until it turns pale coral. Break the salmon into roughly 2cm (¾in) pieces, then set aside to cool.

2 Cook the fusilli following the instructions on the packet, but remove it from the pan when it is al dente. Drain the pasta, reserving about 25ml (1fl oz) of the cooking water. Pour this back into the fusilli along with the olive oil, and season. Transfer to a large bowl and allow to cool to room temperature.

3 Add the remaining ingredients, apart from the salmon, and mix together. Scatter the salmon pieces over the top and serve.

Chicken and olive tagine

....

SERVES 6-8
3 tbsp olive oil
200g (7oz) peeled and sliced
   onions
4 large cloves of garlic,
   peeled and chopped
2.5cm (1in) piece of root
   ginger, peeled and chopped
Salt and ground black pepper
600g (1lb 5oz) chicken meat
400ml (14fl oz) chicken stock
   (see page 51)
Good pinch of saffron
2 tbsp chopped parsley
2 tbsp chopped coriander
16 olives, pitted

This take on a classic Moroccan dish has a real elegance to it despite the fact that it's incredibly easy to make.

1 Pour the olive oil into a large frying pan on a medium heat, then add the onions, garlic and ginger. Season with salt and pepper and fry for about 5 minutes, stirring occasionally, until the onions have almost softened and are a little golden around the edges.

2 Cut the chicken into bite-sized chunks, add to the pan and cook for 2 minutes before adding the stock and saffron. Stir to combine then bring to the boil, reduce the heat and simmer for about 15 minutes or until the chicken is cooked all the way through.

3 Stir in the remaining ingredients and taste for seasoning and serve immediately. This goes very well with couscous.

Chicken, pork and prawn paella

SERVES 10–12

2 tbsp olive oil

250g (9oz) chorizo sausage, chopped into 1cm (½in) chunks

1 large Spanish or red onion, peeled and finely chopped

4 cloves of garlic, peeled and chopped

300g (11oz) chicken meat from the leg or breast, cut into bite-sized pieces

300g (11oz) pork meat from the leg, cut into bite-sized pieces

Salt and ground black pepper

500g (1lb 2oz) paella rice

150ml (5fl oz) dry white wine

1.2 litres (2 pints) chicken stock (see page 51)

4 large very ripe tomatoes, peeled (see tip below) and cut into chunks

1 tsp caster sugar

450g (1lb) peeled raw whole prawns, large ones halved lengthways

150g (5oz) baby spinach, removing any stalks from larger leaves

Juice of ½–1 lemon

1 tbsp chopped parsley

1 tbsp chopped chives

40cm (16in) diameter paella pan or wide, heavy-based frying pan

This rice dish originated in Valencia but can now be found all over Spain and the Balearics. Paella is a wonderful dish for entertaining as it is just as easy to make for 12 people as it is for four, provided you have a pan large enough. Should you ever be in Spain, I would recommend purchasing an authentic paellera, which come in many sizes.

1 Pour the olive oil into the paella pan or frying pan on a medium heat. Tip in the chorizo chunks along with the onion and garlic and cook for 6–7 minutes, stirring regularly, until the oils have come out of the chorizo and the onion is softened and golden.

2 Remove the chorizo, onion and garlic from the pan, leaving any oils behind. Turn the heat up to high, then when the pan is hot, add the chicken and pork and, tossing regularly, cook for 3–4 minutes or until the meat is golden. Season to taste with salt and pepper.

3 Reduce the heat to low, add the rice and stir for 1–2 minutes before adding the cooked chorizo, onion and garlic with the wine, stock, tomatoes and sugar. Continue to cook, uncovered, for 20 minutes, stirring every now and then, until the rice is just cooked. If the paella begins to look a little dry, add some more hot stock.

4 Next add the whole or halved prawns and the spinach and cook for another 2–3 minutes or until the prawns are cooked (opaque and firm to the touch) and the spinach leaves are wilted. Add some lemon juice to taste and half the chopped herbs and taste for seasoning. Scatter the remaining herbs over the top and serve.

RACHEL'S TIP

To peel tomatoes, cut an 'X' in the skin of each one, place in a bowl and cover with boiling water. Leave for 10–15 seconds, then drain, leave to cool and peel off the skin. If you can't get hold of good-quality tomatoes, replace them with a 400g tin of cherry tomatoes.

Beef and red wine stew

....

SERVES 4-6

25g (1oz) butter

300g (11oz) streaky bacon in the piece or 6 rashers, cut into 2cm (¾in) dice

1kg (2lb 3oz) stewing beef, cut into 2cm (¾in) cubes

Salt and ground black pepper

800g (1¾lb) carrots, peeled and sliced

10 small onions, peeled and halved

3 tbsp chopped herbs, such as thyme, rosemary or tarragon

600ml (1 pint) chicken stock (see page 51)

425ml (15fl oz) red wine

500g (1lb 2oz) white mushrooms, sliced

25g (1oz) roux (made with 10–15g (⅓–½oz) each of butter and plain flour; see tip below)

Large flameproof casserole dish

There's nothing better than a big hearty casserole filled with tender meat and delicious veggies, all in a robust red wine sauce. This makes for great winter entertaining, and reheats perfectly. Serve with a big bowl of mashed potato (see page 191) or the Roast Garlic Colcannon on page 244.

1 Preheat the oven to 140°C (275°F), Gas mark 1.

2 Melt half the butter in a casserole dish on a medium heat. Add the bacon and cook for 2–3 minutes until almost golden. Turn up the heat to high and add half the cubed beef and seasoning and cook for 5–6 minutes, tossing regularly, until browned all over. Tip the bacon and beef onto a plate and cook the remaining beef, adding a little more butter if the dish or pan is too dry.

3 Remove the meat from the casserole dish onto the plate, then toss the carrots and onions in the juices on a high heat for 4–5 minutes before adding the herbs and putting the meat back in. Pour in the stock and the wine, cover and bring to simmering point. Place in the oven and cook for 1½–2 hours or until the meat is tender. If you have the time, let it simmer at an even lower temperature – 130°C (250°F), Gas mark ½ – for about 2½–3 hours.

4 Just before the stew has finished cooking, melt the remaining butter in a frying pan on a high heat, add the mushrooms and seasoning and sauté for 3–4 minutes until golden.

5 Take the casserole dish from the oven, remove 2–3 ladlefuls of the sauce and bring to the boil in a small saucepan. Whisk in the roux and allow to boil for 2–3 minutes or until the sauce has thickened. Pour back in the dish and stir in the mushrooms. Taste for seasoning, then serve straight from the casserole dish.

RACHEL'S TIP

A roux is a simple sauce thickener that is made with equal quantities of flour and butter. For the recipe above, melt 15g (½oz) butter in a small saucepan on a medium heat, add 15g (½oz) plain flour and allow to cook for 2 minutes, stirring regularly. Use immediately.

Chinese-style ribs
with coleslaw

....

SERVES 6-8

2kg (4lb 4oz) baby back ribs
   of pork
6 spring onions, trimmed
   and finely sliced, to serve

For the spice mixture
3 tbsp cornflour
2 tbsp light brown sugar
1 tbsp peeled (see page 27)
   and finely grated root ginger
2 tsp Chinese five-spice powder
4 tbsp hoisin sauce
3 tbsp rice wine or dry sherry
Pinch of salt

For the coleslaw
400g (14oz) white cabbage,
   quartered lengthways,
   core removed and leaves
   finely sliced
1 large carrot, peeled and grated
1 onion, peeled and finely sliced
1 stick of celery, trimmed and
   finely sliced
200ml (7fl oz) mayonnaise
   (see page 317)
2 tbsp chopped coriander
   or parsley
Salt and freshly ground pepper

Ribs are one of those foods that demand to be eaten with your hands. It is just not possible to effectively eat a rib with a knife and fork. Perhaps for this reason, as well as the fabulous sweet-sour Chinese flavours, adults and children will happily devour entire piles of these ribs. For the hungrier among your guests, bake some potatoes to serve alongside.

1 Preheat the oven to 220°C (425°F), Gas mark 7.

2 In a bowl, stir together all the ingredients for the spice mixture. Arrange the ribs in a roasting tin in a single layer and rub the spice mixture all over. Place in the oven and bake for 30–35 minutes or until slightly crispy and a deep golden brown.

3 While the ribs are cooking, make the coleslaw. Mix all the ingredients together in a large bowl, seasoning to taste with salt and pepper.

4 Remove the ribs from the oven, scatter with the spring onions and serve with the coleslaw.

Mild lamb curry

4–6 tbsp vegetable oil

1.5kg (3lb 5oz) stewing lamb, cut into 2cm (¾in) cubes

900g (2lb) peeled and sliced onions

8 cloves of garlic, peeled and crushed

2 tsp cumin seeds, ground (see page 25)

2 tsp coriander seeds, ground

2 tsp fennel seeds, ground

1 tsp ground turmeric

1 tsp ground nutmeg

Salt and ground black pepper

800ml (1 pint 9fl oz) coconut milk (or 2 x 400ml tins)

400ml (14fl oz) chicken stock (see page 51)

1 x 400g tin of chopped tomatoes

Juice of 2 limes

4 tbsp chopped mint

Lime wedges, to serve

Large saucepan or casserole dish

This curry isn't spicy and the coconut milk makes it so creamy that our children love it too.

1 Pour about 4 tablespoons of the vegetable oil into a large saucepan or casserole dish on a medium heat. Add the lamb and fry on all sides for 3–4 minutes, stirring frequently.

2 Add the remaining oil, if necessary, then tip in the onions, garlic and spices and add seasoning. Cook for 15 minutes, stirring occasionally, until the onions are soft and beginning to brown.

3 Add the coconut milk, stock and tomatoes, stir well and reduce the heat to low. Gently simmer, uncovered and stirring regularly, for 1¼–2 hours or until the meat is meltingly tender.

4 When the lamb is cooked, stir in the lime juice and chopped mint, taste for seasoning and then serve immediately with some lime wedges.

Slow-roast ginger and citrus shoulder of pork

....

2–3kg (4lb 4oz–6½lb)
    shoulder of pork on the
    bone, with the rind still on
Sea salt

For the marinade
8 cloves of garlic, peeled and
    crushed or finely grated
1 tsp ground star anise
2 tbsp peeled (see page 27) and
    finely chopped root ginger
Finely grated zest of 2 oranges
    and juice of 1 orange
150g (5oz) light soft brown
    sugar
75ml (3fl oz) sherry vinegar
4 tbsp chopped coriander
Juice of 1 large lemon
1 tsp salt
1 tsp ground black pepper

Although this is not a quick supper, it is still perfect for an informal meal. It really isn't difficult to prepare and, once cooked, it is an unfussy dish. The shoulder is a cut of meat that requires slow cooking. The marinade imparts its sweet, citrus notes to the pork, while the slow cooking breaks down all the fat and fibres to leave incredibly flavourful and succulent meat. This recipe is delicious served with broccoli and Celeriac Purée (see page 48).

1 Using a craft knife or a very sharp knife, score the rind of the pork, making incisions (about 5mm/¾in deep) all across the surface of the meat in a criss-cross pattern.

2 Next make the marinade by simply mixing all the ingredients in a bowl. Place the pork shoulder in a sealable plastic bag and pour in the marinade, rubbing it into the pork and into any seams or cuts. Chill in the fridge overnight or for at least 12 hours.

3 Preheat the oven to 220°C (425°F), Gas mark 7.

4 Place the pork shoulder on a roasting tray and pour over any of the marinade that hasn't soaked in. Place in the oven and cook for 10 minutes, then reduce the heat to 110°C (225°F), Gas mark ¼, and cook, basting with the juices from time to time, for 12 hours or until the meat feels completely soft and yielding. Take the pork out of the oven and turn the heat up to 220°C (425°F), Gas mark 7. Sprinkle the rind generously with sea salt then pop it back into the oven and cook for a further 10 minutes to crisp up the skin.

5 Remove from the oven, place on a baking tray or carving board and allow to rest for at least 30 minutes. Put in the oven with the heat turned off. While the meat is resting, degrease the cooking juices (see page 226), then pour them back into the roasting tin in which the pork was cooked. Set on a medium heat and cook for about 5 minutes to reduce the liquid and concentrate the flavours. Carve the meat into thick slices or chunks and serve with the sauce.

Spiced poached pears

....

SERVES 6
VEGETARIAN
300ml (½ pint) red wine
110g (4oz) caster sugar
1.5cm (2in) cinnamon stick
1 clove
Juice and finely grated zest
of 1 orange
6 firm (but not rock-hard)
pears

A spicy version of classic poached pears, these are lovely with vanilla or cinnamon ice cream, or try with a tangy blue cheese.

1 Pour the wine and 300ml (½ pint) water into a large saucepan and add the sugar, cinnamon stick, clove, orange juice and zest. Place on a medium heat and stir until the sugar dissolves.

2 While the sugar is dissolving, peel the pears, leaving the stalks on, and place upright in the saucepan. They should fit snugly, but if they fall over because the pan is too big, place a folded strip of greaseproof paper or baking parchment around them.

3 Cover the saucepan with a lid and bring to the boil, then reduce the heat and allow to simmer on a low heat for 30–40 minutes. Spoon the red wine syrup over the pears once or twice during this time.

4 To test whether the pears are ready, gently press one with your finger: there should be a little bit of give without being too soft to the touch. Remove from the heat and discard the cinnamon and clove. Spoon the syrup over the pears once more and put into the fridge to chill overnight.

5 When you are ready to serve, take the pears out of the syrup and cut a slice off the bottom of each pear – this will ensure they stand upright on the serving plates. Serve each pear with some spicy syrup drizzled over.

Ginger and treacle pudding

....

SERVES 8-10
VEGETARIAN

250g (9oz) butter, softened,
  plus extra for greasing
150g (5oz) caster sugar
4 tbsp treacle/molasses
2 eggs
Grated zest and sieved
  juice of 1 orange
200ml (7fl oz) milk
250g (9oz) plain flour
2 tsp baking powder
1 tsp ground cinnamon
75g (3oz) crystallised ginger,
  finely chopped
Icing sugar, for dusting

This moist, delicious pudding can be made a few days in advance and heated gently before serving. It is yummy served with Orange Ice Cream (see page 258) or whipped cream mixed with some grated orange zest.

1 Preheat the oven to 180°C (350°F), Gas mark 4, and line a 30 x 20 x 6cm (12 x 8 x 2½in) ovenproof dish or deep baking tin with non-stick baking paper.

2 Cream the butter in a large bowl or in an electric food mixer until soft. Add the sugar and treacle and beat until the mixture is light and fluffy. Beat in the eggs, one at a time, then whisk in the orange zest and juice and milk. Sift over the flour, baking powder and ground cinnamon, then fold in with the chopped ginger.

3 Spoon the mixture into the baking tin and bake for 40 minutes or until a skewer inserted into the centre comes out clean. Allow to cool for a few minutes before cutting the pudding into squares. Place each square onto a serving plate and dust with icing sugar.

Apricot crumble

....

SERVES 6
VEGETARIAN

110g (4oz) wholemeal flour
25g (1oz) plain flour
75g (3oz) porridge oats
110g (4oz) butter, cubed
250g (9oz) demerara or light
  soft brown sugar
600g (1lb 5oz) fresh apricots,
  halved and stones removed
100g (3½oz) flaked almonds,
  toasted (see page 25), to
  decorate

23 x 25cm (9 x 10in)
  ovenproof dish

This delicious crumble is wonderful served with homemade custard or vanilla ice cream.

1 Preheat the oven to 180°C (350°F), Gas mark 4.

2 To make the topping, place the flours in a large bowl, add the oats and mix together. Using your fingertips, rub the butter into the flour and oatmeal mixture until it resembles coarse breadcrumbs. Add 110g (4½oz) of the sugar and mix well.

3 Place the apricots, cut side up, in the ovenproof dish. Sprinkle over the remaining sugar and then the crumble mixture to cover the fruit. Cook for 30–40 minutes or until golden and bubbling Serve the crumble warm from the oven, scattering a few toasted almonds on top.

Cherry custard pudding

....

SERVES 6-8
VEGETARIAN
250ml (9fl oz) double or
   regular cream
1 generous tbsp caster
   sugar or vanilla sugar
2 tbsp Kirsch (optional)
450g (1lb) black cherries,
   pitted

For the custard
200ml (7fl oz) milk
1 vanilla pod, split in
   half lengthways
25g (1oz) cornflour
50g (2oz) caster sugar
3 egg yolks

Large glass bowl or 6-8
   individual glasses

Our lovely German au pair Rebecca Zemeitat made this for us at home. The custard is quite thick so the cherries can be added in layers. It can be made in one large glass bowl or in individual glasses. It can also be assembled earlier in the day and kept covered in the fridge until needed.

1 First make the custard. Pour the milk into a saucepan on a low heat, add the vanilla pod, cornflour and half the sugar, and gently heat, stirring constantly, until the sugar has dissolved.

2 In a bowl, beat the egg yolks with the remaining sugar until pale in colour and creamy in consistency. Slowly pour in the hot milk mixture, whisking as you add it in, then pour back into the saucepan (having washed it first to help prevent the custard sticking and scrambling).

3 Whisk well and cook on a low–medium heat for 2–3 minutes, stirring constantly with a wooden spoon (to get to the mixture in the corners of the pan), until the custard has thickened. Now remove the vanilla pod, scrape out some of the seeds and stir these back into the custard. Remove from the heat and allow to cool.

4 In a separate bowl, whip the cream with the vanilla or caster sugar until slightly thickened, then fold in the Kirsch (if using) and the custard.

5 Pour half of the custard cream into a serving bowl, or divide the mixture between individual glasses. Add a layer of cherries, then pour the remaining mixture on top and add the rest of the cherries. Chill in the fridge for 30 minutes before serving.

MENU IDEAS FOR
CASUAL MEALS

Slow-roast ginger and citrus shoulder of pork with green salad (pages 80 and 239)
Apricot crumble (page 83)

*

Roasted vegetable coconut curry (page 66)
Mild lamb curry with boiled rice and naan bread (page 78)
Ginger and treacle pudding (page 83)

*

Chinese-style ribs with coleslaw and baked potatoes (page 77)
Cherry custard pudding (page 84)

STARTERS

Middle Eastern chilled cucumber soup
Harissa roasted vegetables
Tomato and lentil couscous salad
Pan-fried mackerel with panzanella salad

MAIN COURSES

Southeast Asian grilled fish
Salmon teriyaki
Marinades
Spiced barbecued lamb with potato salad and mint raita
Honey, mustard and ginger pork skewers
Lamb and lentil salad with olives and roast red peppers

SALADS AND SIDE DISHES

Broad bean and pancetta salad
Fennel, orange and hazelnut salad
Sue's aubergine, yoghurt and harissa salad
Beetroot slaw
Garlic and herb mushrooms
Grilled asparagus
Barbecued corn on the cob

DESSERTS

Blueberry and custard tart
Strawberries in rosé wine
Strawberries and blueberries with Grand Marnier
Peaches with mascarpone, walnuts and honey

EATING OUTDOORS

When the weather is nice, it's great to throw open the doors and gather one's friends and family around to enjoy time together outside. Picnics, barbecues, dinners in the garden, even beach parties if you're lucky – there are so many options. These are some of my favourite, sunny recipes for when you just don't want to eat indoors! But don't let a little rain stop you from trying them at any time of year – you might just need to keep under cover...

Middle Eastern chilled cucumber soup

....

SERVES 4-6
VEGETARIAN
1 large cucumber, peeled,
  if you wish, and grated
200ml (7fl oz) single or
  regular cream
200ml (7fl oz) natural yoghurt
2 tbsp white wine vinegar
Small handful of coriander,
  plus small sprigs to serve
1 clove of garlic, peeled and
  crushed or finely grated
1 tbsp finely grated gherkins
Salt and ground black pepper

This is an elegant soup. Each ingredient highlights the cucumber's fresh flavour, perfect for a summer's day.

1 Mix all the ingredients, keeping back 4–6 teaspoons cucumber, together in a large bowl and season to taste with salt and pepper, then chill in the fridge for at least 1 hour before serving.

2 Serve in small chilled bowls with a few coriander sprigs and the remaining cucumber sprinkled on top.

Tomato and lentil couscous salad

....

SERVES 4
VEGETARIAN

5 tbsp olive oil, plus extra
   for drizzling
1 large onion (400g/14oz),
   peeled and sliced
100g (3½oz) Puy lentils
1 tbsp lemon juice
Sea salt and ground black
   pepper
300g (11oz) cherry tomatoes,
   halved widthways
150ml (5fl oz) couscous
150ml (5fl oz) hot vegetable
   stock (see page 50)
2 tbsp each of chopped
   coriander and mint,
   to serve

To serve

3 tbsp thick natural Greek
   yoghurt
1 clove of garlic, peeled and
   crushed or finely grated

The different elements of this salad combine together beautifully, the nutty grains dispersed among the sweet onions and tomatoes and intensely savoury garlic yoghurt. This dish also has the advantage of being able to be made a good few hours in advance.

1 Pour 2 tablespoons of the olive oil into a frying pan on a low heat, add the onion and cook, stirring occasionally, for about 45 minutes until completely soft and caramelised.

2 While the onions are caramelising, cook the lentils. Rinse and place in a saucepan with enough water to cover by 1cm (½in) and simmer for 20–30 minutes until soft. Drain, then add the lemon juice and remaining olive oil and season with salt and pepper.

3 Meanwhile, preheat the oven to 220°C (425°F), Gas mark 7.

4 Place the tomatoes in a roasting tin cut side up, drizzle with a little olive oil and season with salt and pepper, then place in the oven for about 15 minutes or until softened and a little scorched at the edges.

5 In a large bowl, mix the couscous with the hot stock and leave to sit for 5 minutes or until absorbed and soft, then allow to cool. When cooled, mix together with the lentils, tomatoes and onions and stir in the chopped herbs.

6 In a separate small bowl, mix together the yoghurt and garlic and season with sea salt. Disperse teaspoonfuls of the garlic yoghurt throughout the couscous salad without mixing them in and serve.

Pan-fried mackerel with panzanella salad

SERVES 8 FOR A STARTER
AND 4 FOR A MAIN COURSE

2 generous tbsp plain flour
8 mackerel fillets, with the
    skin still on
1 tbsp olive oil

For the panzanella salad
3 slices of ciabatta or white
    bread, preferably a couple
    of days old
4 tbsp extra-virgin olive oil
4–6 ripe tomatoes
12 black olives, such as
    kalamata, pitted
    (see page 38)
8 tinned anchovies,
    drained, rinsed and
    roughly chopped
1 heaped tbsp capers,
    drained and rinsed
2 tbsp torn or roughly
    chopped basil
2 tbsp red wine vinegar
    or balsamic vinegar
Sea salt and ground
    black pepper
Pinch of sugar (optional)
Basil leaves, to decorate

This is inspired by a dish we ate at Over the Moon in Skibbereen, a West Cork restaurant gem. The mackerel is perfectly complemented by the bread salad, its oiliness counterbalanced by the punchy anchovies, olives and capers.

1 First make the panzanella salad. Break the bread into chunks and place in a shallow-sided serving dish then drizzle with the extra-virgin olive oil.

2 Cut the tomatoes in half and squeeze out the seeds – not every single one, but just enough to ensure the bread doesn't get too soggy. Chop the tomato flesh and add to the bread along with the remaining ingredients. Season to taste with salt and pepper; it may also need a pinch of sugar.

3 Next prepare the mackerel. Sprinkle the flour onto a plate and season generously with salt and pepper, then place a griddle pan or frying pan on a high heat. While it is heating, dip the mackerel fillets into the flour to coat both sides, shaking off any excess flour.

4 To cook the fish, add the olive oil to the hot pan. Lay the fish in the pan (or as many that will fit in a single layer – the fillets may need to be cooked in a couple of batches), flesh side down. Cook for just a minute or two on each side, then transfer to individual warmed plates and serve with the panzanella salad decorated with some basil leaves on the side.

Southeast Asian grilled fish

....

2cm (¾in) piece of root
    ginger, peeled (see page 27)
    and sliced thinly
1 stick of lemongrass (outer
    layer removed), bruised
    and sliced
2 spring onions, trimmed
    and sliced
1 red chilli, deseeded
    and sliced
2 tbsp light soy sauce
1 tbsp fish sauce (nam pla)
1 tsp caster sugar
2 mackerel or 1 whole small–
    medium fish (½–1kg/1lb
    2oz–2lb 3oz in total), such
    as sea bream, scaled and
    gutted (ask your
    fishmonger to do this)
1–2 tbsp sunflower oil,
    for frying (optional)

To serve
1 tbsp sesame oil
A few drops of fish sauce
    (nam pla)
Squeeze of lemon or
    lime juice
1 tbsp chopped coriander

Ever since spending a few months travelling around southeast Asia, I've been enamoured with the flavour combinations in their food. These ingredients work fantastically well as they bring an array of salt, sweet, sour and spicy flavours to the fish.

1 Place half of each of the ginger, lemongrass, spring onions and chilli into a food processor, along with all of the soy, fish sauce and sugar, and whiz for 1–2 minutes to form a paste.

2 Score the fish by making cuts about 5mm (¾in) deep at an angle in the skin and rub in the paste. Fill the cavity with the remaining ginger, lemongrass, spring onions and chilli, cover and leave to marinate for 1–2 hours in the fridge.

3 Cook on a moderately hot barbecue – or in a large griddle pan or frying pan brushed with sunflower oil and placed on a medium–high heat – for 3–5 minutes on each side or until the skin is crispy and the fish is opaque all the way through.

4 To serve, drizzle with the sesame oil and fish sauce, squeeze over some lemon or lime juice and scatter over the coriander.

RACHEL'S TIP

If you are cooking this dish for quite a few people, you can lay the fish on an oiled oven tray, drizzle a little oil over the top of each fish, and cook under a hot grill for 3–5 minutes on each side or until the skin is crispy and the fish opaque all the way through.

Salmon teriyaki

....

Teriyaki is a famous Japanese cooking technique. It refers to food that is marinated in sweet soy sauce and grilled in the marinade. This traditional sauce is delightfully simple and utterly delicious.

SERVES 6-8

8 salmon steaks (200g/
  7oz each)
150ml (5fl oz) dark soy sauce
100g (3½oz) caster sugar
50ml (2fl oz) mirin
1 tsp salt
1 tbsp sunflower oil,
  for frying (optional)

1 Put the salmon in a shallow dish. Place the remaining ingredients, except the sunflower oil, in a small saucepan and heat gently until the sugar has dissolved, then remove from the heat and allow to cool. Pour over the salmon, cover and leave to marinate in the fridge for 2 hours.

2 Remove the salmon from the marinade and place on a moderately hot barbecue (or in a griddle pan or frying pan brushed with sunflower oil and set on a medium–high heat), reserving the marinade. Cook, brushing continuously with the marinade, for 2–3 minutes on each side or until the fish is opaque all the way through. Remove to serving plates and pour over any remaining marinade.

Marinades

....

When barbecuing or oven-roasting a piece of meat, it is often necessary to marinate it first. This means soaking it in a flavoured liquid – the 'marinade' – before cooking. As well as herbs and spices, this usually contains an acidic ingredient – such as citrus juice, vinegar, yoghurt, wine or soy sauce – to help tenderise the meat. Usually no salt is included in the marinade as this can draw out much needed moisture during the soaking time, so unless a recipe calls for salt, don't add it until just before cooking. In order for the marinade to really soak into the meat – especially a large joint – it's generally a good idea to score the surface a few times before adding the marinade.

HOW LONG TO MARINATE MEAT

All the marinades that follow are enough for about 1 kg (2lb 3oz) meat, which will serve about 6 people. Once combined with the marinade – in a sealable plastic bag or a covered shallow dish – the meat should be left to marinate in the fridge for at least 2 hours or overnight.

Provençal marinade

....

TO GO WITH BEEF OR LAMB
2 sprigs of thyme
2 sprigs of rosemary
2 bay leaves
4 cloves of garlic, peeled and
    crushed or finely grated
10 whole black peppercorns
150ml (5fl oz) olive oil
50ml (2fl oz) red wine vinegar

1 Put all the ingredients except the vinegar
in a saucepan and place on a medium heat.
Cook until the olive oil just comes to a
simmer then remove from the heat – the
simmering process will allow the flavour
of the herbs to infuse.

2 Add the vinegar and allow to cool, then
combine with the meat.

2 Simply pour into a saucepan, bring to the
boil and cook for 3–4 minutes, then drizzle
over the cooked meat.

Port and orange marinade

....

TO GO WITH BEEF, PORK OR DUCK
2 tbsp peeled and finely chopped root ginger
    (for peeling ginger, see page 27)
4 cloves of garlic, peeled and sliced
Juice of ½ lemon
Juice of 1 orange
100ml (3½fl oz) olive oil
100ml (3½fl oz) port

1 Mix everything together in a bowl,
then combine with the meat.

Char sui marinade

....

FOR PORK, CHICKEN OR BEEF
4 cloves of garlic, peeled and crushed
    or finely grated
2 tbsp light soft brown sugar
2 tbsp peeled and finely chopped root ginger
    (for peeling ginger, see page 27)
2 tbsp runny honey
50ml (2fl oz) light soy sauce
50ml (2fl oz) rice wine or dry sherry
2 tbsp hoisin sauce
2 tsp vegetable oil

1 Mix everything together in a bowl, then
combine with the meat. Don't discard this
marinade after marinating the meat – you
can use it as a sauce.

Smoked paprika and
rosemary marinade

....

TO GO WITH LAMB OR CHICKEN LEGS
2 cloves of garlic, peeled and crushed
    or finely grated
2 tsp smoked paprika
3 tbsp finely chopped rosemary leaves
½ tsp ground black pepper
100ml (3½fl oz) sherry vinegar
2 tbsp olive oil

1 Mix everything together in a bowl,
then rub all over the meat.

Saffron yoghurt marinade

....

TO GO WITH LAMB OR CHICKEN LEGS
2 cloves of garlic, peeled and crushed
1 tsp saffron threads
½ small onion, peeled and finely grated
75ml (3fl oz) natural Greek yoghurt
25ml (1fl oz) olive oil
Juice of 1 lemon
Ground black pepper

1 Mix everything together in a bowl, then combine with the meat.

Greek marinade

....

TO GO WITH LAMB, CHICKEN OR PORK
2 cloves of garlic, peeled and crushed
2 tbsp finely chopped marjoram
Juice of ½ lemon
100ml (3½fl oz) olive oil
Ground black pepper

1 Mix everything together in a bowl, then combine with the meat.

Cider marinade

....

TO GO WITH PORK
2 tbsp raisins
2 tbsp light soft brown sugar
Pinch of ground cloves
1 tsp ground cinnamon
½ tsp cardamom seeds
250ml (9fl oz) cider

1 Put all the ingredients in a saucepan and cook just below simmering point for 5 minutes or until the raisins have expanded slightly.

2 Remove from the heat and allow to cool, then combine with the meat.

Mint yoghurt marinade

....

TO GO WITH CHICKEN OR LAMB
2 tbsp chopped mint
Finely grated zest of 1 lemon
2 tsp each of coriander and cumin seeds, ground (see page 25)
Pinch of cayenne pepper
200ml (7fl oz) natural yoghurt

1 Mix everything together in a bowl, then combine with the meat.

Lemongrass marinade

....

TO GO WITH CHICKEN OR BEEF
4 lemongrass stalks (outer layer removed), finely chopped
Zest of ½ lemon
2 cloves of garlic, peeled and crushed or finely grated
2 shallots, peeled and finely chopped
1 red chilli, deseeded and finely chopped
2 tsp light soft brown sugar
3 tbsp fish sauce (nam pla)
3 tbsp lime juice

1 Mix everything together in a bowl, then combine with the meat.

Spiced barbecued lamb with potato salad and mint raita

SERVES 8-12

1 leg of lamb (2.2–2.5kg/
    5–5½lb), butterflied
    (ask you butcher to do this)
3 tbsp chopped coriander,
    to serve

For the marinade
2 tsp each of coriander
    and cumin seeds
1 tsp green cardamom seeds
2 tsp ground turmeric
1 red chilli, deseeded and
    finely chopped
2 tsp salt
4 tbsp olive oil
1 tbsp white wine vinegar
5 garlic cloves, peeled and
    grated or crushed
1 tbsp peeled (see page 27) and
    finely grated root ginger

To serve
450ml (16fl oz) cucumber,
    tomato and mint raita
    (see opposite)
1 quantity of Indian potato
    salad (see opposite)

A leg of lamb steeped in this wonderfully aromatic marinade is ideal for feeding lots of people, whether cooked on the barbecue or in the oven indoors. The meat can be marinated the day (or even two days) before cooking, making it a really entertaining-friendly dish. Serve with the Indian potato salad and the cucumber, tomato and mint raita (see opposite).

1 First make the marinade. Toast and crush the coriander, cumin and cardamom seeds following the tip on page 25. Mix together with all the other marinade ingredients, then massage into the lamb and place in a sealed plastic bag or a covered dish and leave to marinate in the fridge overnight or for at least 8 hours.

2 Take the lamb out of the bag or dish, reserving the marinade, and place on a hot barbecue, quite far from the coals. It should take about 50–65 minutes to cook, depending on how pink you like it, basted from time to time with the reserved marinade. Alternatively, you can cook the lamb in the oven, preheated to 200°C (400°F), Gas mark 6, where it will take about 1–1½ hours, again basted regularly.

3 Remove the lamb from the oven and allow the meat to rest for at least 15 minutes. Serve with the chopped coriander sprinkled on top, Indian potato salad and a bowl of raita on the side.

Indian potato salad with turmeric, chilli and ginger

SERVES 8–10
VEGETARIAN
2kg (4lb 4oz) new potatoes
Salt and ground black pepper
75ml (3fl oz) extra-virgin olive oil
2 tsp ground turmeric
3 cloves of garlic, peeled and
    crushed or finely grated
3 tsp peeled (see page 27) and
    finely grated root ginger
¼–½ red chilli, deseeded and chopped
Juice of ½ lemon
1 tbsp chopped coriander, to serve

1 Place the potatoes in a large saucepan of boiling, salted water and cook for 20 minutes or until tender. While the potatoes are boiling, pour the olive oil into a bowl and add the remaining ingredients. Stir to mix.

2 When the potatoes are cooked, drain, peel and chop into 2cm (¾in) pieces. While they are still hot, pour over the oil mixture and gently mix. Season to taste with salt and pepper, sprinkle with chopped coriander and serve at room temperature.

Cucumber, tomato and mint raita

MAKES 450ML (16FL OZ)
VEGETARIAN
250g (9oz) natural Greek yoghurt
1 small–medium or ½ large cucumber,
    peeled (optional), deseeded and finely diced
4 large ripe tomatoes, cut into 1cm (½in) dice,
    or 16 cherry tomatoes, halved or quartered
2 tbsp chopped coriander or mint
1 tsp cumin seeds, ground (see page 25)
Salt and ground black pepper

1 Mix all the ingredients together in a bowl, seasoning to taste with salt and pepper.

Honey, mustard and ginger pork skewers

....

MAKES 12 SKEWERS
SERVES 6-8

900g (2lb) lean pork, such
    as pork fillet, trimmed and
    cut into 2cm (¾in) cubes
6cm (2½in) piece of root
    ginger, peeled and cut into
    fine matchstick pieces
    (see page 27)

For the marinade
6cm (2½in) piece of root
    ginger, peeled and
    finely grated
3 cloves of garlic, peeled and
    crushed or finely grated
2 tbsp sunflower or
    vegetable oil
2 tbsp dark soy sauce
1 tbsp runny honey
1 tbsp Dijon mustard
1 tbsp cider vinegar
1 tsp salt
½ tsp ground black pepper

12 metal skewers, or 12
    wooden satay sticks
    (soaked in cold water
    for 30 minutes to prevent
    burning)

In this dish I've spiced up the timeless combination of honey, mustard and pork with a little ginger. The crispy ginger topping isn't essential, but it does add a lovely crunch. The ginger is first boiled to take away some of its heat.

1 First make the marinade by mixing all the ingredients together in a large bowl. Add the pork, mixing it with the marinade so that it is well coated, and place in the fridge for at least 1 hour or even overnight.

2 When you are ready to cook the pork, preheat the oven to 200°C (400°F), Gas mark 6, and make the crispy ginger topping.

3 Place a small saucepan of water on the hob and bring to the boil. Add the ginger pieces and boil for 1 minute, then drain, dry with kitchen paper and place in a single layer on a baking tray or roasting tin. Bake in the oven for 5–8 minutes (depending on how thick they are) until golden. Remove from the oven and allow to cool, then set aside.

4 Remove the pork from the fridge and thread onto the skewers or satay sticks.

5 Heat a griddle pan or frying pan on a medium–high heat until very hot, or allow the barbecue to heat up. Place the skewers on the pan or barbecue grill and cook for 3–4 minutes on each side or until cooked all the way through. Sprinkle each skewer with the crisp ginger topping and serve.

RACHEL ALLEN EATING OUTDOORS

Lamb and lentil salad with olives and roast red peppers

....

This is a fantastic way of using any leftover lamb. Anchovies and lamb might seem like a strange combination, but it's actually a classic. The anchovies don't make it fishy, they just add a fullness and depth to the flavour.

SERVES 8-10
2 red peppers
6 tbsp olive oil, plus 2 tsp for brushing the red peppers
800g (1¾lb) Puy lentils
200g (7oz) olives, pitted (see page 38) and roughly chopped
150g (5oz) cold roast lamb (see page 337), sliced
25g (1oz) anchovies from a tin, drained, rinsed and chopped
1 tsp Dijon mustard
2 tbsp finely chopped tarragon
Salt and ground black pepper
Squeeze of lemon juice

1 Preheat the oven to 220°C (425°F), Gas mark 7.

2 First roast the red peppers. Place in a small roasting tin and brush lightly with 1 teaspoon of olive oil, then cook in the oven for 40–45 minutes or until the skins are blackened and charred and the flesh is soft. Remove from the oven and place in a bowl covered with cling film to cool (this makes the skin easier to peel).

3 While the red peppers are roasting, rinse the lentils thoroughly and place in a saucepan. Add enough water to cover by a few centimetres, cover loosely and bring to the boil, then reduce the heat and simmer for 15–20 minutes or until soft. Drain and set aside to cool for 5–10 minutes.

4 Peel the red peppers, removing all the seeds, and cut the flesh into 2cm (¾in) pieces. Place the pepper pieces in a large bowl and add the lentils, 3 tablespoons of olive oil, pitted olives, lamb, anchovies, mustard and tarragon. Mix together well, seasoning to taste with salt, pepper and lemon juice. Serve slightly warm or at room temperature.

Broad bean and pancetta salad

1 tbsp olive oil
200g (7oz) pancetta or 5
    rashers of streaky bacon,
    cut into 1cm (½in) dice
400g (14oz) shelled fresh
    or frozen broad beans
1 tbsp chopped mint
125g (4½oz) soft goat's cheese

For the dressing
2 tbsp extra-virgin olive oil
1 tsp finely grated lemon zest
1 tbsp lemon juice
Salt and ground black pepper

A gorgeously summery salad, this is perfect for al fresco entertaining. If your broad beans are small – no bigger than your thumbnail – then it may not be necessary to peel off their skins after cooking. You can use a harder cheese, such as feta or pecorino instead of the soft goat's cheese if you prefer.

1 First make the dressing by mixing together all the ingredients and seasoning with salt and pepper.

2 Place a frying pan on a high heat, then once the pan is good and hot, pour in the olive oil, add the pancetta or bacon and fry until crispy and golden. Drain on kitchen paper and set aside.

3 Meanwhile, bring a large saucepan of water to the boil. Add the beans and boil for ½–1 minute or until they are just cooked, then drain. If the beans are quite big, peel them at this stage (they'll pop out of their skins easily); this isn't essential but I think it's well worth it as the skins can be tough.

4 Dress the beans while they are still warm, then leave to macerate for 15–20 minutes. Finally, add the cooked pancetta and the mint to the beans, crumble the cheese over the top and serve.

SALADS AND SIDE DISHES

RACHEL ALLEN

Fennel, orange and hazelnut salad

....

SERVES 6-8
VEGETARIAN
4 oranges
Juice of 1 lemon
2 fennel bulbs
110g (4oz) hazelnuts,
  toasted, peeled (see
  page 29) and chopped
2 tbsp chopped mint

I love this salad – it's fantastically fresh and crunchy, and great as a starter before serving something rich like duck or goose. It's also good served with barbecued meats.

1 Peel the oranges (see tip below) and cut across the width of each fruit to make slices about 5mm (¼in) thick. Squeeze out the juice from any flesh still left on the peel and pour it into a large bowl with the lemon juice, then discard the peel.

2 To prepare the fennel, slice off the tops and the fronds (save the feathery fennel bits for scattering over the salad when serving), then thinly slice lengthways using a sharp knife or a mandolin.

3 Finally, add the orange and fennel slices to the bowl with the lemon and orange juices, and mix together. Scatter with the hazelnuts and the chopped mint and serve on individual plates or a single serving dish. (This can be prepared in advance up to the point of scattering the hazelnuts and chopped mint over the top. Chop the mint closer to the time, however, otherwise it will turn black.)

RACHEL'S TIP
A good way of peeling an orange, especially the thinner-skinned varieties, is to first slice the top and the bottom off the fruit just below the pith and into the flesh (but trying not to cut into the flesh too much). Next stand the orange on a chopping board and, using a small sharp knife, slice off the peel in strips following the curvature of the orange.

Sue's aubergine, yoghurt and harissa salad

....

SERVES 6-8 PEOPLE
VEGETARIAN
3 aubergines
75ml (3fl oz) olive oil
4 tsp cumin seeds, ground
  (see page 25)
Salt
25ml (1fl oz) natural yoghurt
3–4 tsp harissa dressing
  (see page 90)
3 tbsp chopped coriander,
  plus 1 tbsp whole coriander
  leaves, to serve

One of the teachers at the Ballymaloe Cookery School, Sue Cullinane, makes this delicious Middle Eastern-inspired salad. It's warm and spicy, and the roasted aubergines give it a wonderful sweetness.

1 Preheat the oven to 230°C (450°F), Gas mark 8.

2 Cut the aubergines into 2cm (¾in) chunks, then place in a roasting tin. Add the olive oil and cumin and toss to coat. Place in the oven and roast for 10–12 minutes or until soft and golden, then season with salt and allow to cool.

3 Meanwhile, mix the yoghurt, harissa and chopped coriander. Drizzle the mixture over the cooked aubergines and scatter with the whole coriander leaves to serve.

Beetroot slaw

....

SERVES 6-8
VEGETARIAN
100g (3½oz) raw beetroot
100g (3½oz) carrot
100g (3½oz) green leafy
  cabbage, such as Savoy
50g (2oz) raisins
100g (3½oz) pecans, toasted
  (see page 25) and roughly
  chopped
2 tbsp walnut, hazelnut or olive
  oil (in order of preference)
1–2 tbsp lemon juice
Salt and ground black pepper

This is a colourful, crunchy salad that looks great in a big bowl. Watch out when grating the beetroot as it can stain quite easily, so wear rubber gloves (if you want to avoid having cerise-pink hands) and an apron.

1 Peel and grate the beetroot and carrot and quarter the cabbage lengthways. Remove the core and finely slice the leaves.

2 Mix all the ingredients together, seasoning to taste with the lemon juice and salt and pepper.

Garlic and herb mushrooms

....

SERVES 6-8
VEGETARIAN

6–8 large flat or portabello
   mushrooms (1 per person)
60–75g (2½–3oz) garlic and
   herb butter (see below)

Very simple to make and so delicious, these mushrooms are lovely cooked on the barbecue instead of in the oven, and are particularly good with lamb chops or steaks. You can easily make larger quantities of the garlic and herb butter and freeze it for up to two months. It's so handy to have in the freezer, to use for anything from a cooked juicy steak or lamb chops to a simple baked potato. You can then slice off pieces as you need them. Leave out the garlic, if you wish, or feel free to add other ingredients, such as chilli, mustard, olives or sun-dried tomatoes.

1 Preheat the oven to 230°C (450°F), Gas mark 8.

2 Wipe the mushrooms clean, then remove the stem from each mushroom, leaving a small well in the centre of the mushroom. Fill this with 1–2 teaspoons of the garlic and herb butter, then place on a baking tray and cook in the oven for 10–20 minutes or until the mushrooms are cooked through and browned. Alternatively, wrap the mushrooms in foil and cook on a hot barbecue for 20–35 minutes. Serve immediately.

Garlic and herb butter

SERVES 8-10
VEGETARIAN

100g (3½oz) butter, softened
2 tbsp finely chopped parsley
1 tbsp lemon juice (or to taste)
3 cloves of garlic, peeled and
   crushed
2 tbsp chopped herbs, such
   as tarragon, marjoram,
   chives, parsley, watercress,
   rocket or thyme, or a
   mixture of these

1 Beat the butter in a bowl until very soft then add the rest of the ingredients and mix thoroughly.

2 Serve like this or place on a piece of cling film or baking parchment and roll into a sausage shape about 3cm (1¼in) in diameter and store in the fridge or freezer.

Grilled asparagus

....

SERVES 6-8
VEGETARIAN
16 asparagus spears
Salt and ground black pepper
4–6 tbsp olive oil, plus extra
for frying (optional)

A light grilling gives gentle scorch marks to the asparagus and adds just a little smokiness to the flavour.

1 Rub the asparagus all over with olive oil and season with sea salt and pepper.

2 Place on a moderately hot barbecue – or griddle pan or frying pan brushed with oil and set on a medium–high heat – and cook for just about 7–10 minutes, turning regularly.

Barbecued corn on the cob

....

SERVES 6-8
VEGETARIAN
8 corn on the cob
Olive oil, for drizzling
Salt and ground black pepper

Using different flavoured butters is a great way of enlivening corn on the cob. Here are two ideas, but it's fun to experiment.

1 Drizzle the corn with a little olive oil, season with salt and pepper and place on a hot barbecue.

2 Cook for 10–15 minutes, turning every so often, until the kernels are slightly soft and charred in places.

3 Remove from the barbecue and serve by brushing with one of the flavoured butters (see below).

FLAVOURED BUTTERS

Cumin and fresh coriander butter: Mix together 200g (7oz) butter (softened) with 2 teaspoons of ground cumin seeds (for grinding, see tip on page 25) and 2 tablespoons of chopped coriander, seasoning to taste with salt and ground black pepper.

Lemon and marjoram butter: Mix together 200g (7oz) butter with 2 teaspoons each of lemon zest and juice and 2 tablespoons of chopped marjoram, seasoning to taste with salt and pepper.

Blueberry and custard tart

....

SERVES 6-8
VEGETARIAN
375g (13oz) fresh blueberries
2 tsp redcurrant jelly
   (see page 337)
2 tsp water, just boiled

For the sweet shortcrust pastry
175g (6oz) plain flour
100g (3½oz) chilled butter,
   cubed, plus extra for
   greasing
25g (1oz) caster sugar
1 egg, separated and the
   white lightly whisked

For the custard
200ml (7fl oz) milk
1 vanilla pod, split in half
   lengthways
25g (1oz) cornflour
50g (2oz) caster sugar
3 egg yolks
200ml (7fl oz) whipped cream

23cm (9in) diameter loose-
   bottomed shallow tart tin

This is a great dessert for summer entertaining. The pastry can be made a day in advance of filling and serving, and if you'd rather use raspberries, there's nothing to stop you.

1 Begin by making the pastry. Place the flour, butter and sugar in a food processor and whiz briefly until the butter is in small lumps. Add the egg yolk and continue to whiz for another few seconds or until the mixture looks as though it may just come together. (Bear in mind that prolonged processing will only toughen the pastry, so don't whiz it up to the point where it forms a ball of dough.) If the pastry is still too dry, you can add a small amount of the egg white, but not too much as the mixture should be just moist enough to come together. If making by hand, sift the flour and salt into a large bowl. Rub the butter into the flour until the mixture resembles coarse breadcrumbs. Add the sugar and gently mix in using a fork. Drizzle in the egg yolk and lightly stir it in with a knife until the mixture comes together, adding more egg yolk if necessary.

2 With your hands, flatten out the ball of dough until it is about 2cm (¾in) thick, then cover with cling film or greaseproof paper and chill for at least 30 minutes in the fridge.

3 When you are ready to roll out the pastry, butter the tart tin and remove the pastry from the fridge, placing it between two sheets of cling film (each wider than your tart tin). Using a rolling pin, roll out the pastry until it's about 3mm (⅛in) thick and wide enough to line the base and sides of the prepared tin. Make sure to keep it in a round shape as well as large enough to line both the base and sides of the tin.

4 Remove the top layer of cling film, slide your hand, palm upwards, under the bottom layer of cling film, then flip the pastry over (so that the cling film is now on top) and carefully lower it into the tart tin. Press into the edges (with the cling film still

attached) and, using your thumb, 'cut' the pastry on the edge of the tin to give a neat finish. Remove the cling film, prick over the base with a fork and chill the pastry in the fridge for a further 30 minutes or in the freezer for 10 minutes (it can keep for weeks like this in the freezer).

5 Meanwhile, preheat the oven to 180°C (350°F), Gas mark 4.

6 Remove the pastry from the fridge or freezer and line with foil, greaseproof paper or baking parchment, leaving plenty to come over the sides of the tin. Fill with baking beans or dried pulses (you can use these over and over again) and bake 'blind' for 15–20 minutes or until the pastry feels dry to the touch in the base. Remove the foil/paper and beans, brush with a little egg white and return to the oven for a further 5–8 minutes or until the pastry is lightly golden. Remove from the oven and allow to cool.

7 To make the custard, pour the milk into a saucepan on a low heat, add the vanilla pod, cornflour and half the sugar and gently heat for 1–2 minutes, stirring to combine.

8 In a bowl, beat the egg yolks with the remaining sugar until they turn creamy in consistency and pale in colour. Slowly pour in the hot milk mixture, whisking as you add it, then pour back into a clean saucepan. (It's best to use a fresh or cleaned pan to lessen the chance of the sauce sticking and scrambling.)

9 Whisk well and place over a low–medium heat, then cook for 2–4 minutes, stirring constantly with a wooden spoon, until the custard has thickened. Now remove the vanilla pod, scrape out some of the seeds and stir these back into the custard. Remove from the heat and allow to cool. Fold in the whipped cream.

10 To assemble the tart, spoon the cooled custard cream into the pastry case and top with the blueberries. Dissolve the redcurrant jelly in the just-boiled water. Using a pastry brush, gently coat the blueberries with this glaze, taking care not to move the blueberries or disturb the custard. This will give the tart a lovely finishing gloss.

11 To serve, remove the tart from the tin (with the base of the tin still attached, if that's easier) and carefully transfer it to a serving plate or cake stand.

Strawberries in rosé wine

SERVES 4
VEGETARIAN
275g (10oz) strawberries,
  hulled and quartered
  lengthways (or halved
  if they are small)
50g (2oz) caster sugar
4 tbsp rosé or white wine

4 wine glasses or bowls

This is a very simple recipe – a classic French way to dress up strawberries. Of course, this is at its best in summer when strawberries are locally grown and perfectly ripe. Serve the marinated strawberries in champagne flutes or delicate bowls, either on their own or with meringues and cream or shortbread biscuits (see page 58).

1 Place the strawberries in a bowl with the sugar, add the wine and stir gently to combine the ingredients.

2 Cover and place in the fridge for at least 2 hours, preferably overnight. If possible, give the bowl a little swirl once or twice during that time.

3 Serve chilled, divided between the wine glasses or bowls.

Strawberries and blueberries with Grand Marnier

SERVES 4
VEGETARIAN
225g (8oz) strawberries,
  hulled and sliced
75g (3oz) fresh or frozen
  and defrosted blueberries
Juice of 1 orange
4 tsp Grand Marnier or
  Cointreau
Crème fraîche, to serve

4 glasses or decorative bowls

This gorgeous summery dessert is so easy to put together.

1 In a large bowl, gently mix together all the ingredients.

2 Serve in the glasses or bowls with a dollop of crème fraîche.

Peaches with mascarpone, walnuts and honey

....

SERVES 10
VEGETARIAN
Butter, for greasing
10 peaches
6 tbsp mascarpone
6 tbsp runny honey, plus
    extra to serve
75g (3oz) shelled walnuts or
    pecans, toasted (see page 25)
    and chopped

Medium-sized gratin or
    ovenproof dish

Mascarpone is a mild, slightly sweet flavoured soft cheese from Italy. Essential to many Italian desserts, especially tiramisu, here it enriches sweet ripe peaches. This elegant dish is delicious served simply on its own, or with vanilla ice cream.

1 Preheat the oven to 200°C (400°F), Gas mark 6, and butter the gratin or ovenproof dish.

2 Cut a cross at the bottom of each peach and place them into a heatproof bowl. Pour over freshly boiled water to cover and leave for a minute or two. Carefully remove the peaches from the bowl and, using a sharp knife, peel off the skins. Halve and stone each peach, remove the stone and place, cut side up, in the gratin dish.

3 In a separate bowl, mix together the mascarpone and honey, then spoon this into the cavity of each peach, dividing the mixture equally between the peach halves. Cover the dish with foil and bake in the oven for 20–25 minutes or until the peaches are soft.

4 Serve the peaches with a good drizzle of honey and some toasted walnuts or pecans scattered on top.

MENU IDEAS FOR
EATING OUTDOORS

Tomato and lentil couscous salad (page 91)
Southeast Asian grilled fish with fennel, orange and hazelnut salad (pages 94 and 108)
Blueberry and custard tart (pages 114–15)

*

Harissa roasted vegetables (page 90)
Spiced barbecued lamb with potato salad and mint raita and
barbecued corn on the cob (pages 100 and 113)
Strawberries in rosé wine (page 117)

*

Middle Eastern chilled cucumber soup (page 88)
Honey, mustard and ginger pork skewers with
broad bean and pancetta salad (pages 102 and 107)
Peaches with mascarpone, walnuts and honey (page 118)

*

Pan-fried mackerel with panzanella salad with
beetroot slaw, grilled asparagus and
barbecued corn on the cob (pages 92, 110 and 113)
Strawberries and blueberries with Grand Marnier (page 117)

SAVOURY CANAPÉS

Moroccan tomato and yoghurt shots
Spicy pastry straws
Black pudding, blue cheese and beetroot toasts
Caramelised onion, blue cheese and walnut tarts
Gently spiced prawn and bacon skewers
Smoked salmon tartlets
Buckwheat blinis with smoked salmon, crème fraîche and caviar
Crab, chorizo and anchovy toasts
Potato soup with chorizo and parsley pesto
Thai chicken cakes with sweet chilli jam
Duck and Chinese five-spice spring rolls
Mini Yorkshire puddings with peppered steak and onion jam

COCKTAILS

Watermelon margaritas
Elderflower champagne
Negroski
Summer punch
Tropical fruit fizz
Apple, rum and ginger

SWEET CANAPÉS

Mendiants
Chocolate, pecan and meringue squares
Pistachio and cranberry chocolates
Crystallised ginger fudge
Mini coffee cupcakes

CANAPÉS AND SMALL BITES

Canapés and cocktails are a fun way to start a dinner party, especially for a special occasion. You can also have a canapés-only party, including dessert, rather than a sit-down meal. You and your guests can mingle and chat, which isn't always possible sitting at a table, and everyone loves the surprise of what comes out of the kitchen next! Ask a family member or friend to help serve, and remember to have enough large platters or trays so that as one goes around, you're getting the next one ready.

Moroccan tomato and yoghurt shots

....

250g (9oz) very ripe tomatoes
Juice of $\frac{1}{2}$ lemon
2 tsp finely chopped mint
2 cloves of garlic, peeled
   and crushed
Salt and freshly ground pepper
Good pinch of sugar
450ml (16fl oz) natural
   yoghurt

10-12 chilled shot glasses

This is best made in summer with really good red ripe tomatoes. Serve before a meal as a little amuse-bouche – which literally means 'mouth amuser', to get your taste buds tingling. They are pictured here with Spicy Pastry Straws (see page 124).

1 Roughly chop the tomatoes and place in a blender with the lemon juice, mint and garlic. Season with salt, pepper and sugar and blend for 2–3 minutes.

2 Push through a sieve, discarding the pulp, and whisk in the yoghurt. Serve in chilled shot glasses. Alternatively, layer the yoghurt and sieved tomatoes and mint in the shot glasses and serve with a swizzle stick.

Spicy pastry straws

MAKES ABOUT
40 PASTRY STRAWS
VEGETARIAN

Plain flour, for dusting
150g (3oz) ready-made
    puff pastry

Flavouring choices
1 tsp each of ground cumin
    and coriander and sea salt
50g (2oz) Parmesan or
    Parmesan-style cheese,
    finely grated and mixed
    with a pinch of cayenne
    pepper
1 x 25g tin of anchovies,
    drained, rinsed and finely
    chopped and mixed with
    2 tbsp sesame seeds
3 tbsp tapenade (see page 163),
    mixed with 25g (1oz) finely
    grated Parmesan or
    Parmesan-style cheese

These are an ideal finger food to serve with drinks (see the picture on page 123). You can use pre-rolled puff pastry to make them. If you have any leftover pastry scraps after making the Raspberry Millefeuille (see page 304), use them for this!

1 Preheat the oven to 220°C (425°F), Gas mark 7.

2 On a work surface lightly dusted with flour, roll the pastry into a rectangle about 20 x 40cm (8 x 16in) and about 3mm (⅛in) thick.

3 Sprinkle one half of the pastry sheet evenly with your chosen flavouring, then fold over the other half of the pastry to completely cover the scattered ingredients. Roll out the pastry again to the same dimensions as before (20 x 40cm/8 x 16in), so that the scattered ingredients become embedded in it. If it is quite warm and sticky by this stage, you may need to place it on a baking sheet (the metal will help to chill it quickly) and place in the fridge for about 15 minutes.

4 Using a pastry wheel or a knife, cut the pastry into strips about 1cm (½in) wide and 15cm (6in) long and give them a little twist if you like. Place on a baking sheet or two and cook in the oven for about 8 minutes or until golden brown and crisp. Take out of the oven and cool on a wire rack.

RACHEL'S TIP
These can be prepared in advance and frozen while raw. A good way to do this is to tray-freeze them first (i.e. freeze them on a baking sheets/trays). Once they have frozen solid, take them off the sheet or tray (if you need the space in the freezer), carefully transfer them to a plastic bag or box and put back in the freezer (they will keep like this for up to three months). When baked from frozen, they will take only an extra minute or two in the oven to cook.

Black pudding, blue cheese and beetroot toasts

....

MAKES 10 TOASTS

Olive oil, for drizzling
   and frying
10 slices of black pudding,
   7mm–1cm (3/8–1/2 in) thick
10 slices of baguette, 1cm
   (1/2 in) thick
10 slices of blue cheese, 5mm
   (1/4 in) thick
10 slices of pickled beetroot,
   5mm (1/4 in) thick

On a trip to San Sebastian in Spain, we ate a great many excellent pintxos (pronounced 'pinchos'), the local version of tapas, and this recipe was inspired by one of them. The flavours of the blue cheese and black pudding are balanced perfectly by the tangy pickled beetroot. Serve warm, or at room temperature, as little bites to enjoy with drinks, or as a starter.

1 Preheat the grill to hot and place a large frying pan on a medium heat and pour in a small drizzle of olive oil. Add the black pudding slices and cook on both sides for 4 minutes then drain on kitchen paper.

2 Toast the bread on both sides under the grill until golden, then drizzle each side with a little olive oil.

3 On each baguette toast, arrange first a piece of black pudding, then a piece of cheese and finally a slice of pickled beetroot. Serve immediately.

RACHEL'S TIP

If you're entertaining lots of people and need to get ahead, the toasts can be made earlier in the day and just slightly warmed through before serving.

Caramelised onion, blue cheese and walnut tarts

MAKES ABOUT
50 MINI TARTS
VEGETARIAN

4 large onions (about
    400g/14oz each)
6 tbsp olive oil
Salt and ground black pepper
Plain flour, for dusting
300g (11oz) all-butter
    puff pastry
4 tbsp roughly chopped
    walnuts, toasted
    (see page 25)
150g (5oz) blue cheese, cut
    into 1cm (½in) cubes

These are great to serve as canapés with drinks. You can also make them in advance and store them in the freezer. (For convenience tray-freeze them first – see page 124 – before transferring into a freezer bag.) If cooking from frozen, they'll take an extra minute or two in the oven.

1 Preheat the oven to 220°C (425°F), Gas mark 7.

2 Peel the onions, then cut in half lengthways through the root and thinly slice along the width, parallel to the root.

3 To caramelise them, pour the olive oil into a large frying pan on a low heat, add the sliced onions, season with salt and pepper and stir to combine. Cook, uncovered, for 40–50 minutes, stirring occasionally (you may need to scrape the bottom of the pan to remove the lovely sweet golden bits and mix them in with the rest), until the onions are golden, completely soft and sweet. Remove from the heat and set aside. (The onions can be kept in the fridge for up to a week.)

4 On a work surface lightly dusted with flour, roll out the pastry into a rectangle about 20 x 40cm (8 x 16in) in size and 3mm (⅛in) thick. Next cut the rectangle into fifty 4cm (1½in) squares.

5 Arrange the squares on the baking sheets, turn each one over (this helps them to really puff up), then add 1 teaspoon of the caramelised onions in the centre of each square, 2–3 pieces of chopped walnut and a cube of cheese. (The tarts can be frozen – and cooked from frozen – or refrigerated for up to 48 hours, at this point.)

6 Cook in the oven for 7–10 minutes or until golden, crispy and puffed up.

Gently spiced prawn and bacon skewers

....

MAKES 30

30 medium-sized prawns
   or langoustines
6 tbsp olive oil
1 tbsp chopped thyme leaves
1 tbsp chopped rosemary
   leaves
1 tsp paprika
1 tsp ground coriander
1 tsp coriander seeds, ground
   (see page 25)
4 large cloves of garlic, peeled
   and finely chopped
15 rashers of streaky bacon,
   cut in half
Lime slices, to serve

10 metal skewers, or 10
   wooden satay sticks, soaked
   in water for 30 minutes

Prawns and bacon make a delicious combination. Serve two or three on each skewer or satay stick and accompany with some slices of fresh lime.

1 Place the prawns in a freezer bag with the olive oil, herbs, spices and garlic and leave to marinate for about 2 hours.

2 Before cooking, wrap each prawn in half a piece of streaky bacon. Place three prawns on a skewer and cook under a hot grill or on the barbecue, or in a griddle pan on a medium–high heat, for 4–5 minutes on each side or until the bacon is crispy and the prawns are firm all the way through.

3 Serve immediately decorated with a slice of lime.

Smoked salmon tartlets

For the shortcrust pastry (if using)
125g (4½oz) plain flour,
    sifted
75g (3oz) chilled butter,
    cubed, plus extra for
    greasing
Pinch of salt
1 egg, beaten

For the filo pastry (if using)
3 sheets
50g (2oz) butter, melted,
    plus extra for greasing

For the filling
1 egg
125ml (4½fl oz) single or
    regular cream
2 tsp chopped herbs, such as
    chives, parsley, dill or fennel
100g (3½oz) smoked salmon,
    chopped into 5mm (¼in)
    pieces
Squeeze of lemon juice
Salt and ground black pepper

6cm (2½in) pastry cutter and
    a 24-hole mini-muffin tin

You can use either shortcrust or filo pastry for these tartlets. Shortcrust is a little more substantial, while filo is more delicate. These can be made about 24 hours in advance. If you like, you can replace the smoked salmon with smoked mackerel or pre-cooked chicken and/or bacon.

1 If making shortcrust pastry, place the flour, butter and salt in a food processor and whiz briefly until the butter is in small lumps. Add half the beaten egg and continue to whiz for just another few seconds or until the mixture looks as though it may come together when pressed. (Prolonged processing will only toughen the pastry, so don't whiz it up until it is a ball of dough.) You might need to add a little more egg, but not too much as the mixture should be just moist enough to come together. If making by hand, rub the butter into the flour and salt until it resembles coarse breadcrumbs, then add just enough egg to bring the mixture together.

2 With your hands, flatten out the ball of dough into a round about 2cm (¾in) thick, then wrap in cling film or place in a plastic bag and leave in the fridge for at least 30 minutes.

3 While the pastry is chilling, make the filling. Whisk together the egg, cream and herbs, stir in the smoked salmon and lemon juice and taste for seasoning.

4 Preheat the oven to 180°C (350°F), Gas mark 4, and butter the muffin tin.

5 Remove the pastry from the fridge and place between two large sheets of cling film. Using a rolling pin, roll the pastry out until it is very thin (about 3mm/⅛in thick), then remove the top layer of cling film and, using the pastry cutter, cut into 24 rounds. If using

filo pastry, cut the sheets into 72 x 6cm (2½ in) squares (three squares per tartlet).

6 If using shortcrust pastry, lightly push down the pastry rounds into the muffin moulds to form cups. If using filo pastry, take one square, brush with melted butter, then place in a muffin mould.

7 Repeat with another square and place in the same mould, perpendicular to the previous square. Repeat once more so there are there three layers of pastry in each mould. Then repeat for all 24 moulds.

8 Next add the filling. Pour 1–2 tablespoons into each mould, then place the tin in the oven for 15–20 minutes or until the filling has set and the pastry is golden and crisp.

VARIATION

These can also be lovely made without any pastry at all. Just grease the muffin tin with a little melted butter, add a tablespoon or two of the filling straight into each mould and bake for 15–20 minutes or until set. Remove and allow to slightly cool before serving.

Buckwheat blinis with smoked salmon, crème fraîche and caviar

....

MAKES ABOUT 40 BLINIS
VEGETARIAN

50g (2oz) buckwheat flour
100g (3 oz) strong white flour
 tsp salt
1 x 7g sachet fast-acting yeast
2 eggs, separated
150ml (5fl oz) milk, at room
  temperature
150ml (5fl oz) crème fraîche,
  at room temperature
25g (1oz) butter

For the topping
110g (4oz) smoked salmon,
  cut into small slices
200ml (7fl oz) crème fraîche
25g (1oz) caviar
Dill sprigs, to decorate

A traditional Russian treat, these lightly leavened pancakes use buckwheat flour, which has an earthy taste. Topped with caviar and/ or smoked salmon, they marry the luxurious with the rustic. These mini-blinis can be popped in the mouth with your fingers.

1 Sift the two flours and the salt together into a bowl and stir in the yeast.

2 In another bowl, whisk the egg yolks with the milk and crème fraîche, and pour over the flour mixture. Whisk everything together, then cover with cling film or a clean tea towel and leave in a warm place for about 1 hour or until the mixture is bubbling.

3 In a separate, spotlessly clean bowl, whisk the egg whites until they form stiff peaks, then gently fold into the batter. Cover again and leave for a further hour.

4 To fry the blinis, melt some of the butter in a large, non-stick frying pan on a medium heat, using a little kitchen paper to spread the butter around the pan – you need just enough to cover the base. When the pan is hot and the butter beginning to turn brown, add 1 teaspoon of batter per blini and cook for 30–40 seconds or until bubbles appear on top and the underside is golden, then turn oven and fry on the other side until golden.

5 As each blini is cooked, transfer to a wire rack to cool while you cook the remaining batter, adding more butter to the pan as you need it.

6 To serve, top each blini with a slice of salmon, 1 teaspoon of crème fraîche followed by 1 teaspoon of caviar and a piece of dill.

Crab, chorizo and anchovy toasts

....

MAKES 10 TOASTS

10 slices of baguette,
    1 cm (½ in) thick
Olive oil, for drizzling
150g (5oz) crab meat,
    shredded (for how to
    cook a crab, see page 36)
2 tsp mayonnaise (see
    page 317)
2 tsp peeled and finely
    grated onion
1 tsp Dijon mustard
Salt and ground black pepper
Small squeeze of lemon juice
    (optional)
20 slices of chorizo sausage,
    about 5mm (¼in) thick
A few lettuce leaves
10 tinned anchovies, drained
    and rinsed

All the components for these tasty little morsels can be prepared and cooked in advance, but you'll need to assemble them closer to the time you want to eat them – an hour or two beforehand. (Pictured with the Potato Soup with Chorizo and Parsley Pesto, see overleaf.)

1 Preheat the grill to hot and toast the baguette slices on both sides until golden. Drizzle each side with olive oil, and set aside.

2 In a bowl, mix together the crab meat, mayonnaise, grated onion and mustard. Taste for seasoning; it may need a small squeeze of lemon juice. Once made, this can sit in the fridge for up to 24 hours.

3 Place a large frying pan on a medium heat, then add a tiny drizzle of olive oil. Tip in the chorizo slices and fry on both sides for 2–3 minutes or until cooked, then drain on kitchen paper and allow to cool.

4 When you are ready to serve, assemble the toasts by first placing the baguette croutons on a large plate. Arrange a small piece of lettuce on each crouton, followed by two chorizo slices, a small dollop of the crab meat mixture and an anchovy carefully laid across the top to finish.

Potato soup with chorizo and parsley pesto

....

SERVES ABOUT 50
25g (1oz) butter
425g (15oz) potatoes,
    peeled and chopped
150g (5oz) onions, peeled
    and chopped
Salt and ground black pepper
750ml (1⅓ pints) chicken
    or vegetable stock
    (see pages 50–1)
250ml (9fl oz) milk, or
    half milk and half single
    or regular cream

To serve
250g (9oz) chorizo, cut into
    5mm (¼in) cubes
1 tbsp olive oil
100ml (3½fl oz) parsley pesto
    (see below)

This delicious soup an be made in advance and looks wonderful served with the parsley pesto and chorizo (see picture on page 134). Pour into espresso cups to serve as a canapé. Stored in a jar in the fridge, parsley pesto will keep as long as it's always re-covered with oil for a few months.

1 Melt the butter in a large saucepan on a medium heat. Add the potatoes and onions and seasoning, stir well and cover with a butter wrapper or greaseproof paper. Put the lid on the pan, turn down the heat and sweat for 10 minutes, stirring regularly.

2 Add the stock, cover again, bring to the boil then reduce the heat and simmer for 5–10 minutes until the vegetables are soft. Pour in the milk, bring back to the boil and liquidise in a blender (or use a hand-held blender). You may need to add more stock to thin it to a velvety and smooth consistency. Season to taste.

3 Fry the chorizo in the olive oil in a frying pan on a medium heat for 2–3 minutes. Remove from the pan when it is crisp and drain on kitchen paper, reserving the rich-coloured oil left in the pan.

4 To serve, pour the hot soup into espresso cups, drizzle with a little parsley pesto, then top with a few cubes of cooked chorizo and a drizzle of the chorizo oil from the pan.

Parsley pesto

MAKES 150ML (5FL OZ)
VEGETARIAN
25g (1oz) parsley, chopped
25g (1oz) Parmesan or
    Parmesan-style cheese,
    grated
25g (1oz) pine nuts
2 cloves of garlic, peeled
    and crushed
75ml (3fl oz) extra-virgin
    olive oil, plus extra
Good pinch of salt

1 Place all the ingredients except the olive oil in a food processor and whiz together. Add the oil and a good pinch of salt and taste for seasoning.

2 Pour into a screw-top jar (for sterilising jars, see page 42), cover with 1cm (½in) of oil and store in the fridge.

RACHEL'S TIP
I pour this soup into a jug and top up guests as they like.

Thai chicken cakes with sweet chilli jam

....

MAKES 20

Sunflower oil, for greasing
1 lemongrass stalk
500g (1lb 2oz) minced chicken
2 tsp peeled (see page 27) and finely chopped or grated root ginger
4 spring onions, trimmed and finely sliced
1 clove of garlic, peeled and crushed
1 tbsp roughly chopped coriander
½ red chilli, deseeded and finely chopped
75g (3oz) fresh white breadcrumbs
1 egg
2 tbsp fish sauce (nam pla)
Salt and ground black pepper
100ml (3½fl oz) sweet chilli jam (see below), to serve

Nowadays, foods that would once have been considered exotic, tasted only on far away trips to Asia, are easily available and routinely cooked at home. The sweet chilli jam is a perfect accompaniment to the Thai flavours in the chicken cakes. You can make it in advance and it will keep for a few months.

1 Preheat the oven to 200°C (400°F), Gas mark 6, and oil a baking tray with sunflower oil.

2 Prepare the lemongrass by peeling off the outer later and finely chopping the inside of the stalk. Place all the ingredients in a bowl, season with salt and pepper and mix to combine.

3 Wet your hands then shape the mixture into 20 balls each about 2cm (¾in) in diameter. Transfer these to the prepared baking tray and lightly flatten to form small patties.

4 Place in the oven and cook for 10–12 minutes or until lightly browned and cooked through. Remove from the oven and serve with the sweet chilli jam.

MAKES 1 X 400G (14OZ) JAR
VEGETARIAN

25g (1oz) root ginger, peeled (see page 27) and roughly chopped
3 cloves of garlic, peeled
2 red chillies, deseeded
2 tbsp fish sauce (nam pla)
375g (13oz) tomatoes or cherry tomatoes, peeled (see page 74) and chopped
200g (7oz) caster sugar
75ml (3fl oz) sherry vinegar or white wine vinegar

Sweet chilli jam

1 Put the ginger, garlic, chillies and fish sauce into a blender (or use a hand-held blender) and whiz to a purée. Place the purée in a saucepan with the tomatoes, sugar and vinegar and bring to the boil. Reduce the heat and simmer, stirring regularly, for 8–10 minutes or until thick and jam-like in consistency.

2 Place in a sterilised jar (for sterilising jars, see page 42), cover with a lid and allow to cool, or pour straight into a bowl to cool, if serving with the Thai Chicken Cakes (see above).

Duck and Chinese five-spice spring rolls

....

Vegetable oil, for stir-frying and deep-frying

1 tbsp peeled (see page 27) and finely grated root ginger

3 garlic cloves, peeled and finely chopped

100g (3½oz) mushrooms, chopped

150g (5oz) cooked duck, finely shredded

½–1 tsp Chinese five-spice powder

1 tbsp sesame oil

100g (3½oz) green cabbage, such as Savoy, quartered lengthways, core removed and leaves finely chopped

100g (3½oz) carrots, cut into matchsticks

2 tbsp light soy sauce

2 tbsp hoisin sauce

4 spring onions, trimmed and finely sliced

100g (3½oz) cornflour

8 square spring roll wrappers

Spring rolls are the perfect food for entertaining. With each one carefully hand-folded it's like giving guests their own little parcels of delight. Chinese five-spice is widely used in Chinese cuisine, it is most commonly a mixture of star anise, cloves, cinnamon, Sichuan pepper and fennel.

1 Place a large frying pan or wok on a high heat. When it is hot, pour in 2 tablespoons of vegetable oil, then add the ginger and garlic and cook on a high heat for 1 minute. Add the mushrooms, duck, five-spice powder and sesame oil and cook, tossing regularly, for 5 minutes.

2 Add the cabbage and carrots and the soy and hoisin sauces and continue to cook for 1–2 minutes or until the cabbage has just wilted. Next remove the wok or pan from the heat and mix in the spring onions. Taste for seasoning, adding more soy sauce, if necessary, then set aside.

3 To fill the spring rolls, first make the cornflour paste by mixing together the cornflour and 10mlg (3½fl oz) of water. Cut a spring roll wrapper into quarters, making sure to cover the remaining wrappers in a clean damp tea towel while you work so that they don't dry out.

4 Using a pastry brush, paint the wrapper all over with the cornflour paste, then place 1–2 teaspoons of the mixture in a sausage shape near the foot of the wrapper, 2.5cm (1in) in from the edges and base of the sheet. Carefully roll the wrapper with your hands, then fold in the edges, roll again and seal to form a sausage shape. Repeat with the remaining spring roll wrappers.

5 Heat the vegetable oil in a deep-fat fryer to 180°C (350°F).

Alternatively, pour the oil into a large saucepan to a depth of 2cm (¾in) and bring to the same temperature on the hob (checking with a sugar thermometer, or see tip below).

6 Deep-fry only 2–3 spring rolls at a time as you don't want to overcrowd the fryer and adding too many spring rolls at once will reduce the temperature of the oil. Cook for 3–5 minutes or until golden and crispy. Drain on kitchen paper and serve while hot.

RACHEL'S TIP

An easy way of checking if cooking oil is hot enough for deep-frying is to drop in a cube of bread. If it comes back up to the top relatively quickly, the oil is the perfect temperature. If it immediately burns, the oil is too hot.

Mini Yorkshire puddings with peppered steak and onion jam

....

1 sirloin steak (200g/7oz)

Olive oil, for drizzling

1 tsp black peppercorns,
coarsely crushed using
a pestle and mortar
or rolling pin

Sea salt

4–5 tbsp onion jam
(see opposite)

24 small rocket leaves,
to decorate

For the Yorkshire puddings

75g (3oz) strong white
flour, sifted

1 egg

1 egg yolk

150ml (5fl oz) milk

½ tsp salt

Vegetable oil, for oiling

24-hole mini-muffin tin

I love the idea of shrinking a main course into a canapé; here, as bite-sized Sunday roasts! I use strong white flour for Yorkshire puddings because the high gluten content means they really rise in the oven and keep their structure. These Yorkshires should form nice cups for the onion jam and beef to sit in, but if they're fully risen and fluffed on top, you can just poke a little hole in the top.

1 Place all the ingredients for the Yorkshire puddings into a bowl, along with 150ml (5fl oz) water, and whisk together just until it firms a smooth batter. Pour into a jug and set aside.

2 Preheat the oven to 200°C (400°F), Gas mark 6. Add 1 teaspoon of the vegetable oil into each hole of the muffin tin.

3 Meanwhile, place a griddle pan or cast-iron frying pan on a high heat. Put the steak on a plate, drizzle with olive oil then sprinkle the black pepper and some sea salt generously over both sides. Place the steak in the dry pan once it's smoking hot and cook for 2–4 minutes on each side, depending on how well done you like it. Once the steak is cooked, remove from the pan, cover it with foil and allow to rest, somewhere warm, for at least 15 minutes.

4 Place the oiled muffin tin in the oven for about 5 minutes until the oil is just smoking. Remove from the oven and quickly fill each hole about two-thirds full with the Yorkshire pudding batter, then immediately return to the oven and cook for about 20 minutes or until they are risen and golden.

5 While the Yorkshire puddings are cooking, cut the steak into 24 slices, 5mm (¼in) thick, making sure to remove any excess fat.

6 As soon as the puddings are cooked, take them out of the oven and transfer them onto a large serving plate.

7 To serve, add a generous half teaspoon of onion jam and a slice of steak to each and decorate with a small rocket leaf.

50g (2oz) butter

700g (1½lb) red onions,
    peeled and finely sliced

150g (5oz) caster sugar

1 tsp salt

2 tsp ground black pepper

100ml (3½fl oz) sherry
    vinegar or balsamic vinegar

250ml (9fl oz) full-bodied
    red wine

2 tbsp crème de cassis
    (blackcurrant liqueur)

Onion jam

1 Melt the butter in a saucepan on a medium high heat, holding your nerve until it becomes a deep nut-brown colour – this will give the onions a delicious rich flavour but be careful not to let it burn. Add the onions, sugar, salt and pepper and stir well. Cover with a lid, reduce the heat to low and cook for 30 minutes, keeping an eye on the onions and stirring from time to time, until the onions are completely soft and caramelised.

2 Next add the vinegar, red wine and the cassis and cook, uncovered, for another 30 minutes, still on a low heat and stirring every now and then. Pour into a serving bowl to use immediately or place in storage jars (for sterilising jars, see page 42).

Cocktails

....

If you're having a canapé party, you probably want to serve at least one cocktail.
Here are some of my favourites.

Watermelon margaritas
....

SERVES 4-6
VEGETARIAN
450g (1lb) peeled and deseeded watermelon
Juice of 4-5 limes
100ml (3½fl oz) tequila
50ml (2fl oz) Cointreau or Triple Sec
2-3 tbsp caster sugar
Handful of ice cubes
Salt, to serve

4-6 cocktail glasses

1 Place all the ingredients, including the ice,
in a blender or food processor and whiz for
about 1 minute.

2 To serve, scatter a little salt onto a plate,
dip the rim of each chilled glass into the
margarita mixture (to a depth of about 5mm/
¼in), then dip in the salt to form a salted rim.
Divide the drink between the glasses.

Elderflower champagne
....

MAKES 5 LITRES (8¾ PINTS) OR
ALMOST 7 X 750ML WINE BOTTLES
VEGETARIAN
1 large lemon
4 large elderflower heads
500g (1lb 2oz) caster sugar
25ml (1fl oz) white wine vinegar

1 Wash the lemon and remove the peel using
a peeler, then cut in half and squeeze out the
juice, discarding the peeled halves.

2 Rinse the elderflower heads and check for
insects, then place in a very large bowl or
saucepan (in either case just over 5 litres/
8¾ pints in capacity) with the lemon peel and
juice, sugar, vinegar and 5 litres (8¾ pints)
of cold water. Stir to combine, then cover with
cling film or a lid and leave in a cool place for
24 hours, stirring every now and again.

3 Pour the cordial through a sieve and
into sterilised screw-top wine bottles
(for sterilising bottles, see page 42). Secure
the tops and store somewhere quite cool,
but not the fridge. The 'champagne' is ready
after two weeks but will keep for up to two
years. Serve chilled.

Negroski

SERVES 4
VEGETARIAN
110ml (4fl oz) vodka
110ml (4fl oz) sweet red Martini
50ml (2fl oz) Campari
8 ice cubes
Peel of 1 orange, cut using a peeler, to serve

4 cocktail glasses

1 Mix the vodka, Martini and Campari together, pour into a cocktail shaker, add the ice cubes and shake, then strain into the glasses.

2 Decorate each with a twist of orange peel.

Summer punch

SERVE 4-6
VEGETARIAN
300ml (½ pint) lemonade
300ml (½ pint) apple juice
110ml (4fl oz) rum
110ml (4fl oz) Triple Sec or Cointreau
500ml (18fl oz) brandy
A few mint leaves, to serve

4-6 highball glasses

1 Pour all the ingredients into a jug and stir to mix. Serve chilled over ice with a few mint leaves.

Tropical fruit fizz

SERVES 4-6
VEGETARIAN
400ml (14fl oz) lemonade

For the fruit purée
1 mango, peeled and stone removed
600g (1lb 5oz) peeled and deseeded watermelon
200ml (7fl oz) pineapple juice
200g (7oz) fresh or frozen and defrosted strawberries
2 tbsp lemon juice
2 tbsp caster sugar

4-6 highball glasses

1 Place all the ingredients for the fruit purée in a blender or food processor and whiz together for 1-2 minutes. Mix with the lemonade and serve chilled over ice.

Apple, rum and ginger

SERVES 4
VEGETARIAN
600ml (1 pint) apple juice
110ml (4fl oz) rum
1 tbsp peeled (see page 27) and finely grated root ginger

4 highball glasses

1 Simply mix everything together, pour into the glasses and serve chilled over ice.

Mendiants

....

MAKES ABOUT 20
CHOCOLATE DISCS
VEGETARIAN
100g (3½oz) dark, milk
or white chocolate,
broken into pieces

Mendiants are a traditional French treat and make a perfect dessert canapé or to serve with coffee at the end of a meal. They are unbelievably fast and easy to make, yet they look so elegant. The French use different nuts and dried fruits to represent the four mendicant or monastic orders of the Dominicans (raisins), Augustinians (hazelnuts), Franciscans (dried figs) and Carmelites (almonds). You can use these or any of the toppings I've suggested below. The salt flakes in particular create a fascinating taste sensation. These can be made a few days in advance; make sure to store them somewhere cool, but preferably not the fridge as they will 'sweat'.

1 Place the chocolate in a heatproof bowl set over a saucepan of water. Heat the water until it just begins to boil, then remove from the heat and allow the chocolate to melt slowly in the bowl, stirring from time to time.

2 Line a baking tray with baking parchment. Carefully drop a teaspoonful of liquid chocolate on one corner of the paper – it will spread out slightly to form a small disc. Repeat with the rest of the chocolate, then carefully, while the chocolate is still liquid, add any of a variety of toppings (see below). Place somewhere cool to set, then carefully lift them off the paper and serve.

TOPPINGS
Dried fruit such as cranberries, raisins, sultanas or candied peel
Chopped crystallised ginger
Nuts such as shelled whole (or chopped) almonds, hazelnuts,
    pistachios, walnuts or pecans
Pinch of dried chilli flakes
Pinch of ground cinnamon or ginger
Sea salt flakes
A little edible gold leaf!

Chocolate, pecan and meringue squares

....

MAKES 30–36 SQUARES
VEGETARIAN

25g (1oz) raisins
½ tbsp brandy or rum
175g (6oz) dark chocolate,
    broken into pieces
50g (2oz) butter, cubed
½ tbsp golden syrup
25g (1oz) shelled pecans,
    toasted (see page 25)
    and roughly chopped
2 leftover meringue halves,
    broken into small pieces
    (about 150ml/5fl oz in
    volume)

13 x 23cm (5 x 9in) loaf tin

These are delicious served as a sweet canapé. They also make a beautiful gift – just pop into a decorative bag and tie up with some pretty ribbon.

1 Line the loaf tin with baking parchment, allowing the paper to come over the sides of the tin.

2 Place the raisins in a small bowl and pour over the brandy or rum. Stir to coat the raisins and then put to one side.

3 Place a heatproof bowl over a saucepan of barely simmering water on a low–medium heat, then add the chocolate, butter and golden syrup. Gently heat, stirring occasionally, for 4–5 minutes or until they have melted.

4 Remove from the heat and add the raisins, with the brandy or rum, together with the pecans and broken meringue pieces. Mix well, then pour the mixture into the lined tin and gently press down. Chill in the fridge for 2–3 hours or overnight until hardened.

5 Carefully lift the hardened chocolate mixture and paper out of the tin and cut, using a sharp knife, into small squares. Store in an airtight plastic container in the fridge until needed. They will keep for a week or two if you can resist them!

Pistachio and cranberry chocolates

MAKES ABOUT
40 CHOCOLATES
VEGETARIAN

200g (7oz) white chocolate, broken into pieces
75g (3oz) shelled pistachios
50g (2oz) dried cranberries
50g (2oz) milk or dark chocolate, chopped or roughly broken into small pieces

13 x 23cm (5 x 9in) loaf tin

These little chocolates are a real cinch to make and so lovely to serve as a canapé or with coffee as petits fours at the end of a meal, or to give as gifts.

1 Place the white chocolate pieces into a heatproof bowl set over a saucepan of water. Heat the water until it just begins to boil, then remove from the heat and allow the chocolate to melt slowly, stirring it from time to time.

2 While the chocolate is melting, line the loaf tin with one piece of baking parchment, allowing the paper to come over the sides of the tin.

3 When the chocolate has melted, stir in the pistachios and cranberries. Pour into the lined loaf tin and allow to cool.

4 As the white chocolate cools, melt the milk or dark chocolate in the same way in a separate bowl. When the white chocolate has almost set (but not completely, or the top layer of chocolate will not adhere to the white chocolate layer), but is still slightly shiny in places, pour the milk or dark chocolate over the top to make a second layer.

5 Allow to cool completely, then cut into about 40 squares and store in the fridge.

Crystallised ginger fudge

MAKES 64 SQUARES
VEGETARIAN

1 tbsp vegetable oil, for oiling
1 x 375ml tin of sweetened
   condensed milk
100g (3½oz) butter
450g (1lb) soft light brown
   or caster sugar
4 tbsp finely chopped
   crystallised ginger

18 x 18cm (7 x 7in) square cake
tin with 2.5cm (1in) sides

I love these sweet, gingery little mouthfuls. They can be made a couple of weeks in advance and stored in an airtight box. They also make a lovely gift. Your guests will be impressed, as fudge is much easier to make than they (or you) might imagine!

1 Oil the cake tin with a little of the oil, line with baking parchment and oil again.

2 Place the condensed milk, butter and sugar in a saucepan on a medium heat, stir together as the butter melts, and bring to the boil, stirring frequently to prevent the sugar from sticking and burning on the bottom of the pan.

3 Reduce the heat to low and simmer for about 15 minutes, stirring all the time, until a sugar thermometer dipped into the mixture reads 113°C (235°F). Alternatively, drop a ½ teaspoon of the fudge into a bowl of cold water and test it with your fingers. It should be malleable to the touch: too soft and the fudge will not set; too hard and the fudge is overcooked. The fudge should also have darkened in colour to a rich golden brown.

4 Remove from the heat and stir in the crystallised ginger, then sit the bottom of the saucepan in a large bowl of cold water that comes 2–3cm (¾–1¼in) up the outside of the pan. Stir vigorously until the fudge cools down – it will go from smooth, shiny and toffeeish in appearance, to thick, grainy and matt-looking.

5 Scrape the contents of the saucepan into the oiled cake tin – the fudge should be about 1–1.5cm (¾– ⅝in) thick. Allow to cool, then cut into squares.

Mini coffee cupcakes

....

75g (3oz) butter, softened
75g (3oz) caster sugar
2 eggs
2 tsp coffee essence or espresso
    or very strong coffee
125g (4½oz) plain flour
1 tsp baking powder
Chocolate covered espresso
    beans, to serve (optional)

For the icing
200g (7oz) icing sugar, sifted
2 tbsp coffee essence or very
    strong coffee

24-hole mini-muffin tin

I adore this twist on after-dinner coffee. The coffee essence (called Camp in England and Irel in Ireland) is very useful because it provides coffee flavour without adding too much liquid to your cake mixture. If you can't get hold of it, you can always substitute very strong coffee for the essence.

1 Preheat the oven to 180°C (350°F), Gas mark 4 and line the muffin tin with paper cases.

2 Cream the butter in a large bowl or in an electric food mixer until soft. Add the sugar and beat until the mixture is light and fluffy. Whisk in the eggs, one at a time, followed by the coffee essence, then sift over the flour and baking powder and fold in.

3 Divide between the paper cases in the muffin tin and bake in the oven for 8–10 minutes or until risen and springy to the touch.

4 While the cupcakes are baking, make the icing. Place the icing sugar and the coffee essence in a bowl, mix together and add a little water (about ½–1 tbsp) and mix until smooth, adding more water if necessary, it should be spreadable.

5 Remove the cupcakes from the oven and allow to cool on a wire rack, then top each with a generous teaspoonful of icing or pipe a swirl of icing. Serve with a chocolate covered espresso bean placed on top, if you wish.

MENU IDEAS FOR CANAPÉS AND SMALL BITES

*

Moroccan tomato and yoghurt shots (page 122)
Gently spiced prawn and bacon skewers (page 129)
Crab, chorizo and anchovy toasts (page 135)
Duck and Chinese five-spice spring rolls (pages 138–9)
Chocolate, pecan and meringue squares (page 148)

*

Potato soup with chorizo and parsley pesto (page 136)
Caramelised onion, blue cheese and walnut tarts (page 129)
Mini Yorkshire puddings with peppered steak and onion jam (pages 140–1)
Pistachio and cranberry chocolates (page 149)

*

Spicy pastry straws (page 124)
Buckwheat blinis with smoked salmon, crème fraîche and caviar (page 132)
Thai chicken cakes with sweet chilli jam (page 137)
Mendiants (page 146)
Mini coffee cupcakes (page 152)

STARTERS

Scallops with Brussels sprouts, bacon and orange
Asparagus on toast with hollandaise sauce
Warm winter green salad with Caesar dressing, smoked bacon and a poached egg
Tomato, mozzarella and tapenade crostini
Gratins of butternut squash and leek
Halloumi with Greek salad and roasted pitta wedges

MAIN COURSES

Summer pea and mint ravioli
Pan-fried tuna with olive, sun-dried tomato and caper salsa
Poached monkfish with tomato, sherry vinegar and toasted hazelnut salsa
Pan-grilled chicken breasts with basil cream sauce and roast cherry tomatoes
Rack of lamb
Chicken confit
Garlic and herb pork chops
Steak au poivre
Pheasant casserole with chorizo, cream and thyme
Roast duck breasts

SIDE DISHES

Watercress mousse
White bean purée
Pea guacamole
Potato and anchovy gratin
Cucumber with mint
Buttered courgettes
Fluffy mashed potato
Creamy lentils with rosemary and tomatoes
Creamy polenta
Sauteed rosemary potatoes

DESSERTS

Chocolate crèmes brulées
Iles flottantes
Coffee zabaglione with tuiles biscuits
Orange sorbet with Campari

SMALL CELEBRATIONS

(2 – 4 P E O P L E)

There are occasions when you want to put a little extra effort into a special meal, whether for a romantic dinner for two or a quiet celebration with your closest friends. This is your chance to show off a little. The recipes here aren't difficult, but a few just take a little more time or have special ingredients, so be sure to give yourself enough time when planning. You don't have to serve three courses, but for an important occasion you may want to have a little more fun and go for it.

Scallops with Brussels sprouts, bacon and orange

....

SERVES 2

3 rashers of streaky bacon
(100g/3½oz), cut into 2cm
(¾in) dice

100g (3½oz) Brussels sprouts,
outer leaves discarded,
sliced about 5mm (¼in)
thick

Sea salt and ground black
pepper

4 prepared scallops, including
the corals

15g (½oz) butter

1 large orange, peeled,
segmented and juice
reserved (see tip on
page 108)

2 tsp sherry vinegar or lemon
juice

These sprouts are decidedly different. Fried rather than boiled, they retain a crisp crunch and marry beautifully with the salty bacon and rich scallops, while the orange provides sweet citrus notes. If you can, try to use scallops that haven't been frozen, otherwise they may leak too much water and end up poached rather than fried.

1 Place a frying pan on a medium–high heat, add the bacon and cook for about 5 minutes, tossing regularly, until golden and very crispy. Drain on kitchen paper then transfer to a plate and keep warm in a low oven, reserving the fat in the pan.

2 Place the pan back on a medium–high heat and allow to get hot, then add the sprouts, season with salt and pepper and cook, tossing frequently, for about 3 minutes or until the sprouts have coloured and slightly softened. You may need to add 1 tablespoon of water if the sprouts dry out too much. Transfer to a bowl and keep warm in the oven with the bacon.

3 Season the scallops, including the corals, with a little salt and pepper. Place a non-stick frying pan on a medium–high heat (add a small knob of butter if using a pan) and put the scallops directly into it in a single layer. Cook on one side for 1–2 minutes or until light golden, before turning over to cook the other side for the same length of time.

4 In a large bowl, mix together the warm sprouts with the bacon, orange segments and sherry vinegar or lemon juice. Taste for seasoning and divide between plates. Add the scallops and serve.

RACHEL'S TIP

To open the scallops (this can be done earlier in the day and the scallops stored, covered, in the fridge), place each scallop on a board with the flat shell pointing up. Insert the point of a knife between the shells and slice across the underside of the top shell to cut through the internal muscle, then pull the shells apart. Pull off the outer membrane with your fingers, remove the coral, keeping it intact. Dry the scallops and corals on kitchen paper.

Asparagus on toast with hollandaise sauce

....

SERVES 4
VEGETARIAN
16–20 asparagus spears
Good pinch of salt and
    ground pepper
4 slices of bread
Butter for spreading
Hollandaise sauce (see below)

With the welcome arrival of spring comes the first of the new season's asparagus, and my very favourite way to enjoy it is on buttered toast with lashings of hollandaise sauce.

1 Snap off the tough woody part at the bottom of each asparagus stalk and discard. Fill a large saucepan to a depth of 4–6cm (1½ – 2½in) with water, add the salt and bring to the boil. Tip in the asparagus and cook in the boiling water for 4–8 minutes or until tender when pierced with a sharp knife. Drain immediately.

2 While the asparagus is cooking, toast the bread, then spread with the butter and remove the crusts, if you wish. For each person, place a piece of toast on a warmed plate, put 4–5 asparagus spears on top and spoon over a little hollandaise sauce.

Hollandaise sauce

MAKES 75ML (3FL OZ)
VEGETARIAN
1 egg yolk
50g (2oz) butter, diced
Squeeze of lemon juice
Salt and ground black pepper

1 Place a heatproof bowl over a saucepan of simmering water on a medium heat. (The water must not boil. If it does it may heat the sauce so much that it will scramble or curdle – so take the pan off the heat every so often.) Add the egg yolk and 1 tablespoon of cold water and whisk together. Gradually add the butter, a few bits at a time, until each addition has melted and emulsified as it is whisked in, before adding the next.

2 Once all the butter has been incorporated, cook for a couple of minutes more, stirring constantly, until the sauce has thickened enough to coat the back of a spoon. Season to taste with lemon juice and salt and pepper. Remove from the heat, and keep warm if necessary, by covering with cling film and leaving to sit over the warm water, until you're ready to serve.

Warm winter green salad with Caesar dressing, smoked bacon and a poached egg

....

RACHEL ALLEN · SMALL CELEBRATIONS

SERVES 4

4 high-quality eggs
1 tbsp sunflower oil, for frying
8 rashers of smoked streaky
   bacon, cut into 1cm
   (½in) dice
4 handfuls of mixed lettuce
   leaves, including rocket and
   winter greens such as kale,
   spinach, mustard greens
   or small beetroot leaves

For the dressing
175ml (6fl oz) sunflower
   or vegetable oil
50ml (2fl oz) extra-virgin
   olive oil
1 x 50g tin of anchovies,
   drained and rinsed
2 egg yolks
1 clove of garlic, peeled
   and crushed
2 tbsp lemon juice
1 tsp Dijon mustard
Pinch of salt
1 tbsp Worcestershire sauce
1 tsp Tabasco sauce

To serve
50g (2oz) Parmesan cheese,
   grated
1 tbsp chopped chives

This recipe is a gorgeous twist on a classic Caesar salad. The dressing makes more than you will need but it keeps in the fridge for a week, if covered.

1 First make the dressing, which you can do either in a food processor or by hand. Pour both oils into a jug. If making the dressing by hand, mash the anchovies with a fork then place in a bowl with the remaining ingredients and whisk together. As you are whisking, add the mixed oils very slowly and gradually. It will become creamy as the emulsion forms. When all the oil has been incorporated, whisk in 50ml (2fl oz) water to make it the consistency of double cream, then add extra seasoning to taste.

2 Alternatively, place all the ingredients, except the mixed oils, in a food processor and whiz together, then gradually add the oil and the water as above, pouring them in through the feed tube of the machine.

3 To poach the eggs, first place a saucepan of water on a high heat to come to the boil. Meanwhile, pour the oil into a frying pan on a high heat, add the bacon and fry for 3–5 minutes or until golden brown and crispy. Drain on kitchen paper and set aside.

4 While the bacon is frying, tear the mixture of lettuce and winter greens into large bite-sized pieces and place a handful on each plate. Drizzle with 1–2 tablespoons of the dressing and sprinkle with the crispy bacon pieces.

5 Once the egg-poaching water has come to the boil, turn the heat down to low. Crack each egg into the lightly simmering water and poach for 3–4 minutes or until the white is set and the yolk still a little soft. Turn the heat off under the saucepan and carefully lift each egg out one by one, allowing all water to drain from the egg.

6 Arrange one egg in the centre of each salad, sprinkle with grated Parmesan and the chopped chives and serve immediately.

Tomato, mozzarella and tapenade crostini

SERVES 2-4
12 slices of baguette
100ml (3½fl oz) tapenade
   (see below)
4 large ripe tomatoes, cut
   widthways into 6 slices
4 tbsp extra-virgin olive oil
Juice of ½ lemon
Salt and ground black pepper
Pinch of sugar
Handful of chopped basil,
   plus leaves to decorate
2 x 125g balls of mozzarella
   cheese, each cut into 6 slices

The Italian flavours here are a timeless combination and the presentation is sure to impress. Get hold of buffalo mozzarella if you can as it is made only from buffalo milk, which is richer than cow's milk. The flavour is more delicate and the texture much softer. This is best made in the summer with perfectly ripe and sweet tomatoes.

1 Toast the baguette slices, spread 1 teaspoon of tapenade on each slice and arrange three pieces on each individual plate.

2 On a large flat plate spread the sliced tomato out in a single layer, drizzle with 3 tablespoons of the olive oil and the lemon juice, then season with salt, pepper and sugar. Add the basil and toss together gently.

3 Mix together the remaining olive oil with 1 tablespoon of the tapenade, then build three 'towers' on each plate. Add a slice of tomato to each piece of toast, followed by a slice of mozzarella and another slice of tomato. Finish with a small drizzle of the tapenade oil, either on top of the crostini or around the plate, and decorate with the basil leaves.

MAKES 150ML (5FL OZ)
100g (3½oz) pitted black
   olives (for pitting olives,
   see tip on page 38)
1 x 25g tin of anchovies,
   drained and rinsed
1 tbsp capers, drained
   and rinsed
1 tsp Dijon mustard
1 tsp lemon juice
4 tbsp extra-virgin olive oil
Ground black pepper
   (optional)
Salt (optional)

Tapenade

1 Place all ingredients apart from the olive oil into a food processor. Whiz for a minute or two to form a rough paste, then, with the machine still running, pour in the olive oil.

2 Taste for seasoning: you may need pepper but probably won't need salt.

Gratins of butternut squash and leek

SERVES 4
VEGETARIAN

75g (3oz) hazelnuts, toasted and peeled (see page 29)

75g (3oz) fresh white breadcrumbs

75g (3oz) Parmesan or Parmesan-style cheese, finely grated

25g (1oz) butter, melted

Salt and ground black pepper

600g (1lb 5oz) butternut squash, peeled and cut into 1cm ($\frac{1}{2}$in) cubes

4 tbsp olive oil

400g (14oz) leeks, trimmed and finely sliced

25g (1oz) butter

4 cloves of garlic, peeled and finely chopped

25g (1oz) kale or spinach (any large stalks removed before weighing), broken into bite-sized pieces or roughly chopped

100ml ($3\frac{1}{2}$fl oz) dry white wine

$\frac{1}{2}$ tsp Dijon mustard

2 sprigs of thyme

75ml (3fl oz) double or regular cream

For the sauce

50ml (2fl oz) vegetable stock (see page 50)

(ingredients continued overleaf)

This dish is a variation of a dish I've eaten at Denis Cotter's restaurant Café Paradiso in Cork. It is a perfect example of Denis' cooking; vegetarian food that is so flavourful and luxurious that even the most ardent carnivore will want to indulge. Stainless steel rings are certainly worth using for presenting this dish. The end result is an elegantly layered and colourful presentation. However, you can just use individual ovenproof bowls – it will taste just the same.

1 Preheat the oven to 220°C (425°F), Gas mark 7.

2 Roughly crush the toasted hazelnuts with a rolling pin, then combine in a bowl with the breadcrumbs, Parmesan cheese and butter, and season to taste with salt and pepper.

3 Next roast the squash. In a bowl, mix together the squash and olive oil, and season with salt and pepper. Place in a roasting tin in a single layer and cook in the oven for 20–25 minutes or until the squash is soft and slightly golden.

4 While the squash is roasting, cook the leeks. Melt the butter in a frying pan on a medium–high heat, add the leeks and garlic, season with salt and pepper, and cook, stirring frequently, for 2–3 minutes or until the leeks have softened.

5 Stir in the kale or spinach, followed by the wine, mustard and thyme, and cook for a further 2 minutes. Add the cream and let it bubble for another 2 minutes or until the kale is wilted, then transfer to a bowl.

6 Turn the oven down to 180°C (350°F), Gas mark 4.

7 To assemble the gratins, place the metal rings on a baking tray lined with baking parchment, or use four ovenproof bowls also

(continued overleaf)

50ml (2fl oz) dry white wine
150ml (5fl oz) double or
    regular cream
75g (3oz) Parmesan or
    Parmesan-style cheese,
    finely grated

4 stainless-steel rings (such as
    10cm/4in cookie cutters) or
    individual ovenproof bowls

placed on a baking tray. Divide the leek and kale mixture between the rings or bowls and then top with the squash, leaving a gap of about 5mm (¼in) from the top. Add a layer of the hazelnut mixture to fill the rings or bowls. Place in the oven and cook for about 20 minutes or until the top is brown and crispy and the mixture is hot inside.

9 While the gratins are baking, make the sauce. Pour the stock and wine into a small–medium saucepan and set on a high heat. Boil for 2–3 minutes or until the liquid has reduced significantly. Add the cream and boil for a further 2–3 minutes or until it has thickened again, then remove from the heat and stir in the Parmesan, seasoning to taste with salt and pepper.

10 To serve, use a fish slice or spatula to carefully place on plates, then remove the rings (if using). Pour the sauce around each gratin and serve immediately. Otherwise serve in the bowls (if using), with the sauce in a jug.

VARIATION
You can always mix together the leek and kale with the butternut squash before putting them into the metal rings.

Halloumi with Greek salad and roasted pitta wedges

SERVES 4
VEGETARIAN
1 x 250g (9oz) halloumi
  cheese, cut into 4 pieces
2 pitta breads, cut into wedges
Olive oil, for drizzling
Sea salt

For the marinade
1 red or green chilli, deseeded
  and finely chopped
25ml (1fl oz) extra-virgin
  olive oil
1 clove of garlic, peeled and
  finely chopped
1 tsp finely chopped oregano
  or marjoram
Salt and ground black pepper

For the Greek salad
100g (3½oz) baby spinach
  leaves
50g (2oz) cherry tomatoes,
  halved
½ cucumber, peeled,
  deseeded and sliced
50g (2oz) black olives, such
  as kalamata, pitted
  (see page 38)
1 tbsp extra-virgin olive oil
Salt and ground black pepper

Halloumi is a Cypriot cheese with a high melting point, which means you can cook it and get a nice golden crust long before it melts. This marinade adds flavour and interest to the salty cheese. Some people call halloumi 'squeaky cheese' – try eating it and you'll see why!

1 In a bowl, mix together all the ingredients for the marinade. Add the halloumi, mix with the marinade and leave to marinate for 1 hour.

2 Meanwhile, preheat the oven to 220°C (425°F), Gas mark 7.

3 Place the pitta bread wedges in a separate bowl, toss together with enough olive oil to coat and season with sea salt. Spread out flat on a baking tray and cook in the oven for about 5 minutes or until pale golden (keep an eye on them as they cook as they burn quickly).

4 While the pittas are roasting, mix together all the ingredients for the Greek salad, seasoning to taste with salt and pepper.

5 Place a griddle pan or frying pan (cast iron if possible) on a high heat and allow to get very hot. Add the halloumi and fry on each side for just 30 seconds until golden. Divide between individual plates, adding some of the Greek salad and a few roasted pitta wedges to each plate.

Summer pea and mint ravioli

MAKES ABOUT 50 RAVIOLI
SERVES 3-4
VEGETARIAN

For the ravioli
250g (9oz) Italian Tipo '00'
    flour or strong white flour,
    plus extra for dusting
Salt and ground black pepper
2–3 eggs
250g (9oz) frozen peas
    (preferably petits pois)
2 tbsp olive oil
3 tbsp chopped mint
Squeeze of lemon juice

For the Alfredo sauce
25g (1oz) butter
200ml (7fl oz) double
    or regular cream
50g (2oz) Parmesan or
    Parmesan-style cheese,
    grated
Salt and ground black pepper

To serve
15g (½oz) butter
50g (2oz) frozen peas
    (petits pois)
Small handful of mint leaves
    or pea shoots, if available

I think this dish should only be made on a beautiful day with the sun cascading into the kitchen. Unless they are very fresh, frozen peas will have more flavour so they are perfectly fine to use here. Peas are the essence of the season and each ravioli is a tiny pillow of summer. The joy of making fresh pasta is that you can fill ravioli or tortellini with a freshly made filling of your choice. Pasta machines are inexpensive and make the process much, much easier, though you can use just a rolling pin.

1 To make the pasta for the ravioli, first sift the flour and salt together into a bowl. Whisk the eggs together in a separate bowl, then make a well in the centre of the flour and add half the beaten eggs. Mix into a dough using your hands, adding the remainder of the egg only if you need it. The pasta should just come together, but shouldn't stick to your hands; if it does, add a little more flour.

2 Knead in the bowl for a few minutes until smooth, then cover with cling film and set aside to rest for 30 minutes–1 hour to relax. (It will keep for about two days in the fridge.) The dough can also be made in an electric food mixer or food processor, again being careful not to add too much egg.

3 Next make the pea purée for filling the ravioli. Bring a saucepan of water to the boil and add 1 teaspoon of salt. Tip in the peas and boil for about 2 minutes or until just cooked (don't overcook them!), then drain. Place in a food processor with the remaining ingredients (or use a hand-held blender) and whiz for a couple of minutes or until smooth, then season to taste. Set aside to cool.

4 To make up the ravioli, divide the dough into quarters and, using a pasta machine, roll out each piece at a time, starting with the widest setting and ending with the narrowest by which time

(continued on page 170)

you should be able to read the headline print on a newspaper through the pasta. You may need a light dusting of flour if your pasta is slightly wet. You can also use a rolling pin, though it is more labour intensive. As you finish rolling each piece, make sure you cover it with a tea towel as the pasta will quickly dry out.

5 Lay two sheets of pasta on a floured work surface and, with a sharp knife, lightly mark each into a grid (5 squares across and 5 squares down) of 5cm (2in) squares, but don't cut through the dough yet. Place ½ teaspoon of the pea purée in the middle of each square, then use a pastry brush to wet the spaces in between the heaps of purée with a littler water. Lay the second sheet of pasta over the top and use your fingers to press the pasta together around the purée and seal. Be careful to press only in between the mounds of purée and try to ensure each ravioli doesn't contain too much air.

6 Using either a pastry wheel (I like to use a fluted one), a pizza cutter or a sharp knife, cut the ravioli into 25 x 5cm (2in) squares so that each ravioli contains a mound of pea purée. Dust 2 baking trays with flour and place the ravioli on the tray in a single layer. (They can be refrigerated for a few hours or frozen at this point.) Repeat steps 4 and 5 with the remaining two pasta sheets.

7 To make the Alfredo sauce, place the butter and cream in a saucepan on a medium–low heat, and bring to a simmer. Cook for about 5 minutes until the sauce has slightly thickened, then remove from the heat and mix in the grated Parmesan cheese. Season to taste and set aside.

8 In a frying pan on a medium heat, melt the 15g (½oz) butter, then add the 50g (2oz) peas and cook for about 2 minutes, tossing occasionally. Set aside somewhere warm until ready to serve.

9 To cook the pasta, bring a large saucepan of water to the boil and add 2 teaspoons of salt. Add the ravioli and cook for about 2 minutes or until the pasta is just al dente. Drain then place on kitchen paper briefly to get rid of any excess water and divide between warmed bowls. Pour over the Alfredo sauce, then scatter over a few peas and some mint leaves, and serve immediately.

Pan-fried tuna with olive, sun-dried tomato and caper salsa

....

SERVES 4

4 x 150–175g (5–6oz) tuna
  fillets
2 tbsp olive oil
Salt and ground black pepper

For the salsa
100g (3½oz) pitted black
  olives (see page 38)
150g (5oz) pitted green olives
4 tbsp chopped sun-dried
  tomatoes
1 tbsp capers
2 cloves of garlic, peeled and
  crushed or finely grated
8 basil leaves, torn
100ml (3½fl oz) extra-virgin
  olive oil

The colour contrast of this tuna looks beautiful on the plate. The outside is cooked and full of flavour while the inside remains pink, moist and succulent. Served at room temperature, pan-fried tuna goes to perfection with the Salade Niçoise (see page 38). The salsa also complements everything from steak to mackerel.

1 First make the salsa. Place all the ingredients apart from the oil in a food processor and whiz for a few seconds, leaving it still slightly chunky.

2 Pour in the olive oil and whiz for a few seconds until combined. This will keep, covered, in the fridge for a couple of weeks. Let it come back up to room temperature before serving.

3 To cook the tuna, place a large frying pan or griddle pan on a high heat and allow it to get very hot. Brush each side of the tuna fillets with the olive oil and season with salt and pepper.

4 Place on the pan and cook for 2–3 minutes on each side – the centre should still be pink.

5 Remove from the heat and allow the tuna to sit for a few minutes before serving with the salsa.

Poached monkfish with tomato, sherry vinegar and toasted hazelnut salsa

....

SERVES 2-4

450g (1lb) monkfish tails, filleted and trimmed of skin and membrane
1 tsp salt

For the toasted hazelnut salsa
3 large ripe tomatoes, or 20 cherry tomatoes, cut into 1cm (½ in) pieces
2 tbsp peeled and finely chopped red onion
3 tbsp extra-virgin olive oil
2 tbsp chopped coriander or parsley
1 tbsp sherry vinegar or balsamic vinegar
50g (2oz) hazelnuts, peeled, toasted (see page 29) and chopped
Sea salt and ground black pepper

Poached monkfish is quite easy to cook when entertaining as it just needs a few minutes in boiling, salted water, and can be prepared in advance. The salsa is lovely with the monkfish; it's fresh, light and very gently warms through from the hot fish. If you are making the salsa in advance, don't put it in the fridge but keep it at room temperature.

1 Cut the monkfish into 1cm (½ in) slices and refrigerate in a covered bowl until needed.

2 To make the salsa, mix the tomatoes, onion, olive oil, coriander or parsley, vinegar and half the hazelnuts in a bowl, then season to taste with salt and pepper. (The salsa can be made up to about 1 hour in advance.)

2 Bring 1.2 litres (2 pints) of water to the boil in a large saucepan and add the salt. Add the monkfish and simmer very gently for 4–5 minutes or until completely white and no longer translucent.

3 Drain well and place on kitchen paper to dry. Arrange on warmed plates and drizzle over some of the salsa, then scatter with the remaining hazelnuts and serve immediately.

RACHEL'S TIP

If you want to keep the monkfish warm for a short while before serving (up to 10 minutes), remove the fish but don't drain the boiling water from the saucepan. Turn the lid upside down over the pan (off the heat), place a double layer of kitchen paper on the flat, upturned lid and sit the cooked monkfish on top.

Pan-grilled chicken breasts with basil cream sauce and roast cherry tomatoes

....

SERVES 2
2 skinless chicken breasts
1 tbsp olive oil

For the roast cherry tomatoes
About 10 small or cherry
   tomatoes (5 per person)
Olive oil, for drizzling
Sea salt and ground
   black pepper

For the basil cream sauce
175ml (6fl oz) double
   or regular cream
150g (5oz) butter, cut into
   1cm (½in) cubes
Squeeze of lemon juice
2 tbsp sliced or torn basil

The deliciously creamy sauce in this recipe transforms a simple supper of grilled chicken breasts into a luxurious treat. I like to serve this with some supremely fluffy mashed potato (see page 191) to soak up all of the sauce. For the roast tomatoes, try to get hold of cherry tomatoes or small tomatoes that are still attached to the stalk. These look good and the stalk can be cut with scissors into portions before cooking. If the tomatoes are off the stalk, you can cook them whole or cut in half.

1 Preheat the oven to 200°C (400°F), Gas mark 6. Place the tomatoes on a baking tray (if they are cut in half, place them cut side up), drizzle with olive oil and season with salt and pepper. Cook in the oven for about 10 minutes or until the skin is a little blistered and the flesh soft on the inside. Take out of the oven and keep warm until serving – they will sit happily for up to half an hour in the oven with the heat turned off to keep warm before serving.

2 Place a cast-iron griddle pan or a frying pan on a high heat and allow it to get quite hot – it should be just smoking. Rub the chicken breasts with the olive oil, and season with salt and pepper. Place the chicken in the pan serving side down (the side that is cooked first always looks the nicest) and cook for 3–4 minutes or until the one side is a deep golden or has good scorch marks (if using the griddle pan).

3 Turn the chicken over and reduce the heat, continuing to cook for 5–10 minutes or until the chicken is cooked through (it should be opaque in the middle). The chicken can also be browned on one side, then turned over and finished in the oven, preheated to 200°C (400°F), Gas mark 6, for about the same amount of time. This is especially useful if you are making more than 2–3 servings.

4 Meanwhile, make the sauce. Pour the cream into a small saucepan, bring just to boiling point, then reduce the heat and

(continued overleaf)

simmer until it has reduced to about 4 tablespoons and is very thick. Remove from the heat and allow to cool for 30 seconds–1 minute (if the cream is too hot when you add the butter, the mixture will curdle), then whisk in the butter bit by bit. When all the butter has been incorporated, season to taste with salt (if necessary), pepper and lemon juice, and stir in the basil.

5 To serve, place the chicken breasts, whole or sliced, on warmed plates, spoon some sauce over the top or around the edge and place a portion of cherry tomatoes on the side.

RACHEL'S TIP

If the sauce is kept warm, it will keep for a couple of hours. Place in a heatproof ceramic bowl or jug (a metal bowl might get too hot) immersed in a saucepan of hot water. Heat up the water every so often to prevent the sauce from becoming cold, but make sure the water isn't boiling as if it's too hot the sauce will curdle.

Rack of lamb

SERVES 2-4
1 rack of lamb
Salt and ground black pepper

A rack of lamb is so easy and is perfect for serving two to four people, depending on the size of the chops and how many there are of them on the rack. It goes very well with the Watercress Mousse and Potato and Anchovy Gratin (see pages 185 and 188) as lamb tastes gorgeous with anchovies.

1 Preheat the oven to 220°C (425°F), Gas mark 7.

2 Remove the papery skin if it is still attached, then score the fat in a criss-cross pattern with lines 1–2cm (½–¾in) apart, trying not to cut into the meat. Sprinkle with salt and pepper, then place in a roasting tin and cook in the oven for 25–35 minutes, depending on the weight of the lamb and how pink you like it to be.

3 Leave in the oven, covered in foil, with the heat turned off, then cut between the chops and give each person 2–3 each.

Chicken confit

....

SERVES 2

2 chicken legs (including
   the thighs)
1 tbsp thyme leaves
2 bay leaves, broken in half
1 tbsp salt
½ tsp ground black pepper
6 cloves of garlic
8 black peppercorns
500ml (18fl oz) duck or goose
   fat (or olive oil), to cover

*It is usually duck legs that are cooked in this way, but all fowl taste
pretty good cooked in half a litre of duck fat! It adds wonderful moisture
and a rich texture to pheasant, guinea fowl or even pigeon. I usually
double or even treble the quantities (but keeping roughly the same
amount of fat, which just needs to cover the meat in the saucepan)
as it makes no difference to the amount of work involved and it keeps
in the fridge, covered in the fat, for up to a year.*

1 Place the chicken legs in a bowl and sprinkle over the thyme,
1 of the bay leaves, salt and pepper, rubbing the herbs and
seasoning into the meat. Cover and place in the fridge overnight.

2 When you are ready to cook the chicken, preheat the oven
to 110°C (225°F), Gas mark ¼.

3 Remove the chicken legs from the fridge. Discard any liquid from
the bowl and rinse the meat to wash off the salt and pepper. Pat
very dry with kitchen paper, then place in a saucepan large enough
to fit both chicken legs snugly. Add the garlic, peppercorns and
remaining bay leaf to the pan, then pour over enough duck fat to
cover the chicken. (If there is not enough duck fat to cover them,
add a little olive oil to make sure they're covered.)

4 Place in the oven and cook for about 7 hours or until the chicken
is completely tender and easily comes away from the bone.
Remove from the oven and allow to cool.

5 To serve, first remove the chicken from the fat. Place a frying
pan on a medium–high heat, then drop in about 1 tablespoon of
the fat and cook the chicken on each side for 4–5 minutes or until
the skin is crisp and golden in colour and the meat heated right
through. Serve hot with the Creamy Lentils with Rosemary and
Tomatoes and the Crunchy Coriander Roast Potatoes (see pages
192 and 297), or at room temperature, broken into large bite-sized
pieces on a salad, such as the Winter Leaf Salad (see page 273).

RACHEL'S TIP
Once you've used the chicken, reserve the fat as it can be reused,
either for this recipe again or for roasting potatoes.

RACHEL ALLEN   MAIN COURSES

Garlic and herb pork chops

4 large pork loin chops or
   12 small cutlets

For the marinade
50ml (2fl oz) olive oil
Juice of 1 lemon
1 tbsp chopped sage
1 tbsp chopped rosemary
   leaves
25ml (1fl oz) balsamic vinegar
4 cloves of garlic, peeled and
   crushed or finely grated

Sage has such a distinctive flavour that pairs very well with pork. If you can, marinate the chops for at least a couple of hours, as it gives the flavours and oils enough time to penetrate deep into the meat. Try serving with the Creamy Lentils with Rosemary and Tomatoes on page 192.

1 Combine all the marinade ingredients in a large bowl and add the pork chops, turning them in the marinade so that they are coated in the mixture. Cover the bowl with cling film or place in a sealed plastic bag, then refrigerate overnight or for at least 2 hours.

2 Preheat the oven to 220°C (425°F), Gas mark 7.

3 When you're ready to cook, remove the chops from the marinade. Place a cast-iron griddle pan or ovenproof frying pan on a high heat and when it begins to smoke, add the chops. Cook for 2–3 minutes on each side to brown the meat, then roast in the oven for 7–9 minutes or until the pork is cooked through. Remove from the oven and allow to rest for a few minutes before serving.

Steak au poivre

SERVES 4

2 tbsp whole black
   peppercorns
1 tsp sea salt
4 sirloin, rump or fillet steaks
   (150–200g/5–7oz each)
2 tbsp olive oil
50ml (2fl oz) brandy
150ml (5fl oz) beef stock
125ml (4½fl oz) double
   or regular cream
½ tsp Dijon mustard

One of my favourite ways to serve steak is this traditional French bistro method. Pepper, a seasoning that often hides in the background barely noticed, is thrust onto centre stage. Where normally we grind peppercorns into a fine powder, here they are left in larger chunks so you notice the flavour and texture as well as the heat.

1 Use a pestle and mortar to coarsely crush the peppercorns, leaving quite large chunks of pepper. Alternatively, place the peppercorns in a plastic bag and use a rolling pin to coarsely crush them. Tip into a sieve with a bowl underneath and shake out the powdered pepper. You can use the finer pepper grounds for seasoning something else but they would make the steaks too hot if combined with the larger pieces of pepper.

2 Place a frying pan (cast-iron if possible) on a high heat, allowing it to get very hot. While the pan is heating, mix the larger pieces of pepper with the salt, spread this out on a plate and dip each steak into it so that the meat is completely coated in salt and pepper.

3 The pan should be very hot by now, so pour in the olive oil. Add the steaks (cook them in batches if necessary) and cook for 2–4 minutes on each side, depending how rare or well done you like them. Then remove to warmed plates and allow to rest.

4 While the steaks are resting, make the sauce. With the pan still on a high heat, pour in the brandy (taking care as you pour it in as it may flame), boil for 30 seconds, then add the stock, cream and mustard. Whisk to combine and boil for 2–3 minutes or until it thickens slightly. Taste the sauce for seasoning then spoon over the steaks and serve immediately with mashed potato to soak up the sauce.

Pheasant casserole with chorizo, cream and thyme

....

1 tbsp olive oil

350g (12oz) chorizo, cut into slices 8mm (³⁄₈in) thick

275g (10oz) onions, peeled and cut into wedges, or baby onions, peeled and cut in half

1 pheasant, cut into portions, still on the bone

Salt and ground black pepper

4 sprigs of thyme, plus 1 tsp chopped thyme leaves

150ml (5fl oz) chicken stock

125ml (4½fl oz) double or regular cream

4 tsp roux (made with 2 tsp butter and 2 tsp flour – see page 76) (optional)

Medium-sized casserole dish or ovenproof saucepan with a lid

Luxurious comfort food for a cold day, this casserole is intensely flavoured, with a lovely warm kick from the chorizo sausage. Serve over Creamy Polenta (see page 193).

1 Preheat the oven to 150°C (300°F), Gas mark 2.

2 Place a casserole dish or ovenproof saucepan on a medium heat, pour in the olive oil, then add the chorizo and onions and cook for 3–5 minutes or until the oils from the chorizo have drained into the dish and the onions are slightly golden Remove the chorizo and onions and set aside, leaving the oils in the pot.

3 Add the pheasant pieces to the casserole dish or saucepan and fry for about 5 minutes or until golden on both sides, being careful not to burn the pot, then season with salt and pepper. Drain any excess oils from the dish or pan, then add the cooked chorizo and onions, along with the thyme sprigs and the stock.

4 Bring to simmering point on top of the stove, then place in the oven and cook for about 45 minutes or until the meat is tender. The cooking time will depend on how long the pheasant pieces were sautéed.

5 When the casserole is cooked, scoop out the pheasant, onions and chorizo and thyme sprigs. Strain off the cooking liquid and return the meat, onions and thyme sprigs to the pot. Degrease the cooking liquid (see tip on page 226) and pour into a separate saucepan, then add the cream, bring to the boil and boil, uncovered, for about 4 minutes or until the sauce has slightly thickened (if you would like a thicker sauce, you can whisk in a little roux). Add the chopped thyme and taste for seasoning, then pour back over the meat, onions and thyme sprigs in the casserole. Serve bubbling hot.

Roast duck breasts

SERVES 2
2 duck breasts
Salt and ground black pepper

Duck breasts make a glorious meal, their pink juicy flesh topped by a layer of undeniably appealing crispy skin. Take care to ensure the skin is crisp and inviting rather than thick and flabby. The low heat at the start of cooking brings out the excess fat, then the higher temperature of the oven gives that crispiness. These are delicious served with redcurrant jelly, White Bean Purée (see pages 337 and 186) and crispy roast potatoes made using the fat rendered from the duck breasts during cooking.

1 Preheat the oven to 220°C (425°F), Gas mark 7.

2 Score the duck breasts by making cuts, about 1cm (½in) apart, in the fat along the width of the breast, trying not to cut into the meat. Season with salt and pepper, briefly massaging the seasoning into the fat.

3 Place an ovenproof frying pan or griddle pan on a low heat, and immediately add the duck breasts, fat side down. When cooked like this all the excess fat will drain out of the scored skin, leaving you with deliciously crisp skin and only the bare minimum of fat underneath. Cook for 10–20 minutes or until the fat is golden underneath, then turn over, transfer to the oven and cook for 6–8 minutes. It should still be pink inside.

4 Remove from the oven and allow to rest for at least 10 minutes before serving. Serve whole or cut into slices.

Watercress mousse

SERVES 3
VEGETARIAN

25g (1oz) butter, plus extra
  for greasing
125g (4½oz) watercress
  (large stalks removed),
  chopped
1 egg
1 egg yolk
50ml (2fl oz) double or
  regular cream
Small pinch of grated nutmeg
Salt and ground black pepper

Six 5cm (2in) diameter,
  100ml (3½fl oz) ramekins
  or a six-hole muffin tin

These individual mousses are particularly good as a side dish served with lamb, but also work well with chicken or turkey. Remove any large tough stalks from the watercress before cooking.

1 Preheat the oven to 200°C (400°F), Gas mark 6, and butter the ramekins or muffin tin.

2 Melt the butter in a large saucepan on a medium heat, then add the watercress and cook for 2–4 minutes or until the leaves are wilted. Meanwhile, whisk together the eggs and egg yolk in a bowl and set aside.

3 Add the cream to the watercress, then purée in a food processor (or use a hand-held blender), for 2–3 minutes until smooth. When the purée has cooled right down, whisk in the beaten eggs, add the nutmeg and season to taste with salt and pepper.

4 Divide the mixture between the ramekins or muffin tin and place in a bain-marie – a roasting tin filled with enough water to come about halfway up the ramekins or muffin tin. Place in the oven and bake for about 20 minutes or until just set. When you gently press the centre of each mousse, it should be lightly springy to the touch. Serve 2 per person.

VARIATION
Spinach/kale mousse: Replace the watercress with the same quantity of spinach or kale.

White bean purée

....

This rich garlicky purée, scented with rosemary, is wonderful served with Roast Duck Breasts (see page 184).

SERVES 2-4
VEGETARIAN
1 x 400g tin of haricot or
  cannellini beans, drained
  and rinsed, or 125g (4½oz)
  dried beans, soaked and
  cooked (see page 64)
2 tbsp olive oil
1 clove of garlic, peeled and
  crushed or finely grated
2 tsp chopped rosemary leaves
50–75ml (2–3fl oz) vegetable
  stock (see page 50)
Salt and ground black pepper

1 Pour the beans into a saucepan, add the remaining ingredients and season to taste with salt and pepper. Place on a low–medium heat and simmer for 8–10 minutes.

2 Take the pan off the heat and either roughly mash the beans with a potato masher, or place in a food processor and whiz to form a smooth purée. Serve while still warm.

Pea guacamole

....

Not strictly a guacamole, this is a pea purée packed with flavour. It is delicious with the Pan-fried Tuna with Olive, Sun-dried Tomato and Caper Salsa on page 171.

SERVES 4 AS A SIDE DISH
VEGETARIAN
450g (1lb) shelled fresh
  or frozen peas
Salt
2 tbsp extra-virgin olive oil
2 tbsp lime juice
2 tbsp finely chopped
  coriander
½–1 red chilli, deseeded
  and finely chopped
½ tsp cumin seeds, ground
  (see page 25)
½ tsp coriander seeds,
  ground

1 Cook the peas in boiling, salted water for 3–4 minutes for fresh peas, 2–3 minutes for frozen. Refresh under cold water and drain.

2 Place in a food processor with the remaining ingredients and a good pinch of salt (or use a hand-held blender) and whiz for 1–2 minutes or until almost smooth. Taste, adjusting the seasoning if necessary, then put into a bowl, cover and refrigerate until needed. Bring back up to room temperature before serving, if not using immediately.

Potato and anchovy gratin

SERVES 4
Butter, for greasing
1kg (2lb 3oz) potatoes,
    peeled and cut into
    5mm (¼in) slices
3 x 50g tins of anchovies,
    drained and rinsed
Salt and ground black pepper
5 cloves of garlic, peeled and
    finely chopped
400ml (14fl oz) single or
    regular cream
100g (3½oz) Parmesan
    cheese, grated
100g (3½oz) Gruyère
    cheese, grated

18 x 26cm (7 x 10½in)
    gratin or similar-sized
    ovenproof dish

This side-dish is based on the famous Swedish dish 'Jansson's Temptation', though Jansson (a nineteenth-century opera singer) would call for sprats rather than anchovies. It goes very well with meat such as lamb.

1 Preheat the oven to 200°C (400°F), Gas mark 6, and butter the gratin or ovenproof dish.

2 Divide the potatoes into four lots, and the anchovies into two. Arrange a quarter of the potatoes in the bottom of the dish, then place half of the anchovies on top of these, in three lines evenly spaced across the width of the dish. Season with salt (not too much as the anchovies will be quite salty) and pepper.

3 Add another layer of potatoes, then three more lines of anchovies perpendicular to the ones in the previous layer. Season again, then add another layer of potatoes. Next add the chopped garlic, sprinkled evenly across the potatoes, season again, then add the last layer of potatoes. Pour the cream into the dish, then sprinkle the grated cheeses over the top.

4 Cover the dish in foil and place in the oven. After 30 minutes remove the foil and cook for a further 30 minutes or until the potatoes are tender when pierced with a skewer and the surface of the dish is golden brown and bubbling.

Cucumber with mint

....

SERVES 2-3
VEGETARIAN
10g (⅓oz) butter
1 cucumber, peeled, deseeded
   and cut into 1cm (½in) dice
1 tsp white wine vinegar
1 tbsp finely chopped mint
Salt and ground black pepper

It's surprising how delicious cucumber is when cooked. This side dish is fresh and light and is a great accompaniment to fish or chicken.

1 Melt the butter in a frying pan on a low heat, add the cucumber and vinegar and cook, stirring occasionally, for 2–3 minutes or until the cucumber has softened slightly.

2 Stir in the chopped mint, season to taste with salt and pepper and serve while warm.

Buttered courgettes

....

SERVES 2-4
VEGETARIAN
2 courgettes
25g (1oz) butter or 3 tbsp
   olive oil
Salt and ground black pepper

Primarily to go with fish, this dish is extremely quick and simple to prepare. It is delicious as it is, but feel free to add a sprinkling of chopped herbs when serving, such as marjoram, tarragon, basil or mint.

1 Peel the courgettes, then slice in half lengthways and remove and discard the soft inner seeds. Next carefully cut the flesh into 1cm (½in) cubes or slices.

2 To cook, place a frying pan on a high heat. Once hot, add the butter or olive oil and when the butter has melted tip in the courgette pieces. Sauté for 2–3 minutes until just softened, tossing regularly, and season to taste with salt and pepper. Serve immediately.

VARIATION
Buttered cucumber: Replace the courgettes with 1 medium cucumber and then prepare and cook as above.

Fluffy mashed potato

....

SERVES 4
VEGETARIAN

1 kg (2lb 3oz) floury potatoes,
    unpeeled
Salt and ground black pepper
About 150ml (5fl oz) milk,
    or 110ml (4 fl oz) milk and
    50ml (2fl oz) single or
    regular cream
25g (1oz) butter
2 egg whites, lightly beaten

The egg whites in this recipe give the potatoes volume, structure and – most importantly – fluffiness. You can also stir in chopped herbs once mashed; parsley, tarragon, marjoram or chives all work well. I find partially steaming floury potatoes is the best way to cook them. If you want to make this dish in advance, add a little extra milk or, as it will dry out as it sits. It will keep really well, covered, in a warm oven for an hour or so.

1 Place the potatoes in a large saucepan of cold water with a good pinch of salt. Bring to the boil and cook for 10 minutes, then pour all but about 4cm (1½in) of the water out of the pan and continue to cook the potatoes on a very low heat. (Don't be tempted to stick a knife into them as the skins will break and they will just disintegrate and get soggy if you do.)

2 About 20 minutes later, when you think the potatoes might be cooked, test them with a skewer: if they are soft, take them off the heat. Peel the potatoes while they are still hot and mash them immediately, either by hand or using the paddle attachment in an electric food mixer.

3 Bring the milk (or milk and cream) to the boil in a small saucepan. Add the butter and some salt and pepper to the potatoes, but don't add any milk until they are free of lumps. When the potatoes are fully mashed, add the boiling milk (or milk and cream) and stir to a smooth consistency. You might not need all the milk/cream or you might need a little more – it depends on how dry the potatoes are.

4 Next add the egg whites and beat well either with a wooden spoon or in the food mixer with the paddle attachment. Keep going for a couple of minutes or until the mixture is light and fluffy. Add some more salt and pepper if necessary and serve immediately.

Creamy lentils with rosemary and tomatoes

....

SERVES 4
VEGETARIAN

2 tbsp olive oil
½ onion (150g/5oz),
    peeled and finely chopped
1 clove of garlic, peeled and
    finely chopped
3 tsp chopped rosemary leaves
200g (7oz) Puy lentils, rinsed
1 x 400g tin of chopped
    tomatoes
150ml (5fl oz) single or
    regular cream
Salt and ground black pepper
Pinch of sugar

Lentils are often thought of as a cheap source of protein without much excitement for the cook. Yet this couldn't be further from the truth for they have a gloriously earthy flavour that here is enriched with cream and tomatoes, enough to convert even the most ardent lentil hater. These work brilliantly with Chicken Confit or Garlic and Herb Pork Chops (see pages 177 and 179).

1 Pour the olive oil into a large saucepan on a medium heat, add the onion and garlic and cook, stirring occasionally, for about 5 minutes. Stir in 1 teaspoon of the chopped rosemary and continue cooking for a further 5 minutes or until the onion is very soft and lightly golden.

2 Add the lentils, tomatoes and 250ml (9fl oz) of water, cover with a lid, bring to the boil, then reduce the heat and simmer for about 50 minutes or until the lentils are quite soft. Add the cream and remaining rosemary, allowing the cream to bubble for about 3 minutes, then season to taste with salt, pepper and sugar. Serve while warm.

Creamy polenta

....

SERVES 2-4
VEGETARIAN
Salt and ground black pepper
100g (3½oz) medium or
 coarse polenta
25g (1oz) butter
50g (2oz) Parmesan or
 Parmesan-style cheese,
 finely grated

Traditional Italian polenta makes a lovely soothing side dish. Like a good mash, the texture and flavour of polenta accommodates any sauce it meets. This recipe works to perfection with the Pheasant Casserole with Chorizo, Cream and Thyme with which it is photographed on page 183.

1 Place 800ml (1 pint 9fl oz) of water and 1 teaspoon of salt in a large saucepan and bring to the boil. Add the polenta, whisking constantly, then bring back up to the boil and as soon as it begins to bubble, turn the heat down as low as possible. Cook for 30–40 minutes, stirring very frequently (this time with a wooden spoon). The polenta is cooked when it is very thick and porridge-like; the fine grains should be fully softened, not al dente.

2 Stir in the butter, grated Parmesan and season generously with pepper, adding a little more salt if necessary.

Sautéed rosemary potatoes

....

SERVES 2-4
VEGETARIAN
Salt and ground black pepper
500g (1lb 2oz) potatoes, cut
 into 1-2cm (½–¾in) dice
50ml (2fl oz) olive oil
2 cloves of garlic, peeled and
 crushed or finely grated
1 tbsp chopped rosemary

This is a lovely quick way of getting soft and crispy potatoes and would go very well with Chicken Confit and Creamy Lentils with Rosemary and Tomatoes (see page 177 and opposite). If the potatoes are new and small, keep their skins on, otherwise peel them.

1 Place a saucepan of lightly salted water over a high heat and bring to the boil. Add the potatoes and cook for 2–5 minutes (floury potatoes will cook faster) until they have slightly softened, then drain before tipping onto kitchen paper to dry completely.

2 Place a large frying pan over a high heat, add the olive oil and when hot, add the potatoes and cook, tossing frequently, for 3–4 minutes until they begin to turn a light golden. Add the garlic and rosemary and cook for a further 3–5 minutes until the potatoes are golden and crispy. Season with salt and pepper and serve immediately, or keep warm, uncovered, to prevent softening.

Chocolate crèmes brûlées

SERVES 4
VEGETARIAN
4 egg yolks
40g (1½oz) caster sugar
½ tsp vanilla extract
350ml (12fl oz) double
   or regular cream
4 tsp cocoa powder
4 tsp demerara sugar

Four small ramekins or
   similar-sized
   ovenproof dishes

My brother-in-law makes this divine chocolate variation of the classic crème brûlée. It is such a pleasing thing to eat, using your spoon to break the crisp sugar barrier to invade the creamy chocolate custard it protects.

1 Place the egg yolks in a large bowl with the caster sugar and vanilla extract, and whisk until combined.

2 Pour the cream into a saucepan and bring to the boil. As it is heating, whisk in the cocoa powder until the cream is just about to boil. Remove from the heat and slowly pour into the bowl with the egg mixture, whisking constantly.

3 Pour the egg and cream mixture into the saucepan (having washed it first to help prevent the custard sticking and scrambling) and place on a low heat (any hotter and it will scramble easily). Cook the custard, stirring constantly, for a couple of minutes or until it thickens. (Stir first with the whisk, then, as it heats up, change to a wooden spoon so you can get into the corners of the saucepan and avoid uneven cooking.) As the custard starts to 'shiver' on top and comes almost to the boil, remove immediately from the heat. At this point, speed is crucial as the custard could turn into sweet scrambled eggs!

4 Pour the mixture into the ramekins, allow to cool and then cover and place in the fridge to chill for at least an hour (or they will be fine left overnight). Make sure when you are covering them with cling film that you do not touch the surface of the crèmes: you need a skin to form as this is what will hold the sugar on top – so no dipping fingers in to taste!

5 When you're ready to serve, sprinkle 1 teaspoon of demerara sugar over each crème, spreading it out evenly so that it's one grain thick across the whole surface. With a cook's blow-torch on full heat, caramelise the sugar, keeping the flame just over the sugar and moving in slow circular movements, taking take care not to burn the sugar. Alternatively, cook for 20–60 seconds under a very hot grill until the sugar has caramelised and is bubbling. Set aside for a few minutes to allow the caramel to cool and set and then serve.

Îles flottantes

SERVES 4
VEGETARIAN

For the crème anglaise
3 egg yolks
75g (3oz) caster sugar
1 vanilla pod, with a line
   scored down the side,
   or ½ tsp vanilla extract
250ml (9fl oz) milk

For the islands
1 egg white
50g (2oz) caster sugar

For the caramel
50g (2oz) caster sugar

4 glass bowls, wide cocktail
   glasses or champagne cups

Floating in a sea of rich vanilla custard, these meringue islands are the most delicate sweet dumplings imaginable.

1 First make the crème anglaise. In a large bowl, whisk the egg yolks with the sugar until light and thick. Place the vanilla pod (if using) in a saucepan with the milk and slowly bring just up to the boil. Remove the vanilla pod and pour the milk onto the egg yolks and sugar, whisking all the time.

2 Return the mixture to the saucepan with the vanilla extract (if using) and stir over a low heat until it has thickened sufficiently to lightly coat the back of a spoon. (Don't allow it to boil.) Remove the pan from the heat and pour into a bowl, then cover with cling film (to prevent a skin forming) and allow to cool.

3 While the crème anglaise is cooling, you can make the 'islands'. In a spotlessly clean, dry bowl, whisk the egg white until it is nearly at the stiff stage, then add half of the sugar and whisk until the mixture forms stiff peaks. Fold in the remaining sugar.

4 Place a wide, shallow saucepan or roasting tin on the stove and pour in enough cold water to a depth of 3–4cm (1¼–1½in). Bring to simmering point, then turn the heat down to low and use a dessertspoon to scoop up four equal blobs of meringue mixture to place in the water to poach.

5 Allow the meringues to poach for 3 minutes before carefully turning them over to poach for a further 3 minutes. When cooked they will feel spongy if prodded gently with your finger. Remove the islands from the water, then drain on kitchen paper.

6 Make the caramel at the last moment. Put the sugar into a heavy-based saucepan and place on a medium heat. Stir until the sugar dissolves, then continue to stir for 2–3 minutes (don't worry if it begins to look almost lumpy – this will go) or until it turns a golden caramel. Remove from the heat while you quickly divide the crème anglaise between the four bowls or glasses and carefully place an island on top of each portion of custard. Drizzle some hot caramel over each island and serve straight away.

Coffee zabaglione with tuiles biscuits

....

SERVES 4
VEGETARIAN
4 egg yolks
50g (2oz) caster sugar
2 tbsp strong black coffee, such as espresso
1 tsp double or regular cream
3 tbsp Marsala or medium sherry
Tuiles biscuits (see below), to serve

4 small glasses

If you love coffee, you will adore this intense dessert. I like to serve it in glasses with tuiles biscuits on the side. Any leftover tuiles can be stored in an airtight container, where they will keep for a couple of days.

1 Place the egg yolks and the sugar in a heatproof bowl sitting over a saucepan of simmering water on a low–medium heat. Whisk together over the heat until the sugar dissolves. The mixture will be runny at this point: continue to whisk for another 5 minutes or until the mixture thickens and becomes quite pale in colour.

2 Now add the remaining ingredients and whisk again for a further 10 minutes or until the mixture is thick and fluffy. Remove from the heat and allow to rest for 10 minutes before pouring into the sherry glasses and serving with the tuiles biscuits on the side.

Tuiles biscuits

MAKES 17–20 BISCUITS
VEGETARIAN
2 egg whites
110g (4oz) caster sugar
50g (2oz) plain flour, sifted
½ tsp vanilla extract
50g (2oz) butter, melted and cooled

1 Preheat the oven to 180°C (350°F), Gas mark 4. Line two baking sheets with baking parchment.

2 Place the egg whites in a spotlessly clean, dry bowl and whisk for 1–2 minutes or until they are foamy and just turning white. Gently fold in the remaining ingredients.

3 For each biscuit, spoon 1 teaspoon of the mixture onto a baking sheet and gently spread into a circle, about 5cm (2in) in diameter. The biscuits will spread a little while baking, so do leave space between them. Place in the oven and bake for 3–6 minutes or until they turn light golden brown around the edge and still pale in the middle.

4 Remove from the oven and very gently lift off each biscuit from the baking parchment. Lay while still warm over a rolling pin or

(continued overleaf)

the side of a wine bottle to give a curved shape (tuile means 'tile' in French, as in a curved roof tile) and place on a wire rack to cool. If you would prefer flat biscuits, just place the tuiles straight on the wire rack without curving them first. The tuiles need to be warm to be pliable so keep the rest warm on the baking sheets – in the oven with the heat off and the door open – as you mould each biscuit.

RACHEL'S TIP
Take care not to leave the tuiles in a steamy atmosphere as they will soften very quickly; make sure they are stored somewhere dry.

Orange sorbet with Campari

SERVES 3–4
VEGETARIAN
300ml (½ pint) freshly squeezed orange juice (from about 5 oranges)
Finely grated zest of 1 orange
100g (3½oz) caster sugar
3–4 tbsp Campari, to serve

3–4 chilled cocktail glasses

A delightful little twist on my favourite drink, this can be served as a starter, a palate cleanser during the meal before the main course or for dessert.

1 Place a saucepan on a low heat, add the orange juice, zest and sugar and gently warm through, stirring frequently, until the sugar has dissolved. Remove from the heat and allow to cool. Place in an ice-cream machine and churn for 20–30 minutes or until it has thickened.

2 If you don't have an ice-cream machine, place the sorbet in the freezer for 2–3 hours or until it begins to set around the edges, then, using a fork, stir to break up the frozen crystals. Put the lid back on and continue to freeze for a further hour. Remove from the freezer and stir again, then freeze for another hour, remove and stir one final time.

3 Meanwhile, place a bowl in the freezer that will hold all the sorbet. Once the sorbet has thickened, transfer to the frozen bowl, cover and pop straight into the freezer and leave overnight.

4 When ready to serve, place the frozen sorbet in the fridge for about 10 minutes to soften ever so slightly, before scooping into the chilled glasses and topping with about 1 tablespoon (or more if preferred) of Campari. Serve immediately.

MENU IDEAS FOR
SMALL CELEBRATIONS

Serve all menus with a green salad (see page 239)

Warm winter green salad with Caesar dressing, smoked bacon
and a poached egg (page 160)
Rack of lamb with watercress mousse and potato and
anchovy gratin (pages 176, 185 and 188)
Chocolate crèmes brûlées (page 195)

*

Scallops with Brussels sprouts, bacon and orange (page 157)
Chicken confit, creamy lentils with rosemary and tomatoes
and sautéed rosemary potatoes (pages 177, 192 and 193)
Coffee zabaglione with tuiles biscuits (page 199)

*

Tomato, mozzarella and tapenade crostini (page 163)
Summer pea and mint ravioli (page 168)
Orange sorbet with Campari (page 200)

*

Asparagus on toast with hollandaise sauce (page 159)
Roast duck breasts with white bean purée (pages 184 and 186)
Îles flottantes (page 196)

STARTERS

Ballycotton prawn soup with rouille and toasts
Chicken liver pâté with sweet apple relish
Fish mousse with shrimp beurre blanc
Smoked mackerel and goat's cheese soufflé
Decadent mushroom tart
Beef carpaccio
Sesame and mint chickpea pancakes

MAIN COURSES

Summer vegetable stew
Jerusalem artichokes, toasted hazelnuts and goat's cheese with pasta ribbons
Bulgar wheat pilaf
Miso salmon steaks
Fragrant coconut prawns
Fish stew
Pot-roast pheasant with bacon and brandy
Beef Wellington
Roast pork belly with a fennel and garlic rub
Roast loin of lamb with a spicy rub
Coq au vin
Roast duck legs

SIDE DISHES

Lentils with red wine
Braised chicory
Green salad dressings
Spinach and mint orzo
Creamy potato and Gruyère gratin
Ribboned carrots with honey and parsley
Butternut squash and chickpeas with cumin and coriander
Roast garlic colcannon
French beans with lemon and pine nuts
Soy and sesame pak choi

DESSERTS

Maple pecan toffee tart
Blackberry mousse
Raspberry and amaretto tart
Peach jelly pannacotta pots
Tiramisu
Spiced raisin tart
Almond and orange cake
Orange ice cream
Cinnamon ice cream
Gin and tonic lemon sorbet
Choosing a cheese board
Paper-thin crispbreads

DINNER
PARTIES
(4-8 PEOPLE)

Ah, the classic dinner party. Don't let them scare you! They can be as relaxed or dressed-up as you want, and you can ask friends to help or to bring a dish, especially if they love cooking! As with Small Celebrations, you may wish to serve either two or three courses, depending on your time available. You may also wish to have fun decorating your table with more than just candles, or to give people name tags at their place settings (see page 8 for ideas).

Ballycotton prawn soup with rouille and toasts

....

100g (3½oz) tomatoes, chopped

1 carrot (about 100g/3½oz), peeled and chopped

1 onion (about 100g/3½oz), peeled and chopped

1 tbsp olive oil

Salt and ground black pepper

Pinch of sugar

25g (1oz) butter

300g (11oz) peeled prawns (raw or cooked), roughly chopped 100ml (3½fl oz) dry white wine

300ml (½ pint) Crab or Prawn/Shrimp Stock (see page 37) or fish stock

125ml (4½fl oz) single or regular cream

Chervil, to decorate (optional)

For the rouille and toast

1 baguette

25ml (1fl oz) Crab or Prawn/Shrimp Stock (see page 37) or fish stock

4 cloves of garlic, peeled and crushed or finely grated

1 large egg yolk

¼ tsp whole saffron strands

75ml (3fl oz) olive oil

This is a heavenly and quite rich soup that is great to serve as a starter for a dinner party. The sweetness of the prawns in the soup gets a good garlicky kick from the rouille.

1 Place the tomatoes, carrot and onion in a large saucepan with the olive oil. Season with salt, pepper and sugar, and gently sweat, covered, on a low heat for 40–45 minutes, stirring regularly, until the carrot is completely soft.

2 While the vegetables are cooking, make the rouille. Cut a large slice, about 2cm (¾in) thick, from the baguette, reserving the remainder for later. Break up the slice into chunks and place in a small bowl with the crab or prawns (shrimps) stock.

3 Allow the bread to soak up the stock so that it becomes completely mushy. Add the garlic, egg yolk and saffron and mix together. Then, whisking all the time, add the olive oil very slowly, as though you were making mayonnaise. Indeed, the rouille should look like a thick, deep yellow mayonnaise. Place in a bowl and set aside. (You could make the rouille in advance as it will keep, covered, in the fridge for a couple of days.)

4 Preheat the grill to hot. Cut the remaining baguette into slices about 1cm (½in) thick and toast on both sides under the grill until light golden.

5 To finish making the soup, melt the butter in another saucepan on a medium heat. When it starts to foam, add the prawns and cook for about 2 minutes until cooked through. Next add the wine, stock and the cooked tomato mixture, then simmer, still on a medium heat, for about 10 minutes.

6 In a blender (or use a hand-held blender), liquidise the soup until it's smooth, then stir in the cream and season to taste.

7 Serve the soup hot. Spread a generous amount of the rouille on each piece of toast and either place in the bowl of soup as croutons decorated with chervil leaves, or eat as an accompaniment.

Chicken liver pâté
with sweet apple relish

....

SERVES 4-6

250g (9oz) chicken livers
110g (4oz) butter
50g (2oz) peeled and finely
    chopped shallots
2 cloves of garlic, peeled
    and finely chopped
2 tsp chopped thyme leaves
75ml (3fl oz) port
25ml (1fl oz) brandy
Salt and ground black pepper
250ml (9fl oz) sweet apple
    relish (see opposite),
    to serve

The combination of port, brandy and thyme gives this rich, smooth pâté bags of flavour –fabulous as a dinner party starter on toast, crusty bread or thin crackers and with a dollop of the sweet apple relish. If you are cooking for larger numbers, this recipe doubles up very easily. It keeps for three days in the fridge.

1 Trim off any greenish or white sinewy bits from the livers.

2 Melt 15g (½oz) butter in a large frying pan on a low–medium heat and, when it starts to foam, add the chicken livers. Cook for 2–4 minutes on each side; cooking time will depend on the thickness of the livers, but they should still be slightly pink inside. Remove the livers to the bowl of a food processor and set aside.

3 Melt a further 15g (½oz) butter in the same frying pan over a medium heat, add the shallots and garlic and cook for 6–8 minutes until slightly golden. Tip in the thyme, port and brandy and continue to cook until the liquid has reduced to approximately 2 tablespoons. (Be very careful when adding the alcohol, as it may flame, so stand well back and make sure you pre-measure it – don't hold the bottle of brandy or port directly over the hob.)

4 Place the shallot mixture in the food processor with the chicken livers, making sure to scrape the pan to get all the juices in. Whiz everything together for a good few minutes until smooth then allow to cool completely. Cut the remaining butter into cubes and add to the chicken livers, whiz together again and season to taste with salt and pepper.

5 Spoon into a bowl, smooth the top and store, covered in cling film, in the fridge. Allow to come up to room temperature before serving with the sweet apple relish.

MAKES 250ML (9FL OZ)
VEGETARIAN

25g (1oz) butter
2 eating apples, peeled,
    cored and chopped into
    5mm (¼in) dice
50g (2oz) caster sugar
25ml (1fl oz) sherry vinegar
75ml (3fl oz) red wine
Pinch of salt

Sweet apple relish

In addition to serving this relish with the chicken liver pâté, opposite, it would also be lovely with the Game Terrine with Celeriac Remoulade or the Venison Sausages with Celeriac Purée (see pages 45 and 48), or serve it with cheese on the cheeseboard. Stored in a sterilised jar, this relish will keep for several weeks.

1 Melt the butter in a saucepan on a medium heat. When it has melted and begins to foam, add the apples and cook for 2–3 minutes or until the apples turn slightly golden around the edges.

2 Add the remaining ingredients, stir thoroughly and cook over a low–medium heat for 5–8 minutes or until reduced and jam-like, the apples cooked through but not mushy.

3 Allow to cool before serving, or store in a sterilised jar (for sterilising jars, see page 42).

Fish mousse with shrimp beurre blanc

SERVES 6

For the shrimp beurre blanc
3 tbsp dry white wine
3 tbsp white wine vinegar
1 tbsp peeled and finely
 chopped shallots
1 tbsp double or regular
 cream
175g (6oz) chilled butter,
 cubed
Freshly ground white pepper
Freshly squeezed lemon juice
A small knob of butter
75g (3oz) cooked shrimps
 or prawns, peeled

For the mousse
175g (6oz) fillets of whiting,
 pollack, cod or haddock,
 skinned and free of bone
 or membrane
½ tsp salt
Pinch of freshly ground
 white pepper
1 egg
Melted butter, for greasing
300ml (½ pint) double or
 regular cream, chilled

Six 100ml (3½fl oz) ramekins

The purpose of a mousse is to take the essence of a flavour and create something that is both light and luxurious at the same time. This is my husband's favourite starter ever; it's been made at Ballymaloe since he was a boy. It's best to have everything as cold as possible to begin with, even the bowl of the food processor, as this helps keep the texture of the mousse as light as possible.

1 To make the beurre blanc, place the wine, vinegar and shallots into a heavy-based saucepan and boil, uncovered, for about 5 minutes to let the mixture reduce to about half a tablespoon.

2 Pour in the cream and boil again until it thickens. Whisk in the chilled butter in little pieces, keeping the sauce just warm enough to absorb the butter.

3 Strain out the shallots, season with white pepper and lemon juice and keep warm in a bowl over hot, not simmering, water. The sauce should not be too thick, only slightly thicker than double cream; if you need to thin it, just add some warm water.

4 Place a frying pan on a medium heat and allow to get hot. Add the knob of butter and toss the shrimps or prawns in the butter for 1 minute until warmed through. Then set aside for a few seconds to slightly cool before stirring through the sauce.

5 Before making the mousse it is best to have everything well chilled to start with, including the bowl of the food processor. Cut the fish fillets into small dice and purée the pieces in the food processor. Add the salt and pepper, then the egg, and continue to purée until the ingredients are well mixed, though not for any

(continued overleaf)

longer or the mixture will curdle and become rubbery in texture. Chill in the fridge for 30 minutes.

6 Preheat the oven to 200°C (400°F), Gas mark 6, and brush the ramekins with melted butter.

7 When the fish has rested for 30 minutes, remove from the fridge, pour in the cream and whiz again in the food processor just until it is well incorporated. Check the seasoning. (The mousse can be prepared to this point several hours ahead. Cover and place in the fridge until needed.)

8 Divide the mousse mixture between the ramekins and place them in a deep roasting tin. Pour enough boiling water in the tin to come halfway up the outside of the ramekins. Cover with a sheet of perforated foil or greaseproof paper (using a skewer or sharp knife to make about 10 holes all over) and transfer to the oven to bake for about 20 minutes. When cooked the mousses should feel just firm in the centre. They will keep perfectly for 20–30 minutes in a low oven.

9 Turn out onto warmed plates then spoon over some shrimp beurre blanc to serve.

Smoked mackerel and goat's cheese soufflé

....

SERVES 6-8

50g (2oz) butter, plus extra for greasing
50g (2oz) plain flour
250ml (9fl oz) milk
4 eggs, separated
100g (3½oz) smoked mackerel, skin removed and flesh chopped
100g (3½oz) soft goat's cheese, broken into 1cm (½in) pieces
2 tbsp chopped chives
1 tsp chopped dill
2 tbsp lemon juice
Salt and ground black pepper
25g (1oz) grated Parmesan cheese

Six 100ml (3½fl oz) or eight 75ml (3fl oz) ramekins

Cheese soufflé is a classic and not nearly as scary a dinner party prospect as you might imagine. This version, with goat's cheese and smoked mackerel, is a fantastic variation on the theme.

1 Preheat the oven to 220°C (425°F), Gas mark 7. Butter the ramekins and place a baking sheet in the centre of the oven to heat up.

2 Melt the butter in a large saucepan on a medium heat, then add the flour and stir for 1 minute, being careful not to let it burn. Turn the heat down and whisk in the milk gradually, stirring until you have a thick white sauce, then remove the pan from the heat.

3 Beat in the egg yolks, then fold in the smoked mackerel, goat's cheese and herbs. Season to taste with lemon juice and salt and pepper. It should taste highly seasoned as adding the egg white will dilute the flavour.

4 Whisk the egg whites in a spotlessly clean, dry bowl until they form stiff peaks, then take 2 tablespoons of the egg white and mix it into the sauce. Very carefully fold in the remaining egg white, making sure not to over-mix it.

5 Divide the mixture between the ramekins, filling each to the top, then scatter with the grated Parmesan. Place the cheese soufflés on the hot baking sheet in the oven and cook for 12–15 minutes or until well risen and golden. Serve immediately.

VARIATION
Twice-baked soufflé: If you have any cheese soufflés left over, tip each out of its ramekin and place in a buttered shallow baking dish. Pour over 50ml (2fl oz) cream per soufflé and bake in the oven, preheated to 200°C (400°F), Gas mark 6, for 6–8 minutes.

Decadent mushroom tart

SERVES 8
VEGETARIAN

For the shortcrust pastry
200g (7oz) plain flour, sifted
100g (3½oz) chilled butter,
    cubed, plus extra for
    greasing
½–1 egg, beaten

For the filling
15g (½oz) butter
100g (3½oz) shallots, peeled
    and finely chopped
200g (7oz) button or large
    flat mushrooms, finely
    chopped
Salt and ground black pepper
25g (1oz) dried mushrooms,
    such as porcini
250ml (9fl oz) boiling water
2 eggs
1 egg yolk
250ml (9fl oz) double
    or regular cream

For the tarragon hollandaise
3 egg yolks
175g (6oz) butter, diced
Squeeze of lemon juice
¼ tsp Dijon mustard
3 tbsp chopped tarragon

23cm (9in) diameter loose-
    bottomed tart tin

Porcini are one of the most prized mushrooms. They are dried for preservation and when rehydrated in water they bestow their powerful, almost meaty flavour to the liquid. This tart uses that liquid and other mushrooms, as well as the porcini themselves, so it is crammed with mushroom flavour. Drizzled with tarragon hollandaise, it becomes the height of luxurious sophistication.

1 Place the flour and butter in a food processor and whiz briefly until the butter is in small lumps. Add half the beaten egg and continue to whiz for another few seconds or until the mixture looks as though it may just come together when pressed. (Prolonged processing will only toughen the pastry, so don't whiz it up until it is a ball of dough.) You might need to add a little more egg, but not too much as the mixture should be just moist enough to come together. If making by hand, rub the butter into the flour until it resembles coarse breadcrumbs then, using your hands, add just enough egg to bring it together. Reserve any leftover egg to use later.

2 With your hands, flatten out the ball of dough until it is about 2cm (¾in) thick, then wrap in cling film or a plastic bag and leave in the fridge for at least 30 minutes.

3 When you are ready to roll out the pastry, butter the tart tin and remove the pastry from the fridge, placing it between two sheets of cling film (each larger in size than your tart tin). Using a rolling pin, roll the pastry out to no thicker than 5mm (¼in). Make sure to keep it in a round shape as well as large enough to line both the base and the sides of the tin.

4 Remove the top layer of cling film, slide your hand, palm upwards, under the bottom layer of cling film, then flip the pastry over (so that the cling film is now on top) and carefully lower it into the tart tin. Press the pastry into the edges of the tin (with the cling film still attached) and, using your thumb, 'cut' the pastry along the edge of the tin for a neat finish. Remove the cling film,

prick over the base with a fork and chill the pastry in the fridge for another 30 minutes or in the freezer for 10 minutes (it can keep for weeks like this in the freezer).

5 Preheat the oven to 180°C (350°F), Gas mark 4.

6 Remove the pastry from the fridge and line with foil, greaseproof paper or baking parchment, leaving plenty over the sides. Fill with baking beans or dried pulses (all of which can be reused repeatedly), then place in the oven and bake 'blind' for 15–20 minutes or until the pastry feels dry in the base. Take out of the oven, remove the baking beans and foil/paper, brush the base of the pastry with any leftover beaten egg, then bake for another 3 minutes or until lightly golden. Remove from the oven and set aside.

7 Next make the filling. Melt the butter in a large frying pan on a medium heat, add the shallots, cover with a lid and cook for 7–8 minutes or until soft but not browned. Stir in the mushrooms, season with salt and pepper and cook, uncovered, for 8–10 minutes or until soft and dark and any juices that have come out during cooking have evaporated.

8 While these are cooking, soak the dried mushrooms in the boiling water for 10 minutes. Drain, reserving the soaking liquid, then finely chop the soaked mushrooms and add to the shallot and mushroom mixture along with the soaking liquid. Continue to cook, stirring occasionally, for about 10 minutes or until the liquid has completely evaporated. Remove from the heat and allow to cool for a few minutes.

9 Meanwhile, whisk together the eggs, egg yolk and cream, then add to the mushrooms. Mix together and then pour into the pre-baked tart case. Place in the oven and cook for about 30 minutes or until the filling has completely set.

10 While the tart is baking make the hollandaise sauce following the instructions on page 159, stirring the mustard and tarragon into the cooked sauce just before seasoning.

11 Remove the tart from the oven, cut into slices while warm and serve with a generous drizzle of the tarragon hollandaise.

Beef carpaccio

....

SERVES 8
350g (12oz) fillet of beef
Extra-virgin olive oil, for
  oiling and drizzling
Rocket leaves (about
  5 per person)
Shavings of Parmesan cheese
  (cut using a peeler)
18 black olives, pitted
  (see page 38) and
  finely chopped
Sea salt and ground black
  pepper

This classic starter uses raw beef (it's perfectly safe if you use good, very fresh quality beef). The fillet is so tender it doesn't need cooking to tenderise, but do try and cut the slices as thinly as possible. When raw beef tastes this good it's almost enough to make me wonder why we ever cook it at all!

1 Chill the meat by placing it on a baking tray in the fridge for an hour or so, then remove and slice widthways as thinly as possible with a very sharp knife.

2 Place each slice on a piece of oiled cling film, then cover with another piece of oiled cling film (you can reuse these for each slice of beef). Roll gently with a rolling pin until the meat is paper thin. Peel the cling film off the top, then flip the meat over onto a plate so that the lower layer of cling film is facing upwards. Gently peel away this piece of cling film. (If you want to prepare this an hour or two in advance, keep the beef slices covered with cling film in the fridge – with cling film between each layer of beef to prevent the slices sticking together – then remove about 20 minutes before serving to bring back up to room temperature.)

3 Scatter the rocket leaves, Parmesan shavings and chopped olives over the beef, then season with salt and pepper. Drizzle with olive oil and serve immediately with crusty bread.

Sesame and mint chickpea pancakes

....

MAKES 6
VEGETARIAN
2 tomatoes, deseeded
  and cubed
½ cucumber, peeled,
  deseeded and sliced
½ red onion, peeled and
  finely sliced
2 tbsp olive oil
1 tbsp sesame seeds, toasted
  (see page 25), to serve

For the dressing
50ml (2fl oz) natural yoghurt
1 tbsp extra-virgin olive oil
1 tsp chopped mint
1 tsp lemon juice
Salt and ground black pepper

For the pancakes
1 x 400g tin of chickpeas,
  drained and rinsed, or 125g
  (4½oz) dried chickpeas,
  soaked and cooked
  (see page 64)
2 tsp chopped mint
2 tsp chopped parsley
2 tsp sesame oil
1 egg
100g (3½oz) fresh white
  breadcrumbs
Juice of ½ lemon

*I absolutely adore the Middle Eastern flavours in this starter.
The pancakes contrast perfectly with the moist and crunchy salad,
while the mint brings a real freshness.*

1 Whisk all the dressing ingredients together, seasoning to taste
with salt and pepper, then stir in the vegetables and set aside.

2 Next make the pancakes. Place the chickpeas in a food processor,
along with the mint, parsley, sesame oil and egg. Whiz for
1–2 minutes to form a rough paste, then add the breadcrumbs,
season with salt and pepper, add the lemon juice and pulse
a few times until everything comes together.

3 Shape into six even-sized pancakes about 6cm (2½in) wide
and 1.5cm (⅝in) thick. Pour the olive oil into a large frying pan
on a medium heat. When the oil is hot, add half the pancakes and
fry on each side for about 3 minutes or until golden brown and
crispy. Repeat with the remaining pancakes, adding a little more
oil first.

4 Place on individual plates with some salad on the side, then
scatter with the toasted sesame seeds.

Summer vegetable stew

SERVES 4-6
VEGETARIAN

350g (12oz) small new
  potatoes, left unpeeled and
  cut into 2cm (¾in) cubes
7 tbsp olive oil
Sea salt and ground black
  pepper
1 red pepper
1 yellow pepper
1 small aubergine, cut into
  2cm (¾in) cubes
200g (7oz) cherry tomatoes,
  halved across the middle
1 onion (300g/11oz in weight),
  peeled and thinly sliced
2 cloves of garlic, peeled and
  finely sliced
1 tbsp sherry vinegar or red
  wine vinegar
3 generous tbsp roughly
  chopped or torn basil

This dish has echoes of a ratatouille, but because in this recipe all the components are roasted, it has a lovely sweet and intense flavour. As with most stews, this is very good reheated when all the flavours have had time to marry and infuse.

1 Preheat the oven to 230°C (450°F), Gas mark 8.

2 In a bowl, mix the potatoes with 2 tablespoons of the olive oil and season with salt and pepper. Place on a large roasting tin with the whole peppers and roast in the oven for 15 minutes.

3 Meanwhile, in the same bowl, mix together the aubergine and tomatoes with 3 tablespoons of olive oil. Season with salt and pepper and set aside.

4 After 15 minutes, add the aubergine and tomatoes to the potatoes and return to the oven. Cook for a further 20–25 minutes or until the aubergine is completely soft and beginning to brown at the edges. Remove the tin from the oven and set aside.

5 The peppers should be completely soft and the skin slightly blackened. Transfer to a bowl and cover with cling film – this makes the skin easier to remove. When the peppers are cool enough to handle, peel them, remove all the seeds and cut the flesh into pieces roughly 2cm (¾in) square.

6 Meanwhile, place a large saucepan on a medium heat and pour in the remaining olive oil. Add the onion and garlic and cook for 10 minutes or until soft and beginning to brown. Add the roasted vegetables, together with the vinegar and basil, and stir gently to combine. Taste for seasoning and serve while warm.

Jerusalem artichokes, toasted hazelnuts and goat's cheese with pasta ribbons

....

SERVES 4
VEGETARIAN
25g (1oz) butter
2 tbsp olive oil
600g (1lb 5oz) Jerusalem
    artichokes, peeled and
    cut into 1cm (½in) cubes
450g (1lb) fresh pasta sheets
    or tagliatelle, or 350g (12oz)
    dried pappardelle or
    tagliatelle
Salt and ground black pepper
2 tbsp chopped mint
4 tbsp chopped parsley
75g (3oz) hazelnuts, toasted,
    peeled (see page 29) and
    chopped
200g (7oz) goat's cheese,
    crumbled
Squeeze of lemon juice

This lovely wintery dish uses one of my favourite veggies, Jerusalem artichokes, which have a natural affinity with hazelnuts and creamy goat's cheese.

1 Place the butter and olive oil in a large frying pan on a high heat. When the butter has melted, add the Jerusalem artichokes and cook for 5–7 minutes, tossing occasionally, until they are cooked through, golden all over and a little crusty.

2 Next cook the pasta. If you are using fresh pasta sheets, first cut them into 2cm (¾in) wide ribbons using a sharp knife or pastry wheel. Place a large saucepan of water on a high heat and bring to the boil. Add 1 teaspoon of salt and the fresh pasta, cook for 2–4 minutes or until just al dente, then drain and place in a large serving bowl. If using dried pasta, cook following the instructions on the packet.

3 Add the cooked Jerusalem artichokes to the pasta, along with the mint, parsley, hazelnuts and goat's cheese. Season to taste with lemon juice and salt and pepper and serve while warm.

Bulgur wheat pilaf

....

SERVES 6–8

VEGETARIAN

2 aubergines (300g/11oz
  each), cut into 2cm (¾in)
  cubes
7 tbsp olive oil
4 tbsp shallots, peeled
  and finely chopped
2 cloves of garlic, peeled
  and finely chopped
350g (12oz) bulgur wheat
600ml (1 pint) vegetable stock
  (see page 50)
150g (5oz) raisins or sultanas
2 tsp cumin seeds, toasted
  and ground (see page 25)
2 tsp coriander seeds, toasted
  and ground (see page 25)
50g (2oz) spinach (any
  large stalks removed
  before weighing),
  roughly chopped
2 tbsp each of chopped
  coriander and mint
2–4 tbsp lemon juice
100g (3½oz) shelled
  pistachios, roughly
  chopped
Salt and ground black pepper
Lemon slices, to serve

Bulgur is made from wheat, most usually durum wheat, and is a whole grain that has been boiled and dried. It is used in Middle Eastern cooking and is very convenient as it only needs to be cooked for a few minutes in stock. The texture is softer than barley, but slightly more resistant than couscous, with its own distinctive flavour. This dish uses bulgur as a base to add various different Middle Eastern flavours, the pistachios giving a lovely Persian crunch.

1 Preheat the oven to 220°C (425°F), Gas mark 7.

2 Toss the aubergines in 3 tablespoons of the olive oil, then spread out in a single layer in a roasting tin or baking tray and roast in the oven for 20–25 minutes or until softened and turning golden.

3 Meanwhile, pour the remaining olive oil into a large saucepan, add the shallots and garlic and cook over a medium heat for 6–8 minutes or until the shallots are soft.

4 Add the bulgur wheat, stock, raisins or sultanas and cumin and coriander. Bring to the boil and stir, then remove from the heat, cover with a lid and allow to sit for 5–10 minutes or until the stock has been absorbed.

5 Stir in the spinach and herbs, allowing the spinach to wilt. Add the aubergines, lemon juice and pistachios, stirring to combine, then season to taste with salt and pepper. Serve warm or at room temperature with some lemon slices.

Miso salmon steaks

200g (7oz) brown or
   white miso paste
200g (7oz) caster sugar
50ml (2fl oz) mirin
4 salmon steaks or fillets
   (150g/5oz each)

Miso is an essential component of the famous Japanese soup and can be used in a variety of dishes. Made from fermented soy, the thick paste has an intense flavour that can be sweetened with sugar. The sweetness marries perfectly with the salmon. You can buy miso in Asian supermarkets or health food stores. Serve with Soy and Sesame Pak Choi (see page 245).

1 Place the miso, sugar and mirin in a saucepan and set on a low heat. Cook, stirring or whisking continuously, until the sugar has dissolved, then remove from the heat.

2 Place the fish in a roasting tin and coat generously with the miso paste. Leave to marinate in the fridge for at least 1 hour (or up to 4 hours).

3 Preheat the oven to 180°C (350°F), Gas mark 4.

4 Transfer the roasting tin to the oven and bake for about 10 minutes or until the fish is just opaque all the way through.

Fragrant coconut prawns

SERVES 4-6
500g (1lb 2oz) peeled raw
  tiger prawns
2 lemongrass stalks
  (outer layer removed),
  finely chopped
2 tbsp peeled and finely
  chopped shallots
2 tsp peeled (see page 27)
  and grated root ginger
2 cloves of garlic, peeled
  and finely chopped
½ mild red chilli, deseeded
  and chopped
1 tsp ground coriander
2 tbsp sunflower oil
200ml (7fl oz) coconut milk
1–2 tbsp fish sauce (nam pla)

For this recipe I like to use tiger prawns but any kind would do. It is wonderfully fragrant in flavour: sweet and creamy from the coconut milk with a mild chilli kick – though you can omit the chilli if you prefer. Serve with boiled or steamed rice.

1 First butterfly the prawns. Using a small sharp knife, cut each prawn in half lengthways, leaving the tail intact and attached.

2 In a bowl, make the prawn marinade by mixing together the lemongrass, shallots, ginger, garlic, chilli, coriander and sunflower oil. Throw in the butterflied prawns and mix well with your hands to coat the prawns with the marinade. Cover the bowl with a plate and place in the fridge for 1 hour.

3 Remove the prawns from the marinade and place any remaining marinade in a large saucepan on a medium heat. Cook for 1–2 minutes, stirring all the time so that nothing burns, then add the coconut milk and the fish sauce. Bring to the boil, then tip in the prawns and simmer for about 3 minutes or until they are cooked (they will go pink). Serve the prawns hot in the sauce.

RACHEL'S TIP
The prawns can be made in advance, and reheated gently, or you can make them up to the point where they go into the marinade and coconut milk mixture, then keep in the fridge for a day and cook closer to the time of serving.

VARIATION
Fragrant coconut chicken: Replace the prawns with 600g (1lb 5oz) raw chicken breast or thigh meat, cut into bite-sized pieces and cooked for 5–10 minutes, or until opaque all the way through.

Fish stew

....

This is a wonderfully aromatic and luxurious fish stew. Use a combination of fish or just one variety if that's all you have to hand. I tend to use salmon, sole and cod, and if I can get good fresh prawns, I'll usually throw some of those in too. This is at its best when served straight away, but it can be gently reheated the next day, being careful not to break up the fish as you warm it through.

SERVES 8

5 tbsp olive oil

600g (1lb 5oz) onions, peeled and chopped

Salt and ground black pepper

3 large cloves of garlic, peeled and crushed or finely grated

2 bay leaves

2 x 400g tins of chopped tomatoes

2 tsp caster sugar

600ml (1 pint) dry white wine

2 x 10g fish or chicken stock cube, crumbled

1 carrot, peeled and studded with 5 cloves

Pinch of saffron strands (optional)

900g (2lb) assorted fish fillets (such as salmon, lemon sole, cod, haddock or pollack)

16–20 whole unpeeled prawns

100ml (3½fl oz) double or regular cream

50g (2oz) butter

300g (11oz) leeks, trimmed and sliced

2 tbsp chopped chives

2 tbsp chopped parsley

1 Place a large saucepan on a medium heat, pour in the olive oil then add the onions and some salt and pepper. Cook for 5–7 minutes, stirring occasionally, until they are softened but not browned.

2 Add the garlic, bay leaves, tomatoes, sugar, wine, stock cube, carrot and saffron (if using), bring to the boil, then reduce the heat and simmer gently, uncovered, for 30 minutes or until the tomatoes are cooked and broken up and the flavours have intensified. Taste for seasoning; it may need a little more sugar, salt or pepper. (The stew can be made in advance up to this point; allow it to cool and store in the fridge for a couple of days.)

3 Cut the fish into 2–3cm (¾–1¼in) chunks. Add the prawns to the sauce and then after 1 minute add the fish chunks. Gently stir in the cream, then continue cooking for a further 7–10 minutes or until the fish is just cooked. Don't cook for too long or the fish will disintegrate.

4 Meanwhile, place a frying pan on a low-medium heat, add the butter and when it has melted tip in the leeks and cook, stirring regularly but trying not to break up the leeks, for 6–8 minutes or until softened but not browned.

5 Finally add the leeks to the stew and stir in the herbs. Remove the carrot and bay leaves and serve immediately.

Pot-roast pheasant with bacon and brandy

....

SERVES 3-4

1 tbsp olive oil

75g (3oz) streaky bacon in the piece, or 4 rashers of bacon, cut into 1cm (½in) dice

1 pheasant

Salt and ground black pepper

50ml (2fl oz) brandy

100ml (3½fl oz) dry white wine

75ml (3fl oz) chicken stock (see page 51)

2 tsp chopped rosemary leaves or marjoram

1 tbsp chopped parsley

Medium-sized flameproof casserole dish

This is an absolutely glorious winter dish. By pot roasting in wine and stock, the pheasant stays both moist and juicy. It goes beautifully with the Roast Jerusalem Artichokes and Creamy Polenta (see pages 295 and 193), and kale too, if you wish.

1 Preheat the oven to 150°C (300°F), Gas mark 2.

2 Heat the oil in a casserole dish into which the pheasant will fit snugly. Toss in the bacon and cook for a 3–4 minutes on a medium–high heat or until it begins to crisp and turn golden, then remove and set aside, leaving any bacon fat in the dish.

3 Season the breast side of the pheasant with salt (but don't add too much as there is bacon to follow) and pepper, and place it breast-side down into the dish. Allow to cook on a medium heat for 2–3 minutes, adding more oil if necessary, until it has turned golden brown on both breasts, then turn it the other way up.

4 Tip the bacon back in, pour in the brandy, wine and stock, and bring to simmering point. Cover the dish with a lid and cook in the oven for 45–60 minutes or until the pheasant is cooked – the legs should feel loose at the joint.

5 Remove the pheasant to a warmed plate and cover with foil and put in the oven, with the heat turned off, to keep warm. Degrease the cooking juices (see below) and pour the liquid into a small saucepan. Reheat, stir in the herbs and taste for seasoning.

6 To serve, carve the pheasant and arrange it on a warmed serving plate, spoon over the sauce and serve.

RACHEL'S TIP

To degrease cooking juices, pour the juices into a separating jug or pour the liquid into a bowl and skim off the melted fat from the surface. It can help to add a few ice cubes: the fat will solidify and float to the surface after a few minutes and you can then scoop it out and discard it.

Beef Wellington

....

SERVES 4

4 beef fillet steaks (about
   150g/5oz each)
Plain flour, for dusting
250g (9oz) ready-made
   puff pastry
2 tsp Dijon mustard
1 egg, beaten

For the duxelles (mushroom stuffing)
2 tbsp olive oil
15g (½oz) butter
100g (3½oz) shallots,
   peeled and finely chopped
250g (9oz) mushrooms,
   finely chopped
Salt and ground black pepper
75ml (3fl oz) dry white wine
75ml (3fl oz) double or
   regular cream
1 tbsp chopped tarragon
2 spring onions, trimmed
   and chopped

This famous dish gets its name from the Duke of Wellington – possibly as a patriotic renaming of the French filet de bœuf en croûte during the Napoleonic Wars, or because Wellington liked beef cooked in this way or possibly because the finished dish was thought to resemble one of his celebrated boots! The duxelles, or mushroom stuffing, is named after a real person too – the seventeenth-century Marquis d'Uxelles. The version of the dish that I make is simpler and less rich than the original as I leave out the pâté. For a dinner party I like to make individual beef Wellingtons – as here. Ribboned Carrots with Honey and Parsley (see page 241) are the perfect accompaniment.

1 First make the duxelles. Place the olive oil and the butter in a large frying pan on a medium heat. When the butter has melted, add the shallots and cook for 10 minutes, stirring occasionally.

2 Tip in the mushrooms, season with salt and pepper and cook for 6–8 minutes, stirring occasionally, then pour in the wine and cream and add the tarragon. Bring to the boil then reduce the heat and simmer, uncovered, for about 10 minutes or until the mixture has thickened. Stir in the spring onions, remove from the heat and spread the mixture out on a plate to allow it to cool.

3 To sear the beef, place a griddle pan or a frying pan on a high heat and, when it is very hot, brown the steaks for 1 minute on each side, seasoning with salt and pepper. Remove from the heat and set aside, allowing the meat to rest for about 20 minutes until cool.

4 Preheat the oven to 220°C (425°F), Gas mark 7.

5 Lightly dust a work surface with flour and roll out the puff pastry into a large rectangle, about 40 x 60cm (16 x 24in) and 3mm (⅛in) thick. (If the work surface isn't large enough, just roll out two smaller rectangles, each about 30 x 40cm/12 x 16in.) Using a

(continued overleaf)

sharp knife, trim the edges of the pastry (reserving the scraps for decorations, if you wish), then cut it into four smaller rectangles – or cut the two smaller rectangles in half – so that you have four rectangles in total, each measuring approximately 20 x 30cm (8 x 12in).

6 Spread about half a teaspoon of the mustard evenly over one side of each piece of pastry, leaving a gap of about 1cm (½in) around the edges, then place a steak in the centre. Divide the duxelles between the four steaks, heaping it neatly on top of each one. Brush the edges of the pastry with a little of the beaten egg, then wrap up the steaks in the pastry as tidily as possible (see the tip below). Turn the parcels over so that the joins are facing down, then brush over the top with the beaten egg.

7 If you wish, you can re-roll the discarded pastry scraps into a thin sheet about 3mm (⅛in) thick, then cut into leaf shapes (or whatever shapes you like) and decorate the top of each parcel, making sure to brush all exposed pastry with the beaten egg. This will give it a lovely golden sheen.

8 Place the beef Wellingtons on the baking tray in the oven and cook for 10 minutes, or until the pastry is golden, before turning the temperature down to 200°C (400°F), Gas mark 6, to cook for another 5–10 minutes, by which stage the pastry should be completely cooked. Take out of the oven and serve immediately.

RACHEL'S TIP

When wrapping the pastry about the beef, you may need to cut off any excess pastry if you feel there is too much. You basically want a single layer of pastry everywhere except for where it joins – too much pastry overlapping will result in a very heavy and doughy beef Wellington.

If I have time, I like to place the beef Wellington parcels in the freezer for about 15 minutes prior to cooking so that the pastry is very cold before going into the oven. They can of course be frozen at this stage – for up to three months.

RACHEL ALLEN DINNER PARTIES

Roast pork belly with a fennel and garlic rub

SERVES 4-6

1kg (2lb 3oz) pork belly,
  rind left on

For the fennel and garlic rub
1 tbsp fennel seeds, toasted
  and ground (see page 25)
8 cloves of garlic, peeled
2 tsp sea salt
2–3 tbsp olive oil

Pork belly needs to cook for a long time in order for (nearly) all the fat to come out and for the crackling to get deliciously crisp and crunchy. Make sure that the rind is still on when you buy it. Buy the best-quality free-range pork that you can. This goes really well with Butternut Squash and Chickpeas with Cumin and Coriander (see page 242).

1 Preheat the oven to 150°C (300°F), Gas mark 2.

2 For the rub, either whiz everything together apart from the olive oil using a hand-held blender, or just finely chop everything by hand and mix together well in a bowl. Add enough olive oil to form a rough paste.

3 Score the rind on the pork belly widthways at 5–7mm (¼–⅜in) intervals along the grain of the meat. Then place the pork belly in a roasting tin and, using a skewer or a small sharp knife, make 5–6 incisions about 1cm (½in) deep into the rind-free sides and the bottom of the meat.

4 Massage the paste into the incisions and scored lines in the fat on the top of the meat. Place in the oven and cook for 3½–4 hours, then turn up the heat to 220°C (425°F), Gas mark 7, and cook for a further 10–15 minutes or until the rind is crisp and crackly.

5 Allow to rest in the oven, with the heat turned off, or somewhere warm for at least 15 minutes before carving and serving. If you would like to serve with gravy, follow the method in Roast loin of lamb in a spicy rub (see page 232).

Roast loin of lamb
with a spicy rub

....

SERVES 4-6

1 generous tsp ground cumin
1 generous tsp ground
    coriander
Sea salt and ground black
    pepper
4–5 tbsp olive oil
1 double loin of lamb, boned
    (1kg/2lb 3oz boned weight),
    rolled and tied with string
    (ask your butcher to do this)
300ml (½ pint) lamb or
    chicken stock (see page 51)

The loin is the most tender cut of lamb with a meltingly soft texture.
It goes perfectly with Spinach and Mint Orzo (see page 240), the flavours
of which marry so well with lamb.

1 Preheat the oven to 180°C (350°F), Gas mark 4.

2 Place the spices and a good pinch each of salt and pepper on a
plate. Rub 2–3 tablespoons of olive oil into the lamb, then roll it
in the spicy seasoning. Place 2 tablespoons of the remaining olive
oil in an ovenproof frying pan or roasting tin and set it on a high
heat. When the oil is hot, add the lamb and sear the meat by
cooking it, turning every 2–3 minutes, until browned all over.
Transfer to the oven and cook for 50–70 minutes, depending
on how well done you like your lamb.

3 When the lamb is cooked, take it out of the oven, cover in foil,
transfer to a warmed serving plate or separate roasting tin and
allow to rest somewhere warm (such as in the oven with the heat
turned off) for at least 15 minutes (preferably between 30 minutes
and a couple of hours).

4 While the lamb is resting, make some gravy. Pour off any excess
fat from the pan or tin (or see the tip on page 226), then place the
pan on a medium heat and deglaze by pouring in the stock,
whisking continuously to dissolve the caramelised juices sticking
to the bottom of the pan. Bring to the boil, seasoning with salt
and pepper if necessary, then pour into a jug to serve straight away
or place in a saucepan and reheat when ready to serve.

Coq au vin

....

SERVES 4–6
3 tbsp olive oil
150g (5oz) streaky bacon
  in the piece, or 4 rashers,
  cut into 2cm (¾in) dice
1 large chicken, jointed into
  8–10 pieces
Salt and ground black pepper
4 tbsp plain flour
25g (1oz) butter
1 x 750ml bottle of red wine
3 tbsp brandy
1 tbsp chopped thyme leaves
1 bay leaf
4 cloves of garlic, peeled and
  crushed or finely grated
250g (9oz) button
  mushrooms, quartered
6 carrots (500g/1lb 2oz),
  peeled and sliced
24 baby onions

Large casserole dish or
  ovenproof saucepan
  with a lid

Classic French bistro fare, coq au vin – a rich stew laced with red wine and Cognac – is traditionally made with a cockerel, although these days a (female) chicken is more usual. Like most stews, this can be made in advance and will taste even better reheated the next day.

1 Place a large casserole dish or ovenproof saucepan on a medium heat, pour in the olive oil, add the bacon and cook for 3–5 minutes or until golden brown and crispy. Remove from the dish and set aside, leaving any bacon fat in the pot.

2 Next season the chicken pieces and toss them in the flour, shaking off any excess. Add half the butter to the casserole dish or saucepan, then brown the chicken a few pieces at a time for 2–3 minutes on each side, remove from the pot and set aside. Deglaze the dish or pan by adding the wine, brandy, thyme, bay leaf and garlic, then boil, uncovered, for 10–15 minutes or until the liquid has reduced by half.

3 Meanwhile, place a frying pan on a high heat and add the remaining butter. When it has melted, tip in the mushrooms, season and cook for 4–6 minutes, tossing frequently, until golden brown, then remove from the heat and set aside.

4 Place the chicken pieces, bacon and mushrooms in the casserole dish or saucepan, add the carrots and the onions, then cover the dish or pan with a lid and gently simmer for 30–45 minutes or until the chicken is tender and the juices should run clear if the meat is pierced with a skewer. Alternatively, cook in the oven, preheated to 150°C (300°F), Gas mark 2, for the same length of time.

5 If there is fat on the surface of the casserole, pour the rich juices into a bowl or jug to degrease them (see page 226), leaving the meat and vegetables in the pot. Gently reheat the juices in a saucepan, then pour back over the chicken and serve from the pot, or in warmed bowls or plates.

To joint a chicken into 8 pieces, place the chicken, breast side up on a chopping board. Using a boning or filleting knife, remove the wishbone (which is at the neck end of the bird – think of it as the collar bone) by cutting behind it to gently loosen it all around, then pull it away from the carcass.

To remove the thigh and drumstick, cut through the loose skin between the leg and breast, then cutting through the ball-and-socket joint attaching the thigh to the body. Repeat for the other side. Try to also remove the oyster piece (which is the tender little oyster-sized morsel) at the base of each thigh, next to the joint.

Separate the drumstick from the thigh by cutting along the thin line of fat – if you cut along this, you will easily cut through another ball-and-socket joint.

Remove the wings by cutting through the ball-and-socket joints where the wing meets the body. Place them on the board and cut off the wing tips and discard (or pop into your chicken stock pot with the wishbone and the carcass).

To remove the breast, place the chicken on the board, breast side up and, starting at the breastbone in the centre, cut along the edge of the bone to loosen the white meat. Use long sweeping movements, removing each breast in one piece. If it is particularly large, you may cut it in half again.

Use the remaining carcass, with the wishbone and the wing tip to flavour the dish if you wish, or use in a stock pot (see page 51).

Roast duck legs

....

SERVES 4
4 duck legs
Salt and ground black pepper

This recipe really couldn't be easier. Serve the duck legs with Lentils with Red Wine and Braised Chicory (see below and page 238). Any leftover duck can be torn into strips and will make a great winter salad.

1 Preheat the oven to 200°C (400°F), Gas mark 6.

2 Place the duck legs skin side up in a small roasting tin, season with salt and pepper and roast in the oven for 1 hour or until the skin is a rich golden brown and the meat comes away from the bone easily.

Lentils with red wine

....

SERVES 4
VEGETARIAN
250g (9oz) Puy lentils, rinsed
3 tbsp olive oil
1 carrot (about 75g/3oz),
    peeled and finely chopped
1 onion (about 200g/7oz),
    peeled and finely chopped
1 stick of celery, peeled and
    finely chopped
2 cloves of garlic, peeled
    and chopped
100ml (3½fl oz) red wine
400ml (14fl oz) vegetable
    stock (see page 50)
Salt and ground black pepper
Chopped chervil or flat
    leaf parsley, to decorate
    (optional)

By treating lentils in this Italian way, similar to a risotto, you elevate a simple pulse to a dish of exquisite flavour. Served with duck and chicory (see page 238) it becomes a foodie match made in heaven.

1 Place the lentils in a saucepan and add about twice the volume of cold water. Bring to the boil on a medium heat, then drain the lentils and set aside.

2 Meanwhile, pour the olive oil into a large saucepan on a low-medium heat, then add the carrot, onion, celery and garlic. Continue to cook for 10–15 minutes or until very soft.

3 Add the lentils and red wine, turn the heat up to medium and cook for 2–3 minutes or until the wine has evaporated. Pour in the stock, bring to the boil, then reduce the heat, cover with a lid and simmer for 20–25 minutes or until the lentils are soft. Season to taste and serve straight away or reheat to serve, decorated with the herbs (if using).

Braised chicory

SERVES 4
VEGETARIAN
2 heads of chicory
25g (1oz) butter
Salt and ground black pepper

Chicory works very well with duck or goose, the slight bitterness perfectly counterbalancing the richness of the meat. Look out for chicory with hardly any trace of green and with tightly packed leaves. This makes a great combination for a main course when served with the Roast Duck Legs and Lentils with Red Wine (see page 236).

1 Preheat the oven to 190°C (375°F), Gas mark 5.

2 Remove the outer leaves from each head of chicory, then trim the base but keep the root intact to ensure the leaves stay together. Slice each in half lengthways.

3 Place a small ovenproof frying pan or saucepan on a medium heat. Once it is quite hot, add the butter, allow it to melt and quickly place the chicory halves cut side down in the pan. Cook for about 5 minutes or until they are golden brown. Turn them over, season with salt and pepper, add 1 tablespoon of water and cover with a lid.

4 Place in the oven and cook for 20–25 minutes or until soft all the way through. If you prefer, this dish can also be cooked on the hob over a very low heat with the lid on (although you may need to add another tablespoon of water).

Green salad dressings

....

SIMPLE DRESSING
3 tbsp extra-virgin olive oil
1 tbsp lemon juice
Pinch of salt and ground
    black pepper

A great salad is often just as simple as some leaves with a dressing, but there are times when you might want to introduce other flavours and textures. Try adding chopped spring or red onions, diced avocado, some olives, toasted pine nuts or seeds such as pumpkin, sunflower or sesame.

1 To make the simple dressing, place all the oil and lemon juice in a jar and shake vigorously to combine. Season to taste with salt and pepper. Alternatively, put the ingredients in a bowl and just stir together.

Ginger, lemon and honey dressing: to the simple dressing ingredients, add 1 small clove of garlic, peeled and crushed, ½ tsp honey, ½ tsp Dijon mustard and ½ tsp finely grated ginger.

Coriander and cumin dressing: mix together 3 tbsp extra virgin olive oil, 1 tbsp red wine vinegar, ½ tsp ground coriander, ½ tsp ground cumin and 1 small clove of garlic, peeled and grated. Season to taste.

Sherry vinegar dressing: mix together 3 tbsp extra virgin olive oil, 1 tbsp sherry vinegar, 1 tbsp finely chopped coriander, ½ tsp wholegrain mustard. Season to taste.

Spinach and mint orzo

SERVES 4–6
VEGETARIAN

50g (2oz) butter
1 onion, peeled and chopped
Salt and ground black pepper
4 large cloves of garlic,
    peeled and chopped
1 tsp ground cumin
1 tsp ground coriander
225ml (8fl oz) double or
    regular cream
200g (7oz) orzo
250g (9oz) button
    mushrooms, sliced
3 tbsp chopped mint
6 spring onions, trimmed
    and finely sliced
200g (7oz) spinach (any large
    stalks removed before
    weighing), chopped,
    or baby spinach
1 tsp Dijon mustard

Orzo is a type of pasta that is shaped like large rice grains. Cooked until just al dente, the texture is lovely. Spinach and mint are two flavours that work wonderfully with lamb, so you can serve this as a side dish with the Roast Loin of Lamb with a Spicy Rub (see page 232), but it would be just as good with a leg or rack of lamb as well.

1 Melt half the butter in a large saucepan on a low heat, add the onion and season with salt and pepper. Cover the pan with a lid and sweat the onion for 8–10 minutes or until soft but not browned.

2 Add the garlic and spices, turn up the heat and cook, stirring occasionally, for a further 3–4 minutes or until the spices give off a fragrant aroma. Pour in the cream, bring just to boiling point, then reduce the heat again and simmer for 10 minutes or until the cream has thickened.

3 While the sauce is simmering, cook the orzo following the instructions on the packet.

4 Meanwhile, melt the remaining butter in a frying pan on a high heat, Once the butter has melted, add the mushrooms, season with salt and pepper and cook, tossing frequently, for 4–5 minutes or until golden.

5 Add the mushrooms to the sauce, along with the mint, spring onions and spinach, and mustard. Fold in the orzo and serve while warm.

RACHEL ALLEN DINNER PARTIES

Creamy potato and Gruyère gratin

....

SERVES 6-8
VEGETARIAN
Butter, for greasing
1kg (2lb 3oz) potatoes,
    peeled and cut into
    5mm (¼in) slices
3 cloves of garlic, peeled
    and finely chopped
Salt and ground black pepper
400ml (14fl oz) double or
    regular cream
100g (3½oz) Parmesan or
    Parmesan-style cheese,
    grated
100g (3½oz) Gruyère cheese,
    grated

18 x 26cm (7 x 10½in) gratin
    or similar-sized ovenproof
    dish

This is a wonderfully comforting dish, but it's also especially handy for entertaining as it can be prepared a few hours in advance. The recipe can be easily doubled if you're feeding a crowd.

1 Preheat the oven to 200°C (400°F), Gas mark 6, and butter the gratin dish.

2 Pat the slices of potato dry with kitchen paper to remove excess starch. Scatter the garlic over the base of the dish, then arrange the potato slices in layers, seasoning them with salt and pepper as you go and making sure the top layer is neat and tidy. Pour the cream into the dish and sprinkle the grated cheeses over the top.

3 Cover the dish with foil and place in the oven. After 30 minutes, remove the foil then bake for a further 30 minutes or until the potatoes are cooked and the surface of the gratin is golden brown.

Ribboned carrots with honey and parsley

....

SERVES 4
VEGETARIAN
500g (1lb 2oz) peeled carrots
1 tsp salt
25g (1oz) butter
1 tbsp runny honey
3 tbsp chopped flat-leaf
    parsley
Salt and ground black pepper

These long ribbons are an elegant way of presenting the humble carrot. Serve with the Beef Wellington (see pages 229–30) or the Roast Pork Belly with a Fennel and Garlic Rub (see page 231).

1 Use a peeler to cut the carrots into long ribbons. Fill a large saucepan with water, add the salt and bring to the boil. Add the carrots and blanch for 30 seconds then drain.

2 Place a small saucepan on a medium heat, add the butter and honey and, as the butter melts, stir to combine. Drizzle over the carrots, add the parsley and toss to combine. Season to taste with salt and pepper, then serve immediately.

Butternut squash and chickpeas with cumin and coriander

....

SERVES 4
VEGETARIAN

1 butternut squash (1.5–2kg/
  3lb 5oz–4lb 4oz)
10 cloves of garlic, left whole
  and unpeeled
4 sprigs of thyme
7 tbsp olive oil
Salt and ground black pepper
1 x 400g tin of chickpeas or
  150g (5oz) dried chickpeas,
  soaked and cooked
  (see page 64)
4 tsp cumin seeds, roasted
  and ground (see page 25)
4 tsp coriander seeds, roasted
  and ground
Juice of ½ lemon
3 tbsp roughly chopped
  coriander

In this dish, the squash acts as a sweet soft sponge, absorbing the flavours of the herbs and spices that surround it. The chickpeas give a little more body and add their unique nutty flavour. This is lovely served with the Roast Pork Belly with a Fennel and Garlic Rub (see page 231), though it's so substantial I'd happily serve it as a vegetarian main. It is also fab served at room temperature.

1 Preheat the oven 220°C (425°F), Gas mark 7.

2 Peel and deseed the butternut squash and cut the flesh into 2cm (¾in) cubes. Put into a large bowl and thoroughly mix together with the garlic, thyme and 4 tablespoons of the olive oil, then season with salt and pepper. Spread out in a roasting tin, place in the oven and roast for 20–30 minutes or until the squash is soft and tender. Remove from the oven and set aside.

3 Pour the remaining olive oil into a frying pan or large wide saucepan, then squeeze out the flesh from the roasted garlic into the pan, discarding the skins. Place on a medium heat and use a fork to mash in the garlic for 1 minute until heated through.

4 Drain and lightly rinse the chickpeas, then add to the pan. Reduce the heat and cook for 5–7 minutes, stirring frequently.

5 Mix in the cooked squash and ground spices, taking care not to break up the squash as you stir, and continue cooking for 4–5 minutes or until the squash is heated through. Add the lemon juice and coriander and serve.

Roast garlic colcannon

....

Colcannon is a traditional Irish dish made from mashed potato and cabbage or kale. By roasting the garlic in this way, its flesh is tempered and tamed to become sweet and mellow.

1 large head of garlic, left whole and unpeeled
2 tbsp olive oil
Salt and ground black pepper
1 sprig of rosemary
1kg (2lb 3oz) floury potatoes, unpeeled
450g (1lb) Savoy cabbage or kale
250ml (9fl oz) milk
50g (2oz) butter

1 Preheat the oven to 220°C (425°F), Gas mark 7.

2 Place the whole head of garlic in a small ovenproof dish, drizzle with the olive oil, season with salt and pepper and add the sprig of rosemary. Cover with foil and cook in the oven for about 45 minutes or until the garlic has completely softened.

3 Place the potatoes in a large saucepan and cover with cold water. Add a good pinch of salt, cover with a lid and bring to the boil. After 10 minutes strain off two-thirds of the water, put the lid back on the pan and cook over a gentle heat so that the potatoes steam for about 30 minutes until they are tender.

4 Remove and discard the dark tough outer leaves from the cabbage (if using). Wash the rest and cut into quarters, removing the core. Cut the cabbage or the kale across the grain into slices about 7mm (⅜in) thick. Place in another large saucepan, add the milk and simmer for about 4 minutes or until tender.

5 When the potatoes are just cooked, peel and mash them while still warm with the butter and some salt and pepper. Use your fingers to squeeze out the roasted garlic pulp and beat into the potatoes with enough boiling milk from the cabbage to make a fluffy purée. Then drain the cooked cabbage or kale, stir into the mash and taste for seasoning.

6 For perfection, serve immediately in a hot dish with a lump of butter melting on top.

French beans with lemon and pine nuts

....

SERVES 4–6
VEGETARIAN
1 tsp salt
300g (11oz) French beans,
    cut into 3–4cm (1¼–1½in)
    lengths
2 tbsp olive oil
50g (2oz) pine nuts
3 cloves of garlic, peeled and
    finely sliced
Finely grated zest and juice
    of 1 lemon

Here is a particularly good way of adding both flavour and texture to elevate French beans.

1 Bring a saucepan of water to the boil on a medium heat, add the salt and cook the French beans for 3–4 minutes or until just cooked but still a little 'squeaky' when bitten, then drain and set aside.

2 Place another saucepan, or a frying pan, on a medium heat, add the olive oil, pine nuts and garlic, and cook for 1–2 minutes or until golden, then add the drained beans, lemon zest and juice. Serve immediately.

Soy and sesame pak choi

....

SERVES 4
VEGETARIAN
1 tsp salt
400g (14oz) pak choi
    (4 large or 8 small),
    quartered lengthways
25ml (1fl oz) sesame oil
25ml (1fl oz) light soy sauce
1 tbsp black or white sesame
    seeds, toasted (see page 25)

I love that pak choi offers both the fresh crunch of its stems and the softness of its wilted green leaves. This side dish works well with the Miso Salmon Steaks, the Salmon Teriyaki or the Southeast Asian Grilled Fish (see pages 222, 95 and 94).

1 Pour 50ml (2fl oz) water into a large frying pan and place over a medium heat, stir in the salt and add the pak choi. Cook, tossing occasionally, for about 5 minutes or until all the water has evaporated and the pak choi is just cooked – the leaves should be soft but the base of the stalks still slightly crunchy.

2 Place on a serving dish and drizzle with the sesame oil and soy sauce, then sprinkle over the sesame seeds.

Maple pecan toffee tart

SERVES 6–8
VEGETARIAN

For the sweet shortcrust pastry
200g (7oz) plain flour, sifted
100g (3½oz) chilled butter, cubed, plus extra for greasing
1 tbsp icing sugar, sifted
½–1 egg, beaten

For the filling
275g (10oz) shelled pecans, coarsely chopped, plus 3 whole nuts for decorating
250ml (9fl oz) maple syrup
75g (3oz) light soft brown sugar
150g (5oz) butter
75ml (3fl oz) double or regular cream

23cm (9in) diameter loose-bottomed tart tin

This deliciously sweet nutty tart just asks to be served with a cup of strong coffee or espresso at the end of a meal. Serve it on its own or with some whipped cream, perhaps flavoured with a little amaretto liqueur.

1 Place the flour, butter and icing sugar in a food processor and whiz briefly until the butter is in small lumps. Add half the beaten egg and continue to whiz for another few seconds or until the mixture looks as though it may just come together. (Bear in mind that prolonged processing will only toughen the pastry, so don't whiz it up to the point where it forms a ball of dough.) You might need to add a little more egg, but not too much as the mixture should be just moist enough to come together. If making by hand, rub the butter into the flour and icing sugar until it resembles coarse breadcrumbs then, using your hands, add just enough egg to bring it together. Reserve any leftover egg to use later.

2 With your hands, flatten out the ball of dough until it is about 2cm (¾in) thick, then wrap in cling film or a plastic bag and leave in the fridge for at least 30 minutes.

3 When you are ready to roll out the pastry, butter the tart tin and remove the pastry from the fridge, placing it between two sheets of cling film (each larger in size than your tart tin). Using a rolling pin, roll the pastry out to no thicker than 5mm (¼in). Make sure to keep it in a round shape as well as large enough to line both the base and the sides of the tin.

4 Remove the top layer of cling film, slide your hand, palm upwards, under the bottom layer of cling film, then flip the pastry over (so that the cling film is now on top) and carefully lower it into the tart tin. Press the pastry into the edges of the tin (with the cling film still attached) and, using your thumb, 'cut' the pastry

(continued overleaf)

along the edge of the tin for a neat finish. Remove the cling film, prick over the base with a fork and chill the pastry in the fridge for another 30 minutes or in the freezer for 10 minutes (it can keep for weeks like this in the freezer).

5 While the pastry is chilling, preheat the oven to 180°C (350°F), Gas mark 4.

6 Remove the pastry from the fridge or freezer and line with foil, greaseproof paper or baking parchment, leaving plenty to come over the sides. Fill with baking beans or dried pulses (all of which can be reused repeatedly), then place in the oven and bake 'blind' for 15–20 minutes or until the pastry feels dry in the base. Remove from the oven, take out the baking beans and foil/paper, brush the base of the pastry with any leftover beaten egg, then cook in the oven for another 3 minutes or until lightly golden. Remove from the oven and set aside.

7 While the pastry is cooking, place the pecans in a roasting tin or baking tray and bake in the oven for 8–10 minutes or until lightly toasted.

8 Meanwhile, make the rest of the filling. Place the remaining ingredients in a saucepan and bring to the boil, stirring to dissolve the sugar. Continue to boil vigorously for 5 minutes then remove from the heat and stir in the toasted pecans and pour into the pre-baked tart base. Place in the oven and cook for 30–35 minutes or until browned and bubbling. Allow to cool and then put in the fridge to chill before serving.

Blackberry mousse

SERVES 6

450g (1lb) blackberries, plus
   extra to decorate (optional)
110g (4oz) caster sugar
1 rounded tsp powdered
   gelatine
300ml (½ pint) double
   or regular cream

This is a gorgeous autumnal dessert with a wonderful pink colour. It's also a great excuse to go out foraging for blackberries! The shortbread biscuits on pages 58–9 are the perfect accompaniment.

1 Place the blackberries in a large saucepan and add the sugar and 2 tablespoons of water. Cook over a low heat for 10–12 minutes or until the blackberries are soft.

2 Pour the blackberries into a large sieve set over a bowl and push through all the liquefied fruit that you can, leaving the seeds in the sieve. Remember to scrape the underside of the sieve too and add this into the purée in the bowl.

3 Pour 1 tablespoon of water into a small bowl, sprinkle over the powdered gelatine and set aside for 5 minutes.

4 Pour the blackberry purée into a saucepan and add the soaked gelatine. Stir the syrup over a low heat for 2–3 minutes or until the gelatine has dissolved.

5 In a separate bowl, whip the cream until it forms stiff peaks, then gently fold in the purée. Pour into a serving bowl, pretty glasses or, if you have them, old-fashioned tea cups. Cover with cling film and chill overnight or for 2–3 hours until set. You could sprinkle a few blackberries on top just before serving.

Raspberry and amaretto tart

225g (8oz) deep-golden
   amaretti biscuits
125g (4½oz) butter
½ tsp ground cinnamon
250g (9oz) natural Greek
   yoghurt, pushed through
   a sieve
350g (12oz) fresh raspberries
Icing sugar, for dusting
   (optional)

23cm (9in) diameter loose-
   bottomed tart tin

At the height of the raspberry season I can think of few more delightful or indeed any easier ways to present them than this tart. The crunchy texture and almond flavour of the amaretti complement the velvety sharpness of the fruit.

1 To make the tart base, first place the amaretti in a clean plastic bag and crush into fine crumbs using a rolling pin. Alternatively, you can whiz the biscuits in a food processor for a second or two.

2 Melt the butter in a large saucepan over a medium heat, then remove from the hob and stir in the biscuit crumbs. Pour the biscuit mixture into the tin, then use the back of a spoon to flatten it into the base and up the sides of the tin by 3cm (1¼in). (I find using my fingertips for this gives the edges a good finish.) Put the biscuit base in the fridge to chill for 1½–2 hours.

3 When you are ready to serve, mix the cinnamon with the yoghurt, then spoon the mixture into the chilled tart base and simply top with the fresh raspberries, lightly dusted with icing sugar, if wished.

Peach jelly pannacotta pots

....

SERVES 6

Sunflower oil, for oiling

For the peach syrup jelly
110g (4oz) caster sugar
3 peaches, left unpeeled but
    halved and stones removed
1 tbsp powdered gelatine

For the pannacotta
300ml (½ pint) double or
    regular cream
25g (1oz) caster sugar
1 vanilla pod, split lengthways
1 rounded tsp powdered
    gelatine

Six 100ml (3½fl oz) ramekin
    dishes or glasses

This divine dessert is a twist on the classic combination of peaches and cream. The bright translucent fruit jelly looks gorgeous perched on the rich smooth pannacotta.

1 Lightly oil the inside of each ramekin, then carefully line with cling film, allowing extra to hang over the sides for covering the top of the dish when it has been filled, then lightly oil the inside of the cling film.

2 Begin by making the peach syrup jelly. Fill a large saucepan with 300ml (½ pint) water and add the sugar. Set on a medium heat and stir until the sugar is dissolved. Then bring to boiling point, add the halved peaches, then reduce the heat and allow to simmer for 5–8 minutes or until the peaches are soft.

3 Take the pan from the heat, carefully remove the peaches from the syrup and gently peel away their skins, which should slip off easily. Place each peach half, cut side up, in one of the lined ramekins.

4 Pour 2 tablespoons of water into a small bowl, sprinkle over the gelatine and set aside for 5 minutes. Next add the soaked gelatine to the peach syrup in the saucepan and stir over a low heat for 2–3 minutes or until dissolved.

5 Divide the syrup equally between the six ramekins, making sure you keep the peaches as central and upright as possible in each dish, then chill in the fridge for 2 hours to set the jelly.

6 To make the pannacotta, place the cream, sugar and vanilla pod in a saucepan and slowly bring to boiling point, then turn off the heat and allow the vanilla to infuse.

7 Pour 2 teaspoons of water into a clean bowl, add the gelatine and set aside for 5 minutes. Add the soaked gelatine to the hot cream mixture, stirring gently until the gelatine dissolves. (If the cream

has cooled down too much, you may need to reheat it slightly once the gelatine has been added.)

8 Allow to cool to room temperature, remove the vanilla pod then pour the pannacotta over the set peach jelly in the ramekins. Gently cover each dish with the excess cling film hanging over the sides, then place in the fridge to chill for 2–3 hours or overnight until set.

9 To serve, turn each ramekin upside down onto a plate, carefully remove the ramekin and then very gently peel off the cling film.

RACHEL'S TIP
Sometimes creased cling film can leave marks on the pannacotta. So if you would like yours to be completely smooth, very gently smooth the edges with a metal spatula dipped in hot water.

Tiramisu

....

SERVES 6
VEGETARIAN

1 egg yolk
1 tbsp caster sugar
1 tsp vanilla extract
1 x 250g tub of mascarpone
200ml (7fl oz) double or
    regular cream
200ml (7fl oz) strong black
    coffee, such as espresso
2 tbsp brandy
10–12 boudoir biscuits
    (sponge fingers), each
    broken into 3 pieces
1–2 tbsp cocoa powder,
    for dusting

Six medium glasses

This classic Italian dessert is very straightforward to prepare yet looks impressive layered up in individual glasses.

1 Place the egg, sugar and vanilla extract in a large bowl and whisk to a creamy consistency. Add the mascarpone and cream and continue to whisk until smooth and creamy.

2 In a separate bowl, mix together the coffee and brandy. Dip 2–3 pieces of the boudoir biscuits into the coffee and brandy (just long enough to absorb the liquid, but not so long that they fall apart) and put into the bottom of one of the six glasses. Repeat for the remaining glasses.

3 Add 1 tablespoon of the mascarpone and cream mixture to cover the biscuits in each glass. Follow this with another layer of 2–3 biscuit pieces, dipped again in the coffee and brandy, finishing with another layer of mascarpone and cream.

4 Dust each glass with cocoa powder and place in the fridge to chill for at least 1 hour (or up to 24 hours). Take out of the fridge 10 minutes or so before serving (so they aren't too chilled) and dust with a little more cocoa powder to serve.

Spiced raisin tart

....

SERVES 6-8
VEGETARIAN

110g (4oz) butter, plus extra
    for greasing
225g (8oz) digestive biscuits
225g (8oz) raisins
1 tsp cornflour
½ tsp ground cinnamon
110g (4oz) demerara or light
    soft brown sugar

23cm (9in) diameter loose-
    bottomed tart tin

A favourite recipe of my mum's from the 70s, this is fabulously retro. My sister and I used to love eating the leftovers (if there were any!) from my parents' dinner parties. It's great served with the Cinnamon Ice Cream on page 258. Because of the dried fruit and spice filling, it works particularly well as a Christmas dessert. If there's any left over, it's also delicious with a cup of coffee.

1 Start by making the biscuit base. Butter the tart tin, then place the digestive biscuits in a clean plastic bag and, using a rolling pin, crush into fine crumbs. Alternatively, you could whiz the biscuits in a food processor for a minute or two.

2 Melt the butter in a saucepan over a medium heat, remove from the heat and stir in the biscuit crumbs. Pour the mixture into the prepared tin and, using the back of a spoon, flatten the crumbs into the base and up the sides of the tin. (I find using your fingertips gives the sides a good finish.) Place in the fridge to chill for 1½–2 hours.

3 Meanwhile, fill a separate saucepan with 300ml (½ pint) of water and add the raisins. Bring to a simmer and cook for about 10 minutes or until the raisins have plumped up.

4 Place the cornflour in a small bowl, add 2 teaspoons of water and mix to a smooth consistency. Pour this into the cooked raisins and continue to stir gently over a low heat for about 2 minutes or until the liquid thickens slightly.

5 Next add the cinnamon and sugar and continue to stir over a low heat for about 2 minutes or until the sugar has dissolved. Remove from the heat and allow the raisin mixture to cool.

6 Once it has cooled, pour the mixture into the biscuit base and pop the tart back into the fridge for 1–2 hours before serving.

Almond and orange cake

SERVES 6-8
VEGETARIAN

100g (3½oz) butter,
  softened, plus extra
  for greasing
175g (6 oz) caster sugar
3 eggs
Juice and finely grated
  zest of 1 orange
50g (2oz) plain flour
1 tsp baking powder
100g (3½oz) ground almonds

For the syrup
75g (3oz) icing sugar
Juice of 1 orange
1 tbsp Cointreau or
  Grand Marnier

20cm (8in) diameter spring-
  form/loose-bottomed tin

This is a really moist cake that will keep for up to a week – if you can resist eating it! It is divine served with Orange Ice Cream (see page 258) or some whipped cream mixed with a little icing sugar and Cointreau or orange zest.

1 Preheat the oven to 180°C (350°F), Gas mark 4. Butter the tin and line the base with baking parchment.

2 Cream the butter in a large bowl or in an electric food mixer until soft. Add the sugar and beat until the mixture is light and fluffy. Beat in the eggs, one at a time, then whisk in the orange juice and zest. Sift in the flour and baking powder and fold into the cake batter, then fold in the ground almonds.

3 Spoon the mixture into the prepared tin and bake in the oven for 30–40 minutes or until the cake is golden and a skewer inserted into the middle comes out clean.

4 While the cake is baking, make the syrup. Place the icing sugar and orange juice in a small saucepan and stir over a low heat for 1–2 minutes or until the sugar has dissolved. Remove from the heat and add the Cointreau or Grand Marnier.

5 When you remove the cake from the oven, leave it in the tin and use a skewer to make holes, about 2cm (¾in) deep and 3cm (1¼in) apart, across the surface of the cake. Gently drizzle the warm syrup over the top of the cake, allowing it to soak in. Allow to cool slightly before removing it from the tin, and serve warm. This cake is also delicious cold.

Orange ice cream

....

SERVES 6-8
VEGETARIAN
300ml (½ pint) double or
   regular cream
4 eggs, separated
100g (3½oz) caster sugar
Juice and finely grated zest
   of 2 oranges

The beauty of this ice cream is that you don't need an ice-cream machine to make it. It is yummy with the Almond and Orange Cake or used in the recipe for Amaretti with Brandy and Ice Cream (see pages 257 and 300).

1 Pour the cream into a bowl and whisk until thickened. In a separate bowl, whisk together the egg yolks and the sugar until thickened and creamy in colour. Add the orange juice and grated zest and whisk to combine.

2 In a spotlessly clean, dry bowl, whisk the egg whites until they form stiff peaks. Fold the cream into the egg and sugar mixture, then gently fold in the egg whites. Pour into an airtight plastic container with a lid or into a serving bowl and cover with cling film. Freeze overnight.

VARIATION
Lemon ice cream: Make the recipe in the same way, simply replacing the orange juice and zest with the juice and zest of 2 lemons.

Cinnamon ice cream

....

SERVES 6-8
VEGETARIAN
300ml (½ pint) double
   or regular cream
4 eggs, separated
100g (3½oz) caster sugar
1 tsp ground cinnamon

A very easy ice cream to make, and you don't need an ice-cream machine. Delicious on its own and particularly good served with the Spiced Raisin Tart or the Spiced Poached Pears (see pages 256 and 82).

1 In a bowl, whip the cream until thickened. In another bowl, whisk together the egg yolks with the sugar until thickened and creamy in colour. Add the cinnamon and whisk again to combine.

2 In a separate, spotlessly clean, dry bowl, whisk the egg whites until they form stiff peaks. Fold the cream into the egg and sugar mixture, and then gently fold in the egg whites.

3 Pour the mixture into an airtight plastic container with a lid or into a serving bowl. Cover with cling film and freeze overnight.

Gin and tonic lemon sorbet

SERVES 8
VEGETARIAN
250ml (9fl oz) freshly
   squeezed lemon juice
   (from about 4 lemons)
400g (14oz) caster sugar
750ml (1⅓ pints) tonic water

To serve
8 slices of lemon
About 8 tbsp gin

8 chilled cocktail glasses

I love this playful twist on the timeless drink. Like the Orange Sorbet with Campari (see page 200), this can be served as a starter, a palate cleanser during the meal before the main course or even for dessert.

1 Place a saucepan on a low heat, add the lemon juice and sugar and gently warm through, stirring frequently, until the sugar has dissolved. Remove from the heat, stir in the tonic water and allow to cool. Place into an ice-cream machine and churn for 20–30 minutes or until the mixture has thickened.

2 If you don't have an ice-cream machine, place the sorbet in the freezer for 2–3 hours or until it begins to set around the edges, then, using a fork, stir to break up the frozen crystals. Put the lid back on and continue to freeze for a further hour. Remove from the freezer and stir again, then freeze for another hour, remove and stir one final time.

3 Meanwhile, place a bowl in the freezer that will hold all the sorbet. Once the sorbet has thickened, transfer to the frozen bowl, cover and pop straight into the freezer and leave overnight.

4 When ready to serve, place the frozen sorbet in the fridge for about 10 minutes to soften ever so slightly, before scooping into the glasses and topping with a slice of lemon and about 1 tablespoon (or more if preferred) of gin. Serve immediately.

Choosing a cheese board

....

I love to serve a cheese course as part of a dinner party, sometimes before dessert, as is the custom in France; sometimes instead of a dessert course; but more often than not I prefer to serve cheese at the very end of the meal to enjoy with the last of the red wine. People may feel apprehensive about serving a cheese board, uncertain as to what goes with what. They needn't be, as there are no solid rules, but here are a few guidelines.

* I think while a selection can be nice, your money would be better spent on fewer, better cheeses. I would be happier with just a couple of great cheeses from a good cheese shop than a number of mediocre, unripe cheeses.

* A little honey is a nice contrast to the intense savoury flavour of a goat's cheese or blue cheese.

* Some fruit, especially figs or grapes, work well with cheese – hard varieties in particular.

* A fruit paste (such as quince membrillo) is very nice with semi-hard to hard cheeses.

* Fresh bread is delicious with cheese, as are oatcakes, crispbreads (see page 262) or crackers. Serve one or a selection.

* Cheese is much better served at room temperature, so take it out the fridge at least 1 hour before serving.

* It's a good idea to ask your cheesemonger the best way to store each variety as some are best stored, covered, outside the fridge.

Paper-thin crispbreads

375g (13oz) plain flour OR
   225g (8oz) plain flour and
   150g (5oz) wholemeal flour
1 tsp salt
1 tbsp sesame seeds or
   poppy seeds
2 tsp crushed cumin,
   fennel, black pepper or
   coriander seeds or sea salt,
   or herbs (all optional)
1 egg
1 tbsp olive oil
125ml (4fl oz) water

This super-thin crispbread is amazingly versatile and goes really well with any cheese board.

1 Place the dry ingredients in a large bowl and mix together.

2 Whisk the egg in another bowl, add the olive oil and water and mix well. Pour the wet ingredients into the dry ingredients and, using your hands or in the bowl of a food processor, mix to a dough. Knead for 2 minutes until the dough is smooth, then wrap in cling film and set aside to rest for 20 minutes.

3 Preheat the oven to 200°C (400°F), Gas mark 6 (if using a fan oven, see below) and lightly oil several baking trays.

4 Divide the dough into two and roll out each piece until it is about 20cm (8in) wide. Fold the dough in half, then in half again and continue to roll until the dough is paper thin, like pasta, about 1–2mm ($\frac{1}{16}$in) thick. The pieces should be about 45cm (18in) square. You may need to use some flour while rolling out.

5 Cut the dough into rectangles approximately 8 x 14cm (5½in) in size and place in a single layer on the prepared baking trays. If you want to sprinkle sea salt or seeds on top of the crispbreads, then brush the top of the raw crispbreads with olive oil before sprinkling over so that they stick to the surface.

6 Bake in the oven for 10–14 minutes or until pale golden brown and slightly curled up at the edges. They will feel dry when cooked, but will only really crisp up when they have cooled. Check after 8–10 minutes of cooking and if they are golden brown underneath, but still quite pale on top, then turn them over. Allow to cool on wire racks.

RACHEL'S TIP
If you have a fan oven, you can bake the crispbreads on more than one baking tray at a time. Preheat it to 180°C (350°F), Gas mark 4.

MENU IDEAS FOR DINNER PARTIES

Serve all menus with a green salad (see page 239)

Smoked mackerel and goat's cheese soufflé (page 211)
Roast loin of lamb with a spicy rub and spinach and mint orzo (pages 232 and 240)
Almond and orange cake (page 257)

*

Beef carpaccio (page 214)
Miso salmon steaks (page 222)
French beans with lemon and pine nuts (page 245)
Peach jelly pannacotta pots (pages 252–3)

*

Chicken liver pâté with sweet apple relish (pages 206–7)
Roast pork belly with a fennel and garlic rub, butternut squash
and chickpeas with cumin and coriander and ribboned carrots
with honey and parsley (pages 231, 242 and 241)
Spiced raisin tart (page 256)

*

Ballycotton prawn soup with rouille and toasts (page 204)
Roast duck legs with lentils with red wine and braised chicory (pages 236 and 238)
Tiramisu (page 254)

STARTERS

Chilled avocado soup with red and yellow pepper and coriander salsa
Roast wedges of butternut squash with goat's cheese and spinach pesto
Zingy Asian prawns
Lamb cutlets with spinach pesto
Winter leaf salad with pomegranate, apple and walnuts
Smoked fish platter with Ballymaloe cucumber relish

MAIN COURSES

Greek red peppers
Baked beetroot risotto with Parmesan crisps
Zesty pine nut-crusted fish with salsa verde
Soy-poached fish with avocado salsa
Spiced chicken with red pepper and almonds
Conchiglie pasta with chicken livers, bacon and port
Winter herb and sausage pasta
Cassoulet
Beef and wild mushroom lasagne
Roast haunch of venison

SIDE DISHES

Wilted greens with garlic and anchovy breadcrumbs
Roast Jerusalem artichokes
Rosemary and garlic bread
Parsnip, mustard and parsley mash
Crunchy roast coriander potatoes
Potato and mushroom gratin
Cucumbers with tomatoes, cream and mint

DESSERTS

Amaretti with brandy and ice cream
Iced strawberry parfait with strawberry sauce
White chocolate and ginger parfait with dark chocolate sauce
Raspberry millefeuille
Salted caramel chocolate tart
Rhubarb and ginger crumble cake
Passion fruit and orange granita
Chocolate roulade

LARGER GATHERINGS
(8-12 PEOPLE)

I won't lie, cooking for a larger group for a party or get-together takes a little extra planning and effort, so here I've given you recipes that are easier to cook for a bigger group. As ever, remember that cooking for a crowd is great fun, and the satisfaction from having fed so many friends and family goes a long way to making you feel great.

Chilled avocado soup with red and yellow pepper and coriander salsa

....

The vivid colours of this soup make it a perfect dish for a dazzling dinner party.

4 very ripe avocados
15g (½oz) peeled and
    sliced onion
100ml (3½fl oz) French
    dressing (see page 318)
2–4 tsp lemon juice
600ml (1 pint) cold chicken
    or vegetable stock
    (see pages 50–1)

For the red pepper salsa
1 red pepper, deseeded
    and chopped into 3mm
    (⅛in) dice
1 yellow pepper, deseeded
    and chopped into 3mm
    (⅛in) dice
1 red onion, peeled and
    chopped, or 2 spring
    onions, trimmed and
    finely chopped
2 generous tbsp chopped
    coriander (or mint or basil),
    plus some leaves
8 tbsp extra-virgin olive oil
Salt and ground black pepper
Juice of ½–1 lemon

1 Peel and roughly chop the avocados and place in a food processor. Add the onion, French dressing and lemon juice, whiz to a purée, then pour in enough of the stock to bring it to the consistency of thick double cream. Depending on the size of your avocados you may need more or less of the stock to achieve the desired consistency, keeping in mind that it needs to be thick enough so that the salsa will not sink when serving.

2 Taste for seasoning, adding more lemon juice if needed. Push through a sieve then pour into a container for the fridge, cover and chill for ½–1 hour or up to about 4 hours before serving.

3 Meanwhile, make the salsa. Place the red and yellow peppers, onion, chopped coriander and olive oil in a bowl, mixing together and seasoning to taste with salt, pepper and lemon juice.

4 When ready to serve, pour the soup into individual bowls with a spoonful of salsa added to the centre of each and scatter over the coriander leaves.

Roast wedges of butternut squash with goat's cheese and spinach pesto

....

SERVES 8-10
VEGETARIAN

½ tsp black peppercorns
2 butternut squash
4 tbsp olive oil
1 tbsp sherry vinegar
    or balsamic vinegar
Sea salt

To serve
150ml (5fl oz) spinach pesto
    (see page 270)
2 large handfuls of rocket
    leaves
250g (9oz) soft goat's cheese,
    broken into 2cm (¾in)
    chunks
3 tbsp pumpkin seeds, toasted
    (see tip on page 25)

The substantial nature of this dish makes it a hearty vegetarian starter. I'm often surprised at just how sweet butternut can be; the roasting draws out and caramelizes the sugars. The sweetness is countered by the savouriness of the goat's cheese and spinach pesto (see overleaf). It is a beautiful combination on the plate as well as in the mouth. It also makes a delicious accompaniment for roast meat. I like to serve it slightly warm, but it can be served at room temperature too.

1 Make the spinach pesto (see overleaf) and place to one side.

2 Preheat the oven to 220°C (425°F), Gas mark 7.

3 Coarsely crush the peppercorns using a pestle and mortar, or place in a small plastic bag and crush with a rolling pin. Peel the butternut squash using a sharp knife, cut in half lengthways and discard the seeds (or see tip below).

4 Cut the butternut squash into wedges just less than 1cm (½in) at the thickest part. Place in a wide bowl and drizzle with the oil and vinegar, seasoning with a good pinch of sea salt and the pepper. Toss with your hands then tip into a roasting tin or baking tray, making sure to pour in all the oil and seasoning. Spread out into a single layer and roast in the oven for 10–15 minutes or until the squash is tender and a little crisp at the edges. Remove from the oven and allow to cool slightly.

5 To serve, divide the butternut squash between individual plates and scatter the rocket leaves on top. Scatter over the goat's cheese, drizzle with the spinach pesto (1–2 teaspoons per plate) and sprinkle over the pumpkin seeds.

RACHEL'S TIP
If you are feeling ambitious, you can wash the squash seeds, roast them in the oven for about 8 minutes or until golden, then peel them and use in place of the pumpkin seeds.

100g (3½oz) spinach
  (any large stalks removed
  before weighing)
50g (2oz) pine nuts
50g (2oz) Parmesan or
  Parmesan-style cheese,
  finely grated
1 clove of garlic, peeled and
  crushed or finely grated
150ml (5fl oz) extra-virgin
  olive oil, plus extra for
  adding to the jar
Salt and ground black pepper

Spinach pesto

Baby spinach is best for this; if you are using a larger-leafed variety, make sure the leaves aren't too large or tough, and remove any stalks. In addition to the Roast Wedges of Butternut Squash with Goat's Cheese (see page 268), the pesto is also delicious with roasted root vegetables, or roast lamb or chicken. It will keep for a few months stored in a jar in the fridge.

1 Place all the ingredients, except the seasoning, in a food processor, adding only a little of the olive oil at this stage. Whiz together for a minute or two to form a rough paste.

2 Mix in the remaining oil, pouring it in through the tube of the food processor, and add salt and pepper to taste. If the pesto is too thick to drizzle, add a little more olive oil, taking care the pesto does not split.

3 Pour into a sterilised jar (for sterilising jars, see tip on page 42) and cover with a layer of olive oil.

Zingy Asian prawns

SERVES 8-12

600g (1lb 5oz) peeled cooked
   prawns
8 cloves of garlic, peeled and
   crushed
2 tsp peeled and finely grated
   root ginger (see page 27)
2 tbsp chopped mint
2 tbsp chopped coriander
2 tsp finely chopped
   lemongrass
4 tbsp fish sauce (nam pla)
2 tbsp soft light brown sugar
½–1 red chilli, deseeded and
   chopped
Juice of 1 lemon

To serve
1 Cos lettuce
Whole coriander leaves

The combination of mint and coriander in this great southeast Asian starter make it wonderfully light and fresh tasting. Serve it on a sunny summer's day, followed by the Spiced Chicken with Red Pepper and Almonds (see page 284).

1 Place all the ingredients in a large bowl and mix together. Taste for seasoning, adding more fish sauce if it's not salty enough, then leave to marinate for at least 20 minutes before serving.

2 To serve, shred the lettuce and divide between individual plates or bowls, then spoon the prawns on top, scattering over a few coriander leaves.

Lamb cutlets with spinach pesto

SERVES 8
24 lamb cutlets
3 tbsp olive oil
Salt and ground black pepper
150ml (5fl oz) spinach pesto
   (see opposite)

If you can, use a cast-iron griddle pan for cooking the cutlets. The pans are heavy but extremely useful in the kitchen. They can get very hot and the criss-cross marks they leave don't just look great, they really enhance the flavour of the meat.

1 Drizzle the cutlets with olive oil and season with salt and pepper. Place a griddle pan or frying pan on a high heat and allow to get quite hot, then add the cutlets and cook for 2–4 minutes on each side depending on how well done you like them.

2 Allow to rest for a few minutes before serving with a drizzle of the spinach pesto.

Winter leaf salad with pomegranate, apple and walnuts

....

SERVES 8
VEGETARIAN

2 large handfuls of salad
  leaves, such as mustard
  greens, rocket, small baby
  chard, kale, beetroot or
  spinach, larger leaves sliced,
  small leaves kept whole
2 large handfuls of radicchio,
  sliced
4 tbsp chopped walnuts,
  toasted (see page 25)
Seeds from 1 pomegranate
2 small crisp eating apples,
  unpeeled, cored and
  chopped

For the dressing
8 tbsp extra-virgin olive oil
3 tbsp lemon juice
Sea salt and ground black
  pepper

*This is an incredible, multi-flavoured, multi-textured salad, the
slightly bitter flavour of the radicchio is offset by the tangy apple and
pomegranate and the earthy crunchiness of the walnuts.*

1 To make the dressing, pour the olive oil and lemon juice into a
bowl or screw-top jar, season with sea salt and pepper and mix or
shake together. (This will sit happily for a few days in the fridge.)

2 Place all the salad ingredients in a large bowl, pour over the
dressing and toss everything together, then serve immediately.

RACHEL'S TIP
To remove the seeds from a pomegranate, simply cut into
quarters and bend the skins to push out the seeds. Make sure
you discard all of the white inner membrane as it is quite bitter.

Smoked fish platter with Ballymaloe cucumber relish

....

2 fillets of smoked mackerel,
  skinned and cut into slices
  about 1cm (½in) thick
8 slices of smoked salmon,
  cold or hot smoked
1 smoked eel fillet, sliced
  into 8 x 4cm (1½in) batons
1 smoked trout fillet, divided
  into 8 pieces
16 smoked mussels
8 thin slices of smoked tuna
  or hake

To serve
8 lemon wedges
8 tbsp cucumber relish (see
  below)
8 tbsp horseradish sauce (see
  page 341)
8 tbsp sweet dill mayonnaise
  (see page 317)

This is less of a cooking recipe and more of a guide to assembling delicious smoked fish to serve as a starter for a larger dinner party. I've given a few suggestions as to which smoked fish to use; you can serve all six or just one or two, depending on what's available. Smoked fish goes beautifully with sweet-sour flavours – hence the cucumber relish below. Serve with slices of bread – brown (yeast or soda) or rye is best, or a good crusty white loaf.

1 Simply divide the portions of fish between individual plates or servings plates for guests to help themselves, adding a wedge of lemon, 1 tablespoon each of the cucumber relish and horseradish sauce and a drizzle of the mayonnaise.

RACHEL'S TIP
When storing smoked fish in the fridge, make sure it is covered, and make sure to take it out of the fridge at least 10 minutes before serving.

MAKES ABOUT 1 LITRE
(1¾ PINTS)
VEGETARIAN
900g (2lb) cucumber, unpeeled
1 medium onion, peeled,
  halved and very thinly sliced
350g (12oz) caster sugar
1 tbsp salt
225ml (8fl oz) cider vinegar
  or white wine vinegar

Ballymaloe cucumber relish

1 Using a food processor or mandolin, slice the cucumber and place in a large bowl with the onion.

2 Add the remaining ingredients and mix well to combine.

Greek red peppers

SERVES 8
VEGETARIAN
600g (1lb 5oz) feta cheese,
    crumbled into 5mm–1cm
    (¼–½in) pieces
2 red onions, peeled and diced
300g (11oz) cherry tomatoes,
    quartered
50g (2oz) capers, drained,
    rinsed and chopped
6 tbsp chopped mint
Salt and ground black pepper
Pinch of sugar
8 peppers (red or yellow),
    halved lengthways,
    retaining the stalks,
    and deseeded
150g (5oz) fresh white
    breadcrumbs
75ml (3fl oz) olive oil

A substantial, yet refined, main course, peppers can be stuffed with a huge variety of fillings. Here the breadcrumbs provide crunch and the salty feta balances the sweetness of roasted peppers.

1 Preheat the oven to 180°C (350°F), Gas mark 4.

2 In a large bowl, mix together the feta, onions, tomatoes, capers and mint and season with salt and pepper and a pinch of sugar. Divide this mixture between the pepper halves.

3 Top with the breadcrumbs and drizzle with olive oil, then place in the oven and bake for 45–55 minutes or until the peppers are soft and the crumbs on top are deep golden and crunchy.

Baked beetroot risotto
with Parmesan crisps

....

SERVES 8–12
VEGETARIAN

For cooking the beetroot
1kg (2lb 3oz) beetroot,
    unpeeled
2 tbsp olive oil, plus
    extra for roasting
Salt and ground black pepper
2 tsp balsamic vinegar

For the Parmesan crisps
100g (3½oz) Parmesan or
    Parmesan-style cheese,
    finely grated

For cooking the risotto
2 tbsp olive oil
2 onions (300g/11oz in total),
    peeled and finely chopped
Salt and ground black pepper
700g (1½lb) risotto rice, such
    as Arborio or Carnaroli
300ml (½ pint) dry
    white wine
2 litres (3½ pints) chicken
    or vegetable stock
    (see pages 50–1)
150g (5oz) Parmesan or
    Parmesan-style cheese,
    finely grated
100g (3½oz) butter, diced

With its amazing deep pink colour, this is a fun-looking dish with a seriously delicious taste. A risotto cooked in the traditional way can be a pain to prepare for a party. You have to be on hand to stir the stock constantly into the rice when you'd much rather be dazzling your guests with witty repartee. This baked recipe offers an easy alternative to all that stirring. For added convenience, the beetroot can be cooked up to two days in advance and the Parmesan crisps kept for up to eight hours if stored in an airtight box.

1 Place the beetroot in a large saucepan of water, bring to the boil then reduce the heat and simmer covered loosely for about 30 minutes or until the beetroot is very tender when pierced with a sharp knife and the skins feel loose to the touch.

2 Drain the beetroot and peel off the skins with your fingers (you may want to wear some rubber gloves for this), then place half the beetroot in a food processor, add the 2 tablespoons of olive oil and whiz to form a smooth purée. Season to taste with salt and pepper and set aside.

3 Cut the other half of the cooked beetroot into bite-sized chunks, or wedges if you prefer, and set aside.

4 Preheat the oven to 180°C (350°F), Gas mark 4.

5 To make the Parmesan crisps, arrange the grated cheese in about 20 small disc-shaped mounds (3–4cm/1¼–1–1½in in diameter and 2–3mm/⅛in thick) on a baking sheet lined with baking parchment. (You can do this very easily by using a round cookie cutter as a stencil.) Cook for 6–8 minutes or until the cheese has melted and is golden in colour. Take out of the oven and carefully

(continued overleaf)

remove the paper, with the crisps still on it, from the baking sheet. After 2–3 minutes they will be crisp and can be removed from the paper and kept in a dry place for up to 2 hours before serving.

6 To roast the beetroot pieces, place in a bowl with some olive oil and the balsamic vinegar, mix to combine, season with salt and pepper and then arrange in a roasting tin and cook for about 30 minutes in the oven preheated for the crisps (or preheated separately, to the same temperature) or until the edges have started to darken and caramelise.

7 With the beetroot in the oven, you can start the risotto. Pour the olive oil into a casserole dish or an ovenproof saucepan and place on a medium heat. Add the onions, cover with a lid and cook for about 6–8 minutes or until the onions are soft but not browned, then season with salt and pepper.

8 Next add the rice, stirring for 1–2 minutes until it begins to slightly 'hiss'. Pour in the wine and cook for 1–2 minutes, stirring constantly, until most of it has evaporated. Add the stock, stir well and bring to simmering point. Cover again with the lid and place in the oven for about 15 minutes or until the rice is al dente, then remove from the oven and allow to stand for 2 minutes. Gently reheat the beetroot purée in a saucepan, stir in the Parmesan and butter, taste for seasoning and then stir vigorously for about a minute to combine everything.

9 To serve, divide the risotto between warmed plates and scatter with the roasted beetroot pieces and the Parmesan crisps.

Zesty pine nut-crusted fish with salsa verde

....

SERVES 8
Vegetable oil, for oiling
(optional)
250g (9oz) fresh white
breadcrumbs
3 tbsp finely chopped herbs,
such as tarragon, basil,
mint or parsley
150g (5oz) pine nuts, toasted
(see page 25)
Finely grated zest of
1½ lemons
Good pinch of salt
75g (3oz) butter
8 round white fish fillets
(about 150g/5oz each),
skin removed

For the salsa verde
3 handfuls of parsley leaves
Grated zest and juice of
2 lemons
6 cloves of garlic, peeled
and crushed
3 tbsp capers, drained
and rinsed
150ml (5fl oz) olive oil
Salt and ground black pepper

Pine nuts are such a versatile ingredient, they can add texture and depth to anything from couscous or salads to pestos and even tarts. Here they're added to a crust that provides a gorgeous flavour and a pleasing crunchy contrast to the soft fish, but it also protects the fish's delicate flesh from the oven's direct heat, ensuring it doesn't overcook or dry out. Salsa verde keeps in the fridge for weeks if stored in an airtight container.

1 Preheat the oven to 200°C (400°F), Gas mark 6. Oil a baking tray with vegetable oil or line with baking parchment.

2 Place the breadcrumbs in a food processor, along with the herbs, pine nuts, lemon zest and salt, and whiz together for a minute or two to combine. Melt the butter in a saucepan on a medium heat, then add the breadcrumb mixture and stir well to combine – it should be quite moist, but if it isn't, then add some more butter.

3 Next place each portion of fish skinned side down on the prepared baking tray and cover with the breadcrumb mixture. Place in the oven and cook for 10–15 minutes or until the breadcrumb topping is crisp and golden and the fish is opaque all the way through.

4 While the fish is cooking, make the salsa verde. Place the parsley, lemon zest, garlic and capers in a food processor (having first cleaned the bowl) and whiz until finely chopped. Mix in the lemon juice and olive oil, adding more oil if you want it to be a bit more runny, and season to taste with salt and pepper (it might not need salt, as capers can be quite salty).

5 Remove the cooked fish from the oven and serve warm with some salsa verde on the side.

Soy-poached fish with avocado salsa

....

SERVES 8
8 round white fish fillets
(150–175g/5–6oz each),
such as grey mullet,
salmon or pollack

For the poaching liquid
300ml (½ pint) chicken stock
(see page 51)
1 tbsp soy sauce
1 tbsp fish sauce (nam pla)

For the avocado salsa
2 avocados, peeled, stone
removed and flesh cut
into 1cm (½in) cubes
8 spring onions, trimmed
and sliced
12 cherry tomatoes, quartered
2 tsp peeled and finely grated
root ginger (see page 27)
½ cucumber, diced
Juice of 1 lime
4 tsp runny honey
Salt and ground black pepper
Lime slices, to serve

This recipe is light and delicate. Poaching is a way of cooking fish to ensure it doesn't dry out. It's also convenient for entertaining because the fish can sit in the poaching liquid for about quarter of an hour after cooking before serving.

1 Pour the ingredients for the poaching liquid into a saucepan, bring to a gentle simmer and place the fish in the liquid. (It's important not to let the liquid boil as this may damage the fish.) Simmer for 6–8 minutes or until the fish is just opaque all the way through and remove from the heat. (The fish can be kept in the poaching liquid at this stage, for up to 15 minutes, but turn off the heat before the fish is completely cooked as it will go on cooking in the hot poaching liquid.)

2 While the fish is poaching, make the avocado salsa, carefully mixing all the ingredients together in a bowl and seasoning with salt and pepper.

3 To serve, divide the salsa between plates and place the pieces of fish on top. Add a slice of lime and drizzle a tablespoon or so of the poaching liquid around each plate.

Spiced chicken with red pepper and almonds

....

SERVES 8–12

6 tbsp sunflower oil
1.2kg (2lb 10oz) skinless and boneless chicken thighs or breasts
2 tbsp lemon juice
4 tbsp chopped coriander

For the paste
2 onions, peeled and roughly chopped
4 tsp peeled (see page 27) and chopped ginger
4 cloves of garlic, peeled
2 red peppers, deseeded and roughly chopped
4 ripe tomatoes (about 350g/12oz)
150g (5oz) blanched almonds
2 tsp deseeded and finely chopped red chilli
1 tsp ground cardamom
Good pinch of salt
2 tsp caster sugar

This is a wonderfully light dish and very easy to make if you have lots of people to feed. The sauce can be made in advance and then the chicken cooked and added to it when you are ready to serve the dish. The sauce can also be frozen.

1 To make the paste, place all the ingredients in a food processor, then whiz together for 1–2 minutes to make a rough paste. (This can be kept in the fridge for 3–4 days.)

2 To cook, place a large frying pan on a medium heat, pour in the sunflower oil and when hot add the paste. Cook, stirring occasionally, for 7–10 minutes or until the paste has slightly thickened. Add the chicken and lemon juice, cover with a lid and cook, stirring occasionally, for a further 10–12 minutes or until the chicken is cooked through. Stir in the chopped coriander, taste for seasoning, adding salt and pepper and more lemon juice if needed. Serve hot with boiled rice.

VARIATION

Spiced fish with red pepper and almonds: Replace the chicken with 600g (1lb 5oz) of round white fish, such as pollack or haddock, cut into bite-sized pieces and cooked in the paste and lemon juice for about 4 minutes or until the fish is opaque.

RACHEL ALLEN LARGER GATHERINGS

Conchiglie pasta with chicken livers, bacon and port

SERVES 8

3 tbsp olive oil, plus extra for
    adding to the cooked pasta
225g (8oz) streaky bacon in
    the piece or 9 rashers,
    chopped into 1cm
    (½in) cubes
300g (11oz) peeled and
    chopped onions
2 bay leaves
7 cloves garlic, peeled and
    finely chopped
300g (11oz) minced beef
2 tbsp tomato paste
150ml (5fl oz) port
150ml (5fl oz) red wine
Salt and ground black pepper
1kg (2lb 3oz) dried conchiglie
    shells, fusilli or farfalle
25g (1oz) butter
225g (8oz) chicken livers,
    cut into 2cm (¾in) cubes
Freshly grated Parmesan
    cheese, to serve

This gutsy variation on the classic ragu uses shell-shaped pasta, which is widely available. The port gives a rich sweetness to balance the chicken livers. If you don't have port, just substitute with the same quantity of red wine – the finished dish will be equally delicious.

1 Pour the olive oil into a large saucepan on a high heat, add the bacon and cook, stirring occasionally, for 2–3 minutes or until the bacon is golden and crispy and the fat has rendered out. Remove the bacon to a plate, draining on kitchen paper and leaving the cooking oil in the pan. Turn the heat down to medium–low, and add the onions. Cook, stirring occasionally, for 5–7 minutes or until soft and only slightly golden.

2 Next add the cooked bacon, along with the bay leaves, garlic, minced beef, tomato paste, port and red wine. Mix together, season with salt and pepper, bring to the boil, then reduce the heat and simmer for about 15–20 minutes or until the liquid has almost completely evaporated.

3 While the sauce is cooking, cook the pasta following the instructions on the packet until al dente, then drain, reserving about 75ml (3fl oz) of the cooking water. Add a splash of the cooking water to the pasta with a small dash of olive oil and set aside. (The extra liquid will prevent the pasta sticking and going mushy; add a little more liquid if this soaks in – there shouldn't be any excess water but neither should the pasta get too dry.)

4 Melt the butter in a frying pan on a medium heat. Add the chicken livers and cook, stirring occasionally, for 2–4 minutes or until the livers have browned but retain a trace of pink on the inside. Add the livers to the mince mixture and cook for 1 minute. Taste for seasoning then toss with the cooked drained pasta and serve warm with lots of freshly grated Parmesan over the top.

Winter herb and sausage pasta

....

SERVES 8-12

2 tbsp olive oil

200g (7oz) smoked streaky bacon in the piece or 8–10 rashers, cut into 2cm (¾in) dice

300g (11oz) peeled and chopped onions

600g (1lb 5oz) sausage meat, broken into chunks about 1cm (½in) or sausages snipped into pieces

2 x 400g tins of chopped tomatoes

Good pinch of freshly grated nutmeg

300ml (½ pint) single or regular cream

4 tbsp chopped marjoram or 1 tbsp chopped sage or rosemary leaves

800g (1¾lb) dried pasta, such as fusilli or farfalle

Juice of 1 lemon

50g (2oz) Parmesan cheese, grated

This delicious comforting pasta dish is a serious family favourite. It's ideal for a simple, stress-free dinner party. The sauce can also be made in advance and stored in the fridge for a day or two.

1 Pour the olive oil into a large saucepan on a medium heat, add the bacon and onion and sweat together for 6–8 minutes until the bacon and onion are slightly golden. Add the sausage meat and sauté for 3–4 minutes to slightly brown the sausage meat.

2 Stir in the chopped tomatoes and the nutmeg and simmer for 20 minutes, uncovered, over a low heat. Next add the cream and marjoram or sage/rosemary and cook for a further 7–10 minutes.

3 Just after you've added the cream, cook the pasta following the instructions on the packet.

4 When the sauce has finished cooking, stir in the lemon juice. Finally, mix in the hot cooked pasta and serve with grated Parmesan sprinkled over the top.

Cassoulet

....

SERVES 10

3 tbsp olive oil

350g (12oz) streaky bacon in the piece (not rashers), cut into 2cm (¾in) cubes

2 large onions (700g/1½lb), peeled and thinly sliced

8 cloves of garlic, peeled and crushed or finely grated

4 cooked confit duck legs

4 thick (1.5–2cm/⅝–¾in) lamb shoulder chops (about 800g/1¾lb in total), cut in half but without removing the bone

450g (1lb) meaty sausages, such as Toulouse

2 x 400g tins of tomatoes

250ml (9fl oz) chicken stock (see page 51)

2 tsp sugar

150g (5oz) fresh white breadcrumbs

Salt and ground black pepper

2 tbsp chopped parsley, to serve

For cooking the beans

500g (1lb 2oz) dried haricot beans, soaked overnight in enough cold water to cover by a few centimetres

1 carrot, peeled and halved

1 onion, peeled and halved

1 bay leaf

1 sprig of rosemary

Large casserole dish or oven-proof saucepan with a lid

This classic French dish is the ultimate meal in a pot: a variety of meats – lamb, duck, bacon, sausages – in a richly flavoured tomatoey bean sauce. It is perfect for feeding a crowd; in fact, if you have a saucepan large enough, you can make it for 30 people as easily as ten. You can use Chicken Confit (see page 177) or raw duck legs instead of duck confit, if you wish.

1 First cook the beans. Drain them, discarding their soaking water, then place in a large saucepan with plenty of fresh cold water, to cover, and add the remaining ingredients. Bring to the boil, then reduce the heat and simmer for 40–60 minutes (timing will depend very much on the age of the beans) or until soft. Alternatively, use 4 x 400g tins of haricot beans, drained and rinsed, instead.

2 Preheat the oven to 110°C (225°F), Gas mark ¼.

3 Pour the oil into a casserole dish or ovenproof saucepan on a medium heat, add the bacon and fry for about 10 minutes, stirring occasionally, until it is golden and most of the fat has rendered out. Next add the onions and garlic and continue to cook for about another 10 minutes, stirring occasionally, until the onion is soft and a little golden.

4 Add the rest of the ingredients, including the beans at this stage apart from the breadcrumbs, to the dish and season well with salt and pepper, then scatter all the breadcrumbs over the top in a roughly even layer. Bring the mixture to simmering point, then cover with a lid and cook in the oven for 3½–4 hours or until all the meat is completely tender.

5 When the meat is cooked, preheat the grill to hot. Remove the lid from the casserole dish and transfer the cassoulet – being careful not to disturb the breadcrumbs – to the grill. Grill for 5–10 minutes or until the breadcrumbs are crispy. Sprinkle the chopped parsley over the top and serve.

Beef and wild mushroom lasagne

....

SERVES 8-10

1 tbsp olive oil

2 onions, peeled and chopped

800g (1¾lb) minced beef

150ml (5fl oz) red wine

1 tbsp chopped rosemary

1 x 400g tin of tomatoes

3 cloves of garlic, peeled and chopped

Salt and ground black pepper

25g (1oz) butter

400g (14oz) mixed wild mushrooms, such as enoki, chanterelles, ceps, shiitake, oyster and field, sliced

250g (9oz) streaky bacon in the piece, or 12 rashers, cut into 2cm (¾in) dice

500g (1lb 2oz) no-soak lasagne sheets (about 30 sheets)

25g (1oz) each of Gruyère and Parmesan cheese, grated

For the béchamel sauce

1.2 litres (2 pints) milk

1 carrot, trimmed and peeled

1 bay leaf or ½ onion, peeled

2–3 tbsp roux (made with 1½ tbsp butter and 1½ tbsp plain flour, see page 76)

225g (8oz) Gruyère cheese, grated

2–3 tsp Dijon mustard

Lasagne or ovenproof dish about 30 x 25cm (12 x 10in), with 5cm (2in) sides

This is fabulous for feeding lots of people; it's rich, creamy and all it needs to go with it is a crunchy green salad and some Rosemary and Garlic Bread (see page 295). The lasagne can be made in advance and frozen after it has been assembled (allow it too cool completely first and thaw before baking), or just stored in the fridge for up to two days. You can use button mushrooms if you can't get wild ones.

1 Pour the oil into a large saucepan on a medium heat, add the onions and cook for 5–8 minutes until softened but not browned. Then add the beef, red wine and rosemary and cook for a further 5 minutes, stirring occasionally, until the beef starts to brown. Next add the tomatoes and garlic and season with salt and pepper. Rinse the tin with a little water and add to the tomatoes. Continue to cook on a medium heat for 30–40 minutes, stirring occasionally, until the tomatoes have completely softened and the mixture has thickened slightly.

2 Melt the butter in a large frying pan on a high heat, then add the mushrooms, season with salt and pepper and cook for 7–10 minutes, tossing regularly. When the mushrooms are cooked and turning golden, check the seasoning, then remove from the pan and set aside.

3 Using the same frying pan, still on a high heat and adding a little oil, fry the bacon until golden and crisp (remember that the bacon will crisp further as it cools), then set aside.

4 Preheat the oven to 200°C (400°F), Gas mark 6, then make the béchamel sauce.

5 Pour the milk into another large saucepan, add the carrot, bay leaf or half an onion, then place on a low heat and bring slowly to the boil. Allow to simmer gently for about 3–4 minutes, for the

(continued overleaf)

flavours to infuse, then remove and discard the bay leaf and the vegetables. Next bring the milk to the boil and whisk in the roux. Continue whisking for a minute or two while the mixture gently boils – the sauce should be thick but 'pourable'.

6 Remove from the heat and, while the mixture is still hot, whisk in the Gruyère and mustard and season with salt and pepper to taste. Place a quarter of the sauce in a bowl and stir the mushrooms into the sauce in the pan.

7 To assemble the lasagne, first spread a little of the sauce over the base of the dish to prevent the pasta from sticking to it. Then arrange a layer of lasagne sheets. (This will be roughly five sheets, depending on the shape of your dish or indeed of the lasagne sheets.) Place half the bacon on top of the pasta, followed by half of the meat in a layer on top of the bacon. Add another layer of lasagne sheets, then all the mushroom sauce mixture, another layer of lasagne, then the remaining bacon, followed by the rest of the meat. Top this with another layer of lasagne and the remaining quarter (without the mushrooms) of the béchamel sauce. Be careful to cover all the pasta with the sauce – any uncovered sheets will become unpleasantly dry during cooking. Scatter over the grated Gruyère and Parmesan cheese, then cook in the oven for 30–40 minutes or until the top is golden brown and bubbling.

Roast haunch of venison

SERVES 8–12

8–10 rashers of streaky bacon
1 haunch of venison (at least 2kg/4lb 4oz in weight)

For the gravy
500ml (18fl oz) beef stock
1 tbsp redcurrant jelly (see page 337)
2 tsp roux (made with 1 tsp plain flour and 1 tsp butter – see page 76) (optional)

The haunch, at the top end of the deer's leg, is quite often bought boned but, if possible, cook it with the bone in for the maximum flavour. If it is boned, however, place a sprig of rosemary in the centre and roll it up, tying it with string.

1 Preheat the oven to 220°C (425°F), Gas mark 7.

2 Lay the bacon rashers on a piece of cling film, then cover with another piece of cling film. Roll them out to flatten them slightly so they are nice and thin. Put the venison in a roasting tin and cover with the flattened rashers. Place in the oven and cook for 20 minutes, then reduce the heat to 180°C (350°F), Gas mark 4, and cook for a further 15 minutes per 500g (1lb 2oz).

3 While the venison is cooking, baste it by spooning any fat and juices back over the meat every 10 minutes. When the venison is cooked, remove it from the roasting tin (which you will need for making the gravy) and place on a warmed serving plate covered with foil. Leave it to rest somewhere warm – such as in the oven with the heat turned off – for at least 20 minutes while you make the gravy.

4 Pour the juices from the roasting tin into a bowl to degrease them (see tip on page 226), then pour them back into the tin and bring to the boil on the hob using a whisk to incorporate any sticky bits from the base of the tin. Pour into a small saucepan, then add the stock and the redcurrant jelly. Bring to the boil and, if you wish, thicken slightly with the roux. Taste the gravy, adjusting the seasoning if necessary, and pour into a warmed jug.

5 To serve, carve the venison into thin slices and pour the hot gravy over the top.

Wilted greens with garlic and anchovy breadcrumbs

....

SERVES 8–12

150ml (5fl oz) olive oil

6 cloves of garlic, peeled and finely sliced

12 tinned anchovies, drained, rinsed and finely chopped

110g (4oz) fresh white breadcrumbs

400g (14oz) greens, such as kale, mustard greens, spinach or rocket, large stalks removed and the leaves roughly sliced

Salt and ground black pepper

The crispy crunchy breadcrumbs give a great contrast to the moist greens. The anchovies don't taste fishy, they just add a salty fullness to the flavour of this great side dish.

1 Pour 100ml (3½fl oz) of the olive oil into a large frying pan and place on a medium heat. When the oil is hot, add the garlic and anchovies and cook for 1–2 minutes, stirring frequently, until very lightly browned. Add the breadcrumbs and cook for a further 2–3 minutes or until golden and crispy, then remove to a bowl.

2 Next fry the greens. Pour the remaining olive oil into the pan still on a medium heat and when it's hot, add the greens, season with salt and pepper (bearing in mind that the anchovies will be quite salty) and cook for about 3–4 minutes, tossing frequently, until wilted.

3 Place the cooked greens in a serving bowl, then scatter the anchovy, garlic and breadcrumb mixture over the top. Serve immediately.

RACHEL'S TIP

If you are making this with very large kale leaves, you may need to blanch them first, otherwise they won't be tender enough. To do this, simply cook them in a saucepan of boiling water (with a good pinch of salt) on a high heat for about 2–3 minutes or until just beginning to wilt, then drain and cook as above.

Roast Jerusalem artichokes

....

SERVES 8–12
VEGETARIAN
1kg (2lb 3oz) Jerusalem
  artichokes, unpeeled
6–8 tbsp olive oil
Salt and ground black pepper
A few sprigs of rosemary or
  thyme (optional)

These knobbly pink- or white-skinned root vegetables are of no relation to the globe artichoke, which comes into season in the summer. As well as being very good for you (high in iron and inulin, a natural probiotic), Jerusalem artichokes are so versatile. They can be eaten raw, finely sliced in salads, or cooked in soups, mashed or roasted. If well scrubbed, they can be eaten with the skins on – which is how I love to roast them – for maximum nutritional benefit.

1 Preheat the oven to 200°C (400°F), Gas mark 6.

2 Scrub the artichokes very thoroughly and cut in half. Place in a roasting tin or on a baking tray and toss with enough olive oil to coat them completely, then season with salt and pepper and toss with the herbs (if using). Spread out in a single layer and roast in the oven for about 20 minutes or until golden brown and soft.

Rosemary and garlic bread

....

SERVES 8
300g (11oz) butter
12 cloves of garlic, peeled
  and crushed or finely grated
4 tbsp chopped rosemary
  leaves
2 baguettes

Almost comfort food defined, this is ideal to serve with the Beef and Wild Mushroom Lasagne on pages 291–2.

1 Preheat the oven to 180°C (350°F), Gas mark 4.

2 Melt the butter in a saucepan on a medium heat and add the garlic and rosemary. Stir-fry for 1 minute then remove from the heat.

3 Slice the baguettes in half horizontally, then drizzle the cut sides generously with the garlic and rosemary butter. Place on a baking sheet and bake in the oven for 15 minutes or until golden brown.

Parsnip, mustard and parsley mash

....

SERVES 8–10
VEGETARIAN

1.5kg (3lb 5oz) parsnips
Salt and ground black pepper
100g (3½oz) butter
1 tsp Dijon mustard
3 tbsp chopped parsley

I sometimes like serving a mash that's a little different to the standard potato. Parsnips are a very robust vegetable, they will stand up to and accommodate even big flavours like mustard. Older, larger parsnips have a better and stronger flavour, but it's worth removing their inner core, as the texture can be too woody and fibrous, particularly for a mash. The wintery nature of this dish makes it an ideal side to the Roast Haunch of Venison on page 293.

1 First peel the parsnips, then cut off the tops and tails, cut them into wedges and remove the inner core. Next cut the wedges into roughly 2cm (¾in) chunks .

2 Place the parsnips in a large saucepan and pour over enough boiling water just to cover them. Add a pinch of salt and cook on a medium heat for 15–20 minutes or until they are quite soft. By the time the parsnips have cooked, most of the water will have evaporated; there is no need to add more. I like to cook them like this as I prefer all the goodness to stay in the parsnip and not to throw it all away down the sink in the cooking water.

3 When the parsnips are cooked, drain them, pouring off any excess liquid. Then mash together with the butter, mustard and parsley. You can either mash by hand or using a food processor, depending on how smooth you want it. Season to taste with salt and pepper and serve.

Crunchy roast coriander potatoes

....

SERVES 8
VEGETARIAN
2 tbsp coriander seeds
900g (2lb) peeled floury
  potatoes (weight
  when peeled)
Sea salt and ground black
  pepper
6–8 tbsp olive oil or warmed
  duck fat
1 tbsp balsamic vinegar

A golden layer of crunch enveloping soft, floury potato is surely one of the most divine foods. The coriander makes these roast potatoes perfect for special meals. Duck or goose fat will give the best crunch to roast potatoes, but olive oil can work almost as well. It's very important to par-boil them and slightly roughen the edges before roasting. The frayed edges fry in the oil and properly crisp up. These make a lovely accompaniment to the Roast Haunch of Venison on page 293.

1 Preheat the oven to 220°C (425°F), Gas mark 7.

2 Crush the coriander seeds with a pestle and mortar or place in a small plastic bag and use a rolling pin to crush them. Cut the potatoes into large bite-sized chunks.

3 Half fill a saucepan with water, add a good pinch of salt and bring to the boil. Add the potatoes to the pan and boil for about 5–7 minutes or until almost cooked but still relatively hard in the centre. Drain and place in a roasting tin, with the crushed coriander and some salt and pepper. Slightly press with a potato masher to break the potatoes up ever so slightly.

4 Drizzle the olive oil or warmed duck fat over the top, making sure all the potato pieces are coated in it, and place on a high heat to sizzle for 1 minute, then transfer to the oven and cook for 20 minutes until golden and crispy. Take out of the oven and drizzle with the balsamic vinegar to serve.

Potato and mushroom gratin

....

SERVES 8-10
VEGETARIAN

900g (2lb) waxy potatoes,
    peeled and thinly sliced
25g (1oz) butter, softened
3 cloves of garlic, peeled and
    crushed or finely grated
Salt and ground black pepper
450g (1lb) flat or button
    mushrooms, finely sliced
    (any large mushrooms cut
    in quarters first)
550ml (19fl oz) single
    or regular cream
50g (2oz) Parmesan or
    Parmesan-style cheese,
    finely grated

25 x 35–40cm (10 x 14–16in)
    gratin or similar-sized
    ovenproof dish

The mushrooms flavouring this gratin make it ideal as an autumnal potato dish. Rich and creamy, it goes perfectly with the relatively lean Roast Haunch of Venison (see page 293).

1 Preheat the oven to 180°C (350°F), Gas mark 4.

2 Place the sliced potatoes on a clean tea towel on your worktop and pat them dry to remove any excess starch. Grease the gratin dish generously with butter and sprinkle the garlic over it. Arrange half the potatoes in the bottom of the dish (as nobody will see this layer, they don't have to be tidily arranged, just fairly even in thickness), season with salt and pepper and add the sliced mushrooms. Season again and finish with a layer of overlapping potatoes (more neatly arranged this time).

3 Bring the cream almost to boiling point and pour over the potatoes. Sprinkle over the cheese and bake in the oven for about 1½ hours or until the gratin is crisp and golden brown on top with the cream bubbling up around the edges. If it is in danger of getting too browned during cooking, loosely cover it with foil, greaseproof paper or baking parchment.

Cucumbers with tomatoes, cream and mint

....

SERVES 4-6
VEGETARIAN
15g (½oz) butter
1 onion (100g/3½oz), peeled and sliced
1 cucumber, peeled and cut into 1cm (½in) dice
4 very ripe tomatoes, peeled (see tip on page 74) and sliced
Good pinch of sugar
Salt and ground black pepper
50ml (2fl oz) double or regular cream
1 tbsp chopped mint

Not many people cook cucumbers, but they are delicious, especially when served in this way. This light dish makes a refreshing accompaniment for roast chicken or fish. You can even use it as a sauce for pasta. Feel free to replace the mint with other herbs, such as basil, tarragon, coriander, dill or fennel.

1 Place a large saucepan on a medium heat, add the butter and when it melts and starts to foam, add the onion, cover the pan with a lid and cook for 8–10 minutes or until the onion is soft but not browned.

2 Add the cucumber and mix well with the onion, then replace the lid and cook for 2 minutes. Next add the tomatoes and the sugar, and season with salt and pepper. Cover the pan again and cook for 2–3 minutes or until the cucumbers are almost tender, then remove the lid and simmer, uncovered, for 10–15 minutes until the tomatoes are completely soft and the mixture has thickened slightly. Next add the cream and continue to simmer for another 5 minutes.

3 Sir in the mint then taste for seasoning. Serve immediately or store in the fridge until needed (it will keep for a few days) and gently reheat.

Amaretti with brandy
and ice cream

....

SERVES 8–12
VEGETARIAN
4 amaretti, crushed
4 tsp brandy
1 litre (1¾ pints) ice cream
  of choice, such as vanilla,
  chocolate or orange
  (see page 258)
Cocoa powder, for sprinkling

8–12 champagne flutes or
  wine glasses

*My mum's friend Pia serves this dessert at her birthday parties.
It's really easy to put together for lots of people. Simply line up the
champagne flutes and get set! When you're buying amaretti for this
dish, go for the golden crunchy ones rather than the soft variety.*

1 Place half the crushed amaretti in the champagne flutes
or wine glasses, then cover with the brandy.

2 Add scoops of ice cream and top with the remaining crushed
biscuits and a sprinkling of cocoa powder. Serve immediately.

Iced strawberry parfait
with strawberry sauce

SERVES 8-10
VEGETARIAN

450g (1lb) strawberries,
   hulled and halved
50g (2oz) caster sugar
250ml (9fl oz) double or
   regular cream
6 individual meringues
   (about 500ml/18fl oz in
   volume), roughly broken
   up into 2–3cm (¾–1¼in)
   pieces
2–3 tsp Cointreau or Grand
   Marnier

13 x 23cm (5 x 9in) loaf tin

With its lovely pink colour, this wonderful dessert is just the thing for a summertime lunch or dinner. It can be made in advance and the strawberries can be substituted with raspberries if you prefer.

1 Line the loaf tin with a double layer of cling film, allowing extra to come over the sides as this will be wrapped over the top as a lid later.

2 Place the prepared strawberries in a saucepan with the caster sugar and 50ml (2fl oz) water. Cover the saucepan with a lid, bring to the boil, then reduce the heat and simmer on a low heat for 6–8 minutes or until the strawberries are soft. Remove from the heat and allow to cool, then purée in a blender or food processor and put to one side.

3 In a large bowl, whip the cream until thick, then fold in the meringues and half of the strawberry purée. Spoon the mixture into the prepared loaf tin and cover with the extra cling film. Put in the freezer overnight or until frozen.

4 Add the Cointreau or Grand Marnier to the remaining strawberry purée and taste, adding more liqueur if you wish.

5 Take the parfait out of the freezer and place in the fridge 10 minutes before serving, to soften it very slightly. Turn it out onto a serving dish and slice into individual portions. Serve with a drizzle of strawberry purée.

White chocolate and ginger parfait with dark chocolate sauce

....

SERVES 8-10
VEGETARIAN

225g (8oz) white chocolate, chopped

600ml (1 pint) double or regular cream

125ml (4 ½fl oz) milk

10 egg yolks

15g (½oz) caster sugar

125ml (4½fl oz) sweetened condensed milk

1 tsp vanilla extract

75g (3oz) crystallised or stem ginger, finely chopped

For the dark chocolate sauce

200ml (7fl oz) double or regular cream

125g (4½oz) dark chocolate, chopped into small bits

13 x 23cm (5 x 9in) loaf tin

Crystallised ginger and white chocolate – or any chocolate, for that matter – are a match made in heaven. If you don't like ginger, however, just leave it out as the combination of white and dark chocolate is divine on its own. This dessert is perfect for entertaining as it can be made in up to two weeks in advance.

1 Line the loaf tin with a double layer of cling film, allowing extra to come over the sides as this will be wrapped over the top as a lid later.

2 Place the white chocolate and 300ml (½ pint) of the cream in a heatproof bowl over a saucepan of simmering water on a low heat. Stir gently until the chocolate has melted and the mixture is smooth. Put to one side.

3 Heat the milk and the remaining cream in a saucepan, stirring all the time, until it is just about to boil, then take off the hob.

4 In a large bowl, whisk the egg yolks and the caster sugar until thick and pale. Then, while continuing to whisk, pour the hot cream and milk mixture gradually into the yolks.

5 Pour the egg mixture into the saucepan and cook over a gentle heat, stirring constantly, until the mixture coats the back of a spoon. Remove from the heat and add the melted chocolate, the condensed milk and vanilla extract. Mix well and allow to cool.

6 Spread the ginger over the bottom of the loaf tin to cover completely. Gently pour the parfait mixture on top of the ginger and cover the top with the extra cling film. Freeze overnight.

7 To make the chocolate sauce, pour the cream into a small saucepan and bring to the boil, then removed from the heat and add the chocolate bits, stirring as they melt.

8 Put the parfait in the fridge 10 minutes before serving. Then turn out of the loaf tin and serve in slices with a drizzle of the chocolate sauce.

RACHEL ALLEN   DESSERTS

Raspberry millefeuille

SERVES 8
VEGETARIAN
500g (1lb 2oz) puff pastry
Plain flour, for dusting
300ml (½ pint) double or
    regular cream
150g (5oz) raspberry jam
350g (12oz) fresh raspberries,
    plus 50g (2oz) raspberries
    to decorate
Icing sugar, for dusting

This is a wonderfully light dessert of puff pastry layered with cream and raspberry. It looks very grand and impressive, so do serve it at the table as it looks best before it is sliced. Alternatively, cut the pastry into smaller rectangles before cooking, to make eight individual millefeuilles.

1 Preheat the oven to 220°C (425°F), Gas mark 7.

2 Divide the puff pastry into four equal pieces, as each piece will be rolled and baked separately. On a work surface lightly dusted with flour, roll out each piece to 20 x 32cm (8 x 13in), making sure it is nice and thin – about 2mm (⅛in).

3 Trim the edges with a knife dipped in hot water (to give a nice neat edge) before carefully lifting into the tin. Prick the pastry all over with a fork and chill in the fridge for 10–15 minutes.

4 Bake in the oven for about 7–8 minutes or until crisp and golden in colour. (The pastry will shrink a little while baking.) Remove from the oven and allow to cool on a wire rack while you roll out and bake the next pastry layer. You may need to do this in batches, but the pastry will sit perfectly in the fridge once cut while you're baking the other sheets. Repeat until all four layers are baked and have been set aside to cool.

5 In a bowl, whip the cream until thick, then place in the fridge if you are not using it immediately.

6 To assemble the millefeuille, first place one pastry layer on a serving plate and spread with a third of the whipped cream, then cover the cream with half the raspberries. Carefully spread the raspberry jam over the second pastry layer, then place on top of the previous layer and spread with another third of the whipped cream.

7 Add another layer of pastry and spread the remaining cream and raspberries on top of this. Finish with the last layer of pastry (I like to save the best-looking one for the top), dusting liberally with icing sugar and extra raspberries for decoration. Bring to the table to serve, cutting into squares as neatly as possible.

Salted caramel chocolate tart

....

SERVES 8–10
VEGETARIAN

For the sweet shortcrust pastry
200g (7oz) plain flour
100g (3½oz) chilled butter,
    cubed, plus extra for
    greasing
1 tbsp icing sugar
½–1 lightly beaten egg

For the caramel
225g (8oz) caster sugar
100g (3½oz) chilled butter,
    cubed, plus extra for
    greasing
100ml (3½fl oz) double or
    regular cream
1 heaped tsp sea salt flakes

For the chocolate layer
100g (3½oz) caster sugar
2 eggs
2 egg yolks
250g (9oz) dark chocolate
150g (5oz) butter, cubed

23cm (9in) diameter x 3.5cm
    (1¼in) deep loose-
    bottomed tart tin

The exquisite combination of salt, chocolate and caramel has risen to the height of pastry fashion in the past few years. Here there is soft yielding chocolate and a sticky caramel layer, all encased within a buttery-sweet pastry. It takes some time to make, but as soon as you experience that first taste you will understand why it's all worth it. The tart is delicious on its own or with whipped cream.

1 Place the flour, butter and icing sugar into a food processor and whiz briefly until the butter is in small lumps. Add half the beaten egg and continue to whiz for another few seconds or until the mixture looks as though it may come together when pressed. (Prolonged processing will only toughen the pastry, so don't whiz it up until it is a ball of dough.) You might need to add a little more egg, but not too much as the mixture should be just moist enough to come together. If making by hand, rub the butter into the flour and icing sugar until it resembles coarse breadcrumbs then, using your hands, add just enough egg to bring it together. Reserve any leftover egg to use later.

2 With your hands, flatten out the ball of dough until it is about 2cm (¾in) thick, then wrap in cling film or place in a plastic bag and chill in the fridge for at least 30 minutes.

3 When you are ready to roll out the pastry, butter the tart tin and remove the pastry from the fridge, placing it between two sheets of cling film (larger in size than your tart tin). Using a rolling pin, roll the pastry out to no thicker than 5mm (¼in). Make sure to keep it in a round shape as well as large enough to line both the base and the sides of the tin.

4 Remove the top layer of cling film, slide your hand, palm upwards, under the bottom layer of cling film, then flip the pastry over (so that the cling film is now on top) and carefully lower it

(continued overleaf)

307

into the tart tin. Press the pastry into the edges of the tin (with the cling film still attached) and, using your thumb, 'cut' the pastry along the edge of the tin for a neat finish. Remove the cling film, prick over the base with a fork and chill the pastry in the fridge for another 30 minutes or the freezer for 10 minutes (it can keep for weeks like this in the freezer).

5 Meanwhile, preheat the oven to 180°C (350°F), Gas mark 4.

6 Remove the pastry from the fridge and line with foil, greaseproof paper or baking parchment, leaving plenty to come over the sides. Fill with baking beans or dried pulses (all of which can be reused repeatedly), then place in the oven and bake 'blind' for 15–20 minutes or until the pastry feels dry in the base. Remove from the oven, take out the baking beans and foil/paper, brush the base of the pastry with any leftover beaten egg, then cook in the oven for another 3 minutes or until lightly golden. Remove from the oven and set aside.

7 Meanwhile, make the caramel. Put the sugar and 75ml (3fl oz) water into a heavy-based saucepan over a low heat and stir until the sugar dissolves. Add the butter, stirring to melt, increase the heat to medium and allow to bubble away, stirring occasionally, for about 15 minutes or until the mixture is a light toffee colour. Mix in the cream and sea salt and boil for another 2–3 minutes until slightly thickened. Allow to cool.

8 To make the chocolate layer, whisk the sugar, eggs and egg yolks until thickened and creamy in colour. Gently melt the chocolate and butter together in a bowl over a saucepan of simmering water (the bowl should not touch the water), leave to cool for a minute and then add to the sugar and egg mixture, whisking until smooth and glossy.

9 Spread the caramel over the cooled pastry base and spoon over the chocolate mixture, spreading it evenly. Bake for about 20 minutes or until it is almost set but still a bit wobbly. Allow to cool in the tin for 40–45 minutes before removing from the tin and serving in slices.

Rhubarb and ginger crumble cake

....

SERVES 8-10
VEGETARIAN
Butter, softened, for greasing
400g (14oz) rhubarb,
    trimmed and cut into 2–
    3cm (¾–1¼in) chunks
100g (3½oz) demerara or
    light soft brown sugar
½ tsp ground ginger
Icing sugar, for dusting

For the crumble topping
100g (3½oz) plain flour
¼ tsp baking powder
75g (3oz) chilled butter, cubed
75g (3oz) light soft brown
    sugar
25g (1oz) flaked almonds

For the cake sponge
100g (3½oz) butter, softened
100g (3½oz) caster sugar
2 eggs
½ tsp ground ginger
2 tbsp milk
175g (6oz) plain flour
Pinch of salt
1 tsp baking powder

23cm (9in) diameter spring-
    form/loose-bottomed tin

Rhubarb and ginger is one of my favourite flavour pairings. The gentle spiciness of the ginger perfectly marries with the sweet-sour nature of rhubarb. This is a twist on the traditional treatment for rhubarb that is somewhere between a crumble and a cake.

1 Preheat the oven to 180°C (350°F), Gas mark 4. Butter the tin and line the base with baking parchment.

2 Place the rhubarb, sugar and ginger in a saucepan with 2 tablespoons of water and simmer on a low heat, with the lid on, for about 4–6 minutes or until the rhubarb is tender but not mushy. Remove from the heat, take off the lid and allow to cool.

3 To make the crumble topping, first sift the flour and baking powder into a bowl. Using your fingertips, rub in the butter until it resembles coarse breadcrumbs. Add the sugar and flaked almonds and mix to combine, then set aside in the fridge while you make the sponge.

4 Now make the cake sponge. Cream the butter in a large bowl or in an electric food mixer until soft. Add the sugar and beat until the mixture is light and fluffy. Beat in the eggs, one at a time, then whisk in the ginger and milk. Sift over the flour, salt and baking powder and fold into the cake batter.

5 Spoon the batter into the prepared tin, spreading it out evenly, then gently spoon the stewed rhubarb on top. Sprinkle the crumble topping over the rhubarb and bake in the oven for 45–50 minutes or until golden and cooked in the centre.

6 Allow the cake to cool slightly before removing the tin, then place on a serving plate. Dredge with icing sugar and serve slightly warm or at room temperature with some whipped cream.

DESSERTS

RACHEL ALLEN

Passion fruit and orange granita

....

This is perfect served after a long summer dinner party when you feel like something really fresh-tasting but not too filling. Use passion fruit that are nice and ripe and full of flavour. You can tell whether they are ripe as the skins will be a bit wrinkled.

150g (5oz) caster sugar
1 tbsp lemon juice
8 passion fruit
500ml (18fl oz) freshly
    squeezed and sieved
    orange juice (from about
    5 large oranges)

8-10 wide champagne glasses
    or dessert bowls

1 First make the syrup. Fill a saucepan with 150ml (5fl oz) of water and add the sugar and lemon juice. Place on a low heat and stir until the sugar has dissolved. Increase the heat and bring to the boil. Allow to boil for 3 minutes, then remove from the heat and allow to cool.

2 Meanwhile, cut each passion fruit in half and scoop out the pulp and seeds into a sieve placed over a bowl. Use a spoon to press the pulp against the sieve and extract as much juice as possible, remembering to scrape underneath the sieve too. Put the seeds to one side, if you want to use them in the granita and/or for decoration.

3 In a large bowl, mix together the passion fruit juice and 2 tablespoons of the seeds (or you can leave the seeds out, if you prefer). Add the orange juice and the syrup and stir to mix. Pour the mixture into an airtight plastic container and put the lid on.

4 Place in the freezer for 2-3 hours or until it begins to set around the edges, then, using a fork, stir to break up the frozen crystals. Put the lid back on and continue to freeze for a further hour. Remove from the freezer and stir again, then freeze for another hour, remove and stir one final time. At this point you can leave the granita to freeze completely overnight.

5 Serve in pretty glasses or champagne flutes, depending on the occasion, and with a few passion fruit seeds sprinkled on top (if using).

Chocolate roulade

....

SERVES 8-10
VEGETARIAN
6 eggs, separated
150g (5oz) caster sugar
50g (2oz) cocoa powder, plus
  extra for dusting (optional)
Icing sugar, for dusting
  (optional)
225ml (8fl oz) double or
  regular cream

For the chocolate mousse
125ml (4½fl oz) double or
  regular cream
125g (4½ oz) dark chocolate,
  finely chopped
2 tbsp brandy or dark rum
  (optional)
2 eggs, separated

20 x 30cm (8 x 12in)
  Swiss roll tin

With its chocolate mousse and cream filling, this roulade is wickedly good. Use crystallised violets to decorate, if you wish. It looks really fabulous at Christmas time dusted with icing sugar and decorated with a sprig of holly.

1 Preheat the oven to 180°C (350°F), Gas mark 4. Line the Swiss roll tin with baking parchment.

2 Place the egg yolks and sugar in a bowl and whisk until the mixture starts to thicken. Whisk in the cocoa powder.

3 In a separate, spotlessly clean bowl, whisk the egg whites until just stiff, then carefully fold these into the chocolate mixture. Pour into the prepared tin and gently smooth the surface. Bake in the oven for 15–20 minutes or until the sponge feels springy to the touch. Remove from the oven and allow to cool in the tin.

4 Next make the mousse. Pour the cream into a saucepan and bring to the boil, then remove from the heat. Add the chocolate pieces to the cream and stir until all the chocolate is melted. Add the brandy or rum (if using) and whisk in the egg yolks.

5 In a clean bowl, whisk the egg whites until stiff. Stir a quarter of the egg whites into the chocolate mixture, then pour the chocolate mixture into the bowl with the remaining egg whites, and fold in gently. Cover the bowl with cling film and chill in the fridge for 1–2 hours to set.

6 When the roulade sponge has cooled, turn it out onto an oblong piece of baking parchment, greaseproof paper or foil liberally dusted with either the cocoa powder or the icing sugar.

7 Carefully peel away the lining paper, now facing up. Spread the chocolate mousse over the roulade sponge. Now whip the cream and spread it over the chocolate mousse.

8 With one long edge facing you, gently roll up the roulade into the shape of a log and transfer to a serving plate with the join facing down. (The roulade will crack as you roll it but don't worry, this is normal.) Dust with a little more cocoa powder or icing sugar (if using), and cut into slices to serve.

MENU IDEAS FOR
LARGER GATHERINGS

Serve all menus with a green salad (see page 239)

*

Smoked fish platter with Ballymaloe cucumber relish (page 275)
Roast haunch of venison, wilted greens with garlic and
anchovy breadcrumbs, roast Jerusalem artichokes and
parsnip, mustard and parsley mash (pages 293–6)
Salted caramel chocolate tart (pages 307–8)

*

Winter leaf salad with pomegranate, apple and and walnuts (page 273)
Cassoulet (page 288)
White chocolate and ginger parfait with dark chocolate sauce (page 303)

*

Roast wedges of butternut squash with goat's cheese and spinach pesto (page 268)
Beef and wild mushroom lasagne (pages 291–2)
Amaretti with brandy and ice cream (page 300)

*

Chilled avocado soup with red and yellow peppers and coriander salsa (page 266)
Zesty pine nut-crusted fish with salsa verde, cucumbers with
tomato, cream and mint and new potatoes (pages 281 and 299)
Iced strawberry parfait with strawberry sauce (page 302)

Egg mayonnaise
Potato and fresh herb salad
Cucumber and dill salad
Tomato and basil salad
Mushroom, lemon and garlic salad
Oignons à la Monégasque
Smoked mackerel with dill mayonnaise
Oysters
Gravalax
Poached whole salmon with basil mayonnaise
Boiled shrimps or prawns with herb mayonnaise
Crab and mayonnaise salad
Dressed mussels and clams
Ballymaloe glazed loin of bacon with spicy mayonnaise
Cold roast chicken with herb stuffing
Roast lamb with redcurrant jelly
Roast pork with apple sauce
Traditional roast rib of beef with horseradish sauce

THE
BUFFET PARTY

Sometimes we have the great occasion to feed a crowd. Maybe you've invited
all your friends around for a blow-out feast, or you're planning a family reunion,
or are hosting an important anniversary as a special gift. Rather than having a
sit-down meal, a cold buffet is your answer unless you're feeling incredibly
brave and have an industrial kitchen, staff and catering equipment to keep
everything hot! The Sunday evening cold buffet a Ballymaloe is an institution
– it has been served for over forty years and between May and September all
the vegetables are picked and prepared just before serving. The recipes in
this section are based on these well-loved Ballymaloe dishes. Many of them can
be prepared in advance, and though you will help serve and top things up
as your lovely creations get devoured, your guests can pretty much help
themselves. For more advice on planning your buffet, see pages 342–3.

Egg mayonnaise

SERVES 4
VEGETARIAN

4 eggs
3–4 tbsp mayonnaise
  (see below)
½ tsp finely chopped chives
Salt and ground pepper

Piping bag fitted with a star
  nozzle (optional)

The chives are essential for the aromatic flavour they bring to this classic dish. The mayonnaise will keep in the fridge for at least a week.

1 Place each whole egg in its shell in a saucepan of boiling water and boil for 10 minutes. Carefully drain and pour cold water over them for 1 minute, then set aside and allow to cool. Peel the shell from each egg (you may find this easier to do under cold running water) and slice in half lengthways.

2 Remove the yolks from the eggs and push through a sieve into a bowl, then mix with the mayonnaise and chives and season with salt and pepper to taste. Fill the piping bag with the mixture and pipe into the hollowed-out egg whites. Alternatively, scoop 2 teaspoons of the mixture into each egg white. Arrange on a serving dish.

RACHEL'S TIP
If you want to make this a few hours in advance, it's best to keep the egg yolk mixture aside covered in the fridge along with the egg whites, bringing back up to room temperature before serving. Pipe/spoon it into the egg whites as close to serving as possible to prevent it drying out.

Mayonnaise

MAKES 300ML (½ PINT)
VEGETARIAN

2 egg yolks
Pinch of salt
1 tsp Dijon mustard
2 tsp white wine vinegar
225ml (8fl oz) oil (I like to use
  200ml/7fl oz) sunflower oil
  and 25ml / 1fl oz) olive oil)
Ground black pepper

1 Place the egg yolks in a bowl, then mix in the salt, mustard and vinegar.

2 Very gradually, whisking all the time (either by hand or using hand-held electric beater), slowly pour in the oil in a thin stream. You should start to see the mixture thickening. Season with pepper and more salt to taste.

VARIATION
Herb mayonnaise: Make the recipe as above, then mix in 2 tablespoons of chopped herbs, such as chives, dill, fennel, tarragon, watercress or rocket.

Potato and fresh herb salad

....

SERVES 6-8
VEGETARIAN

900g (2lb) waxy potatoes,
  unpeeled
Salt and ground black pepper
100ml (3½fl oz) French
  dressing (see below)
8 spring onions, trimmed
  and chopped
2 tbsp chopped mixed herbs,
  such as thyme, parsley
  and chives
125ml (4½fl oz) mayonnaise
  (see page 317)

It's important to dress this salad in two stages. The potatoes should be tossed in the dressing while still warm as they absorb much more flavour that way, yet the mayonnaise must only be folded in when they have cooled otherwise it can split. This dish keeps for up to 24 hours covered in the fridge, but allow it to come up to room temperature before serving.

1 Place the potatoes in a large saucepan and cover with water. Add a good pinch of salt, cover with a lid and bring to the boil, then cook for 20 minutes or until tender.

2 Drain, then peel and cut into 2cm (¾in) chunks and toss (while still warm) with the French dressing, spring onions and herbs. Season with salt and pepper and allow to cool before finally folding in the mayonnaise. Serve at room temperature.

MAKES 100ML (3½FL OZ)
VEGETARIAN

1 small clove of garlic, peeled
1 sprig of parsley
½ small spring onion,
  trimmed
75ml (3fl oz) extra-virgin
  olive oil
25ml (1fl oz) white wine
  vinegar
1 tsp Dijon mustard
Salt and ground black pepper

Classic French dressing

1 Place all the ingredients in a blender and whiz for about 1 minute or until smooth, then season to taste with salt and pepper.

2 Alternatively, crush or finely grate the garlic, finely chop the parsley and spring onion, then place all ingredients in a clean jam jar with a screw-top lid and shake to mix.

Cucumber and dill salad

....

SERVES 6-8
VEGETARIAN

1 cucumber (peeled if you
   wish)
2 tbsp chopped dill
Salt and ground black pepper
Good pinch of sugar
Juice of ½ lemon or 1 lemon,
   cut into wedges

*This brings a wonderful crunch when served with cold roast meats
or smoked fish. It is best made at least 15 minutes before serving,
and will keep in the fridge for a few days and then served chilled.*

1 Using a food processor or mandolin, slice the cucumber very
finely – about 2–3mm (⅛in) thick.

2 Place in a bowl with the chopped dill, seasoning to taste with
a good pinch each of salt, pepper and sugar. Add the lemon juice
just before serving or serve with lemon wedges to squeeze over
the salad.

Tomato and basil salad

....

SERVES 6-8
VEGETARIAN

8–12 vine-ripened tomatoes,
   cut into 5mm (¼in) chunks
   or slices
4 tbsp extra-virgin olive oil
Good squeeze of lemon juice
Salt and ground black pepper
Pinch of sugar
2 tbsp roughly sliced or
   torn basil

*This salad is an example of real ingredients-led cooking. You season with
salt, pepper and sugar, but to ensure this salad tastes as good as it should,
you should use perfectly ripe tomatoes picked in the height of summer.*

1 Arrange the tomatoes in a serving dish and dress with the olive
oil and lemon juice. Season with salt, pepper and sugar and add
the basil.

2 Toss the tomatoes gently to coat in the dressing, and taste for
seasoning. Serve immediately or within 1 hour.

Mushroom, lemon and garlic salad

....

SERVES 6–8
VEGETARIAN

500g (1lb 2oz) mushrooms,
   such as wild mushrooms,
   chanterelles, enoki, oyster
   or button mushrooms,
   or a mixture
4 tbsp olive oil
5 cloves of garlic, peeled
   and crushed
Salt and ground black pepper
Juice of 1 lemon
2 tbsp balsamic vinegar
Lemon wedges, to serve

The garlic and lemon juice in this recipe ensure these mushrooms are full of flavour. This can be made 24 hours in advance, covered and stored in the fridge. Allow to come back up to room temperature before serving.

1 If any of the mushrooms are larger than the size of a small fingernail, then halve or slice them. Slice any button mushrooms.

2 Pour the olive oil into a heavy-based frying pan on a high heat, then add the mushrooms and garlic and season with salt and pepper. Cook for 2–3 minutes, tossing regularly. Add the lemon juice and vinegar and continue to cook for a further 3–4 minutes or until the mushrooms are golden brown.

3 Remove from the pan and allow to cool to room temperature before serving with lemon wedges to squeeze over the salad.

Oignons à la monégasque

....

SERVES 8–10
VEGETARIAN

450g (1lb) baby onions, spring
   onions, young summer
   onions or baby leeks
250ml (9fl oz) tomato purée
110ml (4fl oz) white wine
   vinegar
1 tbsp olive oil
50g (2oz) caster sugar
1 small bay leaf
1 tsp chopped thyme leaves
1 sprig of parsley
75g (3oz) raisins or sultanas
Salt and ground black pepper

This is always on the buffet table at Ballymaloe. It plays at being both a sauce and a vegetable accompaniment and the sweet-sour flavour is ideal for cold meats. The dish keeps for up to two weeks if covered and kept in the fridge.

1 Place all the ingredients in a large saucepan along with 350ml (12fl oz) of water, and season with salt and pepper. Cover with a lid and bring to the boil, then reduce the heat and simmer gently for 1 hour.

2 Remove the lid and continue to cook for a further 30 minutes or until the onions are soft and the sauce has thickened slightly. Allow to cool before serving.

Smoked mackerel
with dill mayonnaise

....

SERVES 10–12
8 smoked mackerel fillets
    (about ½ fillet per person)
250ml (9fl oz) sweet mustard
    and dill mayonnaise
    (see page 326)

Mackerel is one of the ocean's most distinctive tastes. Smoke seems to agree with the mackerel's oily flesh more than maybe any other fish.

1 Cut the fillet of smoked mackerel into slices at an angle about 2cm (¾in) wide. Serve with the sweet mustard and dill mayonnaise on the side.

Oysters

....

SERVES 10
20 oysters
Lemon wedges, to serve
    (optional)
Tabasco sauce, to serve
    (optional)

Oysters are a gorgeous guest at a buffet table. Their frilly pearled shells act as their own stunning presentation plates, and they demand nothing from the cook but careful opening. Open them just before your guests arrive and then place them on ice, away from any heat source or sunlight. It is best not to leave them out for more than 1 hour.

1 To open (shuck) the oysters, see the recipe on page 18, then insert a knife into each opened shell and cut the oyster away from the upper, flat-sided section. Discard the upper shells and place the oysters, in their half shells, on a serving dish.

2 Serve immediately, on their own or with wedges of lemon or a dash of Tabasco sauce.

Gravalax

....

1 salmon fillet, with the skin still on (but scaled) and all bones removed (see tip, below)

3 tbsp chopped dill

3 tbsp sea salt

3 tbsp caster sugar

2 tsp ground white or black pepper

250ml (9fl oz) sweet mustard and dill mayonnaise (see page 326), to serve

I remember eating this as a child in Reykjavik, where my mother is from, with sweet mustard and dill mayonnaise (see page 326 for my version of this) and bread, rye crackers or boiled potatoes. The word gravalax comes from the Scandinavian word grav ('grave' or 'hole in the ground') and lax ('salmon'), harking back to when medieval fisherman used to bury salted salmon in the sand to allow it to ferment. These days the salmon is no longer fermented but 'buried' in a dry marinade of salt, sugar and dill, and cured for two to three days. But don't be put off: the marinade is actually very quick to prepare and, once made, the gravalax will keep very well, covered in the fridge, for up to a week.

1 Cover a baking sheet or long dish with cling film and place the salmon, skin side down, on top of this.

2 In a small bowl, mix together the remaining ingredients and spread over the flesh of the salmon, making sure to cover it completely. Wrap in the cling film and place under a board. Then put some weights on top (such as a couple of packs of butter) and allow to marinate in the fridge for two days. (It can be eaten after 24 hours but the flavour will be even better if the fish is kept in the marinade for an extra day.)

3 Drain the fish, pouring away any liquid and wiping off the excess marinade, then cut into thin slices and serve with a generous drizzle of the mayonnaise. Cucumber relish (see page 275) would also go well with the salmon.

VARIATION

If you are serving lots of people and wish to double the recipe, you can place another salmon fillet, skin side up (or flesh side down), on top of the first fillet, then turn every 12 hours while curing.

(continued overleaf)

325

2 egg yolks
1½ tbsp white wine vinegar
1½ tbsp caster sugar
3 tbsp Dijon mustard
200ml (7fl oz) sunflower oil
2 tbsp chopped dill
Salt

Sweet mustard and dill mayonnaise

This mayonnaise will keep, covered in the fridge, for up to a week.

1 Place the egg yolks, vinegar, sugar and mustard in a small bowl and mix together. Pour the oil in very gradually (too quickly and the mixture will curdle), whisking by hand (or use a hand-held electric beater) all the time. The mixture will begin to look creamy as it emulsifies.

2 Once all the oil has been added, stir in the chopped dill and salt to taste – you want to have a sauce that is both sweet and intensely mustardy in flavour.

Poached whole salmon
with basil mayonnaise

SERVES 10-20, BUT MORE
IF YOU CHOOSE TO HAVE
VARIOUS MEATS OR FISH
ON THE BUFFET TABLE
1 whole salmon 3–4kg
   (6½–8¾lb), gutted and
   descaled, or a large chunk
   of salmon cut through the
   bone with the skin and
   bone still attached
Salt

To serve
Mixed lettuce leaves, such
   as butterhead, Cos, Little
   Gem, lollo rosso
Mixed chopped herbs such as
   chervil, parsley or rosemary
300ml (½ pint) mayonnaise
   (see page 317), mixed with
   2 tablespoons of chopped
   basil

Fish kettle (to fit a whole
   salmon) or a large saucepan
   with a lid

Presented whole, this makes a wonderful centrepiece for a meal. To poach the salmon in one piece, you will need a fish kettle or place a large chunk, still in its skin, snugly in a saucepan and cook as below. Ask your fishmonger to clean, gut and descale the fish for you (or follow the tip below for descaling a fish yourself). If you're cooking the fish whole, then don't remove the head or tail.

1 Put the fish in the pan and pour in enough water to cover it, then remove the fish and set aside. Add 1 tablespoon of salt to every litre (1¾ pints) of water. Cover with a lid and bring to the boil.

2 Once boiling, carefully lower the salmon into the fish kettle or saucepan, replace the lid and allow the water to come back up to the boil. Reduce the heat and simmer gently for 20 minutes, then remove from the heat. Keeping the lid on, allow the fish to cool completely in the poaching water (the fish should be just barely covered by the water).

3 When the salmon is just cold, carefully remove from the fish kettle or saucepan and allow to drain for a few minutes. Place on a serving dish or board. Just before serving, peel off the top layer of skin, leaving the tail and head intact. Serve on a board on its own or surrounded by lettuce leaves and herbs and with a bowl of the basil mayonnaise on the side.

RACHEL'S TIP
To descale a fish, hold it by its tail over an open plastic bag and using a sharp knife at about a 45-degree angle, remove the scales by scraping in the direction of the head.

Boiled shrimps or prawns with herb mayonnaise

....

SERVES 8-10

1kg (2lb 3oz) shrimps
   or prawns
Salt
300ml (½ pint) herb
   mayonnaise (see variation
   on page 317)

One of my favourite things to eat is freshly cooked prawns or shrimps with homemade mayonnaise flavoured with herbs (see page 317), eaten with sweet-and-sour-tasting Ballymaloe Cucumber Relish (see page 275). The fresher your prawns and shrimps, the better they'll taste, so if possible buy them while they are still live and frisky, and cook them as soon as you can. If they are not live, then make sure they are good and fresh – they should not smell 'strong' but simply of the ocean. To get the best flavour from boiled prawns or shrimps, you need to cook them in well-salted water – some people use seawater.

1 To cook the shrimps or prawns, three-quarters fill a large saucepan with water, add the salt and bring to the boil, making sure the water is at a good rolling boil before you tip in the shrimps or prawns. Bring back up to the boil and cook for 2–3 minutes for little shrimps and 1–2 minutes for larger prawns. Make sure not to overcook them, however, or they will turn into a rather sad mush.

2 When they are cooked, shrimps will go from browny grey in colour to bright orangey pink, all trace of black from their heads having disappeared. The best way to tell when prawns are cooked is to take one from the pan once they rise to the top of the water, after a minute or so of boiling, and if it is opaque and firm all the way through, then they are ready to drain. As soon as prawns or shrimps are cooked, drain them and lay out to cool on flat trays to stop them cooking any further. Serve at room temperature with a bowl of herb mayonnaise on the side.

RACHEL'S TIP

I like to cook both prawns and shrimps with their heads still attached. Of course, if you wish, you can cook just the tail of the prawns and if you still have the heads, save them for a stock (see page 37) or a bisque (see page 36).

Crab and mayonnaise salad

SERVES 8–12

900g (2lb) crab meat,
   including brown meat if
   possible (for how to cook
   a crab, see page 36)
3 tbsp mayonnaise
   (see page 317)
50ml (2fl oz) French dressing
   (see page 318)
1–2 tsp Dijon mustard
Salt and ground black pepper
Lemon wedges, to serve

Served this salad as part of a buffet or as a lunch on a perfect summer's day with tomato and basil salad, Ballymaloe Cucumber Relish (see page 275), some lettuce leaves and delicious bread. If you can get hold of the brown meat too (and you will if you are cooking the crabs from scratch yourself, though fishmongers should sell it as well), this is well worth adding for its depth of flavour and sweetness. Any left over will make the most delicious sandwich filling too. This can be kept covered in the fridge for up to 24 hours, but allow it to come up to room temperature before serving.

1 Place all the ingredients in a large bowl and mix together, then season to taste with salt and pepper. Serve with lemon wedges alongside for your guests to squeeze over the crab.

Dressed mussels and clams

....

SERVES 10-12

About 50 mussels
About 50 clams
3–4 tbsp mayonnaise
   (see page 317)
2 tbsp chopped chives

Great fresh shellfish often doesn't need much doing to it. The mayonnaise here is instilled with the essence of the shellfish, the cooking juices, and it serves only to enhance the original flavours of the sea. This dish can keep covered in the fridge for 6-8 hours, but allow it to come up to room temperature before serving.

1 Wash the mussels and clams carefully, removing the beard (the fibrous tuft of hair attached to the shell) from the mussels. Discard any shells that are open or won't close if tapped on a worktop.

2 Place the mussels and clams in a large saucepan with just 1 tablespoon of water. Cover with a tight-fitting lid and cook slowly on a low heat for 4–5 minutes or until they have opened in their own steam. (You should remove individual shells once they've opened.)

3 Remove all the mussels and clams from the pan, saving any cooking liquid. Discard the top shell from each mussel or clam and arrange carefully on a serving dish. Place the mayonnaise in a bowl and mix in enough of the strained cooking juices to make a coating consistency. Mix half the chives into the mayonnaise and spoon the sauce over each mussel and clam. Sprinkle with the remaining chives and serve.

Ballymaloe glazed loin of bacon with spicy mayonnaise

....

SERVES 8-10, BUT MORE
IF YOU CHOOSE TO HAVE
VARIOUS MEATS OR FISH
ON THE BUFFET TABLE
1 loin of smoked or
    unsmoked bacon
    (1.8–2.2kg/4–5lb),
    preferably with the
    rind on
60–80 whole cloves,
    depending on the size
    of the 'diamonds' scored
    into the fat (see below)
450g (1lb) demerara or soft
    brown sugar
50–75ml (2–3fl oz) pineapple
    or orange juice
75ml (3fl oz) mayonnaise
    (see page 317), mixed with
    2 tbsp tomato chutney,
    to serve

The saltiness of bacon cries out for sweetness. The brown sugar caramelises and forms a gorgeous glaze when cooked in an oven at a high temperature.

1 Place the bacon in a large, heavy-based saucepan, cover with cold water and bring slowly to the boil. If the meat is still salty, there will be a white froth on top of the water once boiled. Discard the water, cover the bacon with fresh water and bring to the boil once again.

2 Reduce the heat, cover with a lid and simmer the bacon for 1–1¼ hours (or 15 minutes for every 450g/1lb) until cooked. When the bacon is done a skewer inserted into the centre of the meat will come out easily.

3 Meanwhile, preheat the oven to 240°C (475°F), Gas mark 9.

4 Once the bacon is cooked, remove from the water and allow to drain, then set aside for a few minutes to slightly cool. Peel off the rind with your hands (trying not to remove any fat), then, using a sharp knife, score the fat diagonally to make a diamond pattern (without cutting through the meat) and stud each diamond with a whole clove.

5 Blend the sugar and orange or pineapple juice to a thick paste and spread this over the bacon. Place in a roasting tin or ovenproof dish and roast in the oven for about 20 minutes or until the top has caramelised to a deep golden brown. While the bacon is roasting, baste a couple of times by spooning the syrup and juices over the meat.

6 Take the bacon out of the oven, remove to a carving board and allow to cool. Carve the bacon into slices, arrange on a serving plate with the spicy mayonnaise in a bowl next to it.

Cold roast chicken with herb stuffing

SERVES 4-6, BUT MORE
IF YOU CHOOSE TO HAVE
VARIOUS MEATS OR FISH
ON THE BUFFET TABLE
15g (½oz) butter, softened
1 chicken (1.3–1.8kg/3–4lb)
Salt and ground black pepper

For the stuffing
40g (1½oz) butter
75g (3oz) peeled and
  chopped onion
Salt and ground black pepper
75–100g (3–3½oz) fresh
  white breadcrumbs
2 tbsp finely chopped mixed
  herbs, such as parsley,
  thyme, chives, tarragon
  and marjoram

Cold roast chicken is the basis for various dishes, but it's also delicious to eat on its own. The stuffing is particularly good when served at room temperature as the herby flavours are that much more pronounced. You could use just one or a combination of different herbs in the stuffing.

1 Preheat the oven to 180°C (350°F), Gas mark 4.

2 To make the stuffing, place the butter in a small saucepan on a medium heat, add the onion and season with salt and pepper. Cover the pan with a lid and cook gently for 8–10 minutes or until the onion is soft but not browned. Remove from the heat, then stir in the breadcrumbs and herbs and taste for seasoning. Allow the stuffing to cool completely, then spoon it into the cavity of the chicken.

3 Spread the 15g (½oz) of softened butter onto the breast and the legs of the chicken and season with salt and pepper. Place in a roasting tin and cook in the oven for 1½–1¾ hours (or 20 minutes for every 450g/1lb, plus 20 minutes extra), basting occasionally with the cooking juices and hot fat in the tin.

4 To check whether the chicken is fully cooked, stick a skewer into one of the thighs with a spoon placed underneath to catch the juices – these should run clear. Also, if you gently pull on one of the legs it should feel slightly loose from the carcass. Once cooked, remove from the oven, place on a carving board and allow to sit covered in foil, to keep moist until it cools to room temperature.

VARIATION
Roast turkey with herb stuffing: Follow the recipe above. Cook a 6kg (13lb) turkey for 20 minutes per 450g (1lb) plus 20 minutes extra. Multiply the quantities for the stuffing ingredients by four. This serves 12–16 people.

Roast lamb with redcurrant jelly

....

SERVES 10-12, BUT MORE
IF YOU CHOOSE TO HAVE
VARIOUS MEATS OR FISH
ON THE BUFFET TABLE
1 leg of lamb (2.5–3.5kg/
    5½–7¾lb)
1 large sprig of rosemary,
    leaves stripped from the
    stalk
4–5 garlic cloves, peeled and
    sliced lengthways into
    matchstick thickness
Salt and ground black pepper
250ml (9fl oz) redcurrant jelly
    (see below)

Roast lamb and redcurrant jelly work wonderfully together.

1 Preheat the oven to 220°C (425°F), Gas mark 7.

2 Place the joint in a roasting tin and, with a skewer or the point of a sharp knife, make several incisions (about 1cm/½in deep) every 2.5cm (2in) or so in the top of the lamb. Push a tuft of rosemary leaves into each incision plus a slice or two of garlic, then sprinkle the joint with salt and pepper.

3 Place in the oven and roast for 20 minutes, then reduce the heat to 180°C (350°F), Gas mark 4, and cook for a further 18–20 minutes for every 450g (1lb) depending on how you like it cooked, basting from time to time with the melted fat and cooking juices.

4 Remove the joint to a carving board, cover with foil and allow to cool to room temperature. Then carve into slices and arrange on a serving dish with a bowl of redcurrant jelly on the side.

MAKES 3 X 450G (1LB) JARS
1kg (2lb 3oz) fresh or frozen
    (and defrosted) redcurrants
1kg (2lb 3oz) caster or
    granulated sugar

Redcurrant jelly

It will keep for months in sterilised jars in the fridge.

1 Place the redcurrants and sugar in a large, heavy-based saucepan and stir over a medium heat until the sugar dissolves and the mixture comes to the boil. Continue to boil for 8–10 minutes, stirring only if the mixture appears to be sticking to the bottom of the pan. Skim away any froth that rises to the surface.

2 Pour into a sieve (not an aluminium one as the acidity of the fruit can react with this metal) and allow to drip through. Don't push the pulp through or the jelly will be cloudy; you can stir it gently once or twice just to stop the bottom of the sieve getting clogged with pulp.

3 Pour the jelly straight into hot, sterilised jars (for sterilising jars, see tip on page 42).

Roast pork with apple sauce

....

SERVES 10-12, BUT MORE
IF YOU CHOOSE TO HAVE
VARIOUS MEATS OR FISH
ON THE BUFFET TABLE

1 loin of pork (1.5–2kg/3lb
    5oz–4lb 4oz), with the
    rind still on
2 tsp salt
Ground black pepper
3 sprigs of rosemary, plus
    extra for decorating

For the apple sauce
500g (1lb 2oz) cooking apples,
    such as Bramley or
    Grenadier
About 50g (2oz) caster or
    granulated sugar (quantity
    depending on how tart the
    apples are)

This dish rests entirely on the quality of the pork, so do try to get the best pork you can, and free range if possible. You will really notice the difference in flavour; great pork gives you crispy crunchy crackling and the meat will be both moist and sweet.

1 Preheat the oven to 190°C (375°F), Gas mark 5.

2 Place the pork skin side up on the worktop and, using a very sharp knife or a craft knife, score the rind lengthways (in the direction you'll be slicing when rolled, to make it easier to carve later) at 1cm (½in) intervals, taking care not to cut down into the meat. Rub the salt and pepper all over the rind and into the fat, then sit the piece of pork rind side up on the whole sprigs of rosemary in a roasting tin.

3 Roast in the oven for 2–2¼ hours (or 25 minutes for every 450g/1lb, plus 25 minutes extra). Baste every 30 minutes or so by spooning any fat or juices back over the rind. If, towards the end of the cooking time, the crackling needs to be crisped up, increase the temperature to 230°C (450°F), Gas mark 8 for 10 minutes.

4 Meanwhile, make the apple sauce. Peel and quarter the apples, cutting away the core. Slice the quarters in half and put in a small saucepan with the sugar and 2 tablespoons of water. Cover the pan with a lid, place on a low heat and cook for 6–8 minutes or until the apple has broken down, then beat into a purée. Taste for sweetness, adding more sugar if desired, and set aside to cool.

5 When the pork is cooked, a skewer inserted into the centre (and left in for 10 seconds) will feel very hot when held against the inside of your wrist, and the juices will run clear. Remove to a carving board covered in foil and allow to cool. When putting out on the buffet table decorate with a few sprigs of rosemary.

RACHEL ALLEN   THE BUFFET PARTY

Traditional roast rib of beef with horseradish sauce

....

SERVES 8-10, BUT MORE
IF YOU CHOOSE TO HAVE
VARIOUS MEATS OR FISH
ON THE BUFFET TABLE

1 prime rib of beef
  (2.5–3.5kg/5½–7¾lb),
  on the bone, chine bone
  removed
Salt and ground black pepper
250ml (9fl oz) horseradish
  sauce (see opposite), to serve

A great rib of beef can be the centrepiece of a cold buffet, the star of the show. If possible, this should be something you order in advance from your butcher and it should be a well-hung piece of meat. Beef is hung or aged to improve both its flavour and tenderness. Natural enzymes break down the meat so the potentially tough connective fibres are partially dissolved and proteins are transformed into smaller pieces, making them much more flavourful. In dry aged beef there will also be some moisture loss, which intensifies the flavour. Try to get beef that has been hung for at least 21 days, though some people like meat that has been hung for 28 days or even longer.

1 Preheat the oven to 230°C (450°F), Gas mark 8.

2 Weigh the joint and calculate the cooking time (see opposite). Score the fat with a sharp knife and season generously with salt and pepper. Place the beef in a roasting tin fat side up so that as the fat melts during cooking it will baste the meat. The bones provide a natural rack to hold the meat clear of the fat in the roasting tin. (If you are cooking beef off the bone, then use a trivet or place a few metal spoons in the bottom of the tin.) Roast the beef in the oven for the calculated cooking time, turning the heat down to 180°C (350°F), Gas mark 4, after 15 minutes.

3 To check that the beef is cooked, insert a skewer into the thickest part of the joint, but not too near the bone as this will give a false reading as the bone conducts heat. Leave it there for about 20 seconds and then lay it against the back of your hand. If it still feels cool, the meat is rare, if it is warm it's medium rare, if it's hot it's medium and if you can't keep the skewer against your hand for more than a second, then you can bet it's well done! Also, if you check the colour of the juices that run out, you will find they are clear for well done and red or pink for rare or medium. If you own a meat thermometer, that will eliminate guesswork altogether, but make sure the thermometer is not touching a bone when you are testing. If the thermometer

reads 60°C (140°F) then the beef is rare, 70°C (158°F) is medium and 75°C (167°F) is well done. Once cooked to your liking, remove the beef from the tin, place, covered in foil, on a carving board and allow to cool completely.

4 Once the beef has rested, carve into slices and arrange on a serving plate. Serve with a bowl of horseradish sauce on the side.

CALCULATING COOKING TIMES FOR BEEF

Beef on the bone

Rare	10–12 minutes per 450g (1lb)
Medium	12–15 minutes per 450g (1lb)
Well done	18–20 minutes per 450g (1lb)

Beef off the bone

Rare	8–10 minutes per 450g (1lb)
Medium	10–12 minutes per 450g (1lb)
Well done	15–18 minutes per 450g (1lb)

MAKES 250ML (9FL OZ)
VEGETARIAN
3 tbsp peeled and grated
  horseradish root
3 tsp lemon juice
1 tsp Dijon or ½ tsp
  English mustard
1 tsp caster sugar
¼ tsp salt
Pinch of ground black pepper
225ml (8fl oz) softly whipped
  double or regular cream
  (measured when whipped)

Horseradish sauce

A classic accompaniment to roast beef, horseradish sauce is also excellent with smoked fish, such as mackerel, trout or eel (see page 275). It will keep, covered, in the fridge for 5–6 days.

1 Place the grated horseradish in a bowl with the lemon juice, mustard, sugar, salt and pepper, and mix well together.

2 Fold in the whipped cream, taking care not to over-mix or it will curdle.

3 Serve immediately, with the cooled beef (see above), or store in the fridge until needed.

PLANNING YOUR
BUFFET PARTY

While each of the dishes in this chapter are easy enough to prepare on their own, I won't hide the fact that you will need to think and plan ahead in cooking a variety of dishes when feeding many people. You may also need to borrow trays, bowls, or even refrigerator space from friends and neighbours, but the following guidelines should help you host a successful event.

First off, what to prepare: depending on the size of your crowd, try to serve at two to three different meat dishes (beef, turkey or chicken, lamb, bacon or pork); three to five salads or veggie dishes, including potato, tomato and green salad; and at least two fish dishes (one smoked and one shellfish and/or poached salmon). There will always be people who can or can't eat certain dishes – or who have particular likes and dislikes – so variety is the name of the game. They're bound to like something if you serve enough different foods! Aim to have some leftovers rather than running out of food – plus, it means no more cooking for you for the week to come.

When budgeting how much food to prepare, as a general guideline remember that the more dishes you have on your table, the less you'll need of each dish, since people will be piling their plates with many different things. So don't feel you need to multiply precisely up to the number of guests you have (for example, they may only take a tablespoon or two of a potato dish if they have many meats and salads from which to choose), but do use a common-sense approach to ensure you have enough of each so that nobody gets disappointed. For the more popular dishes

such as egg mayonnaise and potato salads, you may wish to err on the side of generous portions.

For desserts, many of the recipes in this book are perfect for buffets, especially the cold desserts such as roulades, tarts or fruit salads. Choose one or two desserts that can be made a day in advance to help minimise your preparation on the day.

GETTING YOUR BUFFET TABLE READY
Be sure to make your buffet table welcoming for guests with a vase of flowers or a tablecloth, or even candles – but be sure you don't place candles where your guests may need to reach over, unless you want to set them alight!

Think about how your guests will move around the table, and be sure to have everything laid out in a logical order so that they're not carrying things they don't need until the end (like cutlery and glassware). Put the more luxurious foods are at the end of the line – people tend to take the most of whatever is first on the buffet line!

The most useful order is this:
1 Plates
2 Bread
3 Green salad
4 Meats with appropriate sauces
5 Salads
6 Smoked fish
7 Shellfish
8 Cutlery (if not set on the dining table)

Be absolutely sure to put sauces next to their relevant dishes, not at the end of the table. Remember, too, that you don't need to put all the food out at once. Have a plate or bowl of each for people to take from, and keep the rest in a cool place in the kitchen to keep it fresh and to save room on the table.

BRINGING FOOD TO THE BUFFET TABLE

Because your dishes are cold, you will have prepared them all in advance of your occasion. You will need to keep them refrigerated until it's time to bring them to the table, so the following timetable should help you in setting up your dishes:

* 60 minutes prior to guests arriving: meat dishes

* 30 minutes before guests arrive: salads (only dress green salad just before eating, though, or they will go soggy)

* 15 minutes before guests arrive: smoked fish

* Shortly before eating: shellfish.

While you want your guests to have the time for a drink and to mingle before it's time to eat, be sure to get them to the buffet while the food is still fresh. Most of the food will happily sit (covered) for up to an hour after your guests arrive, but shellfish should be kept in the fridge until ready to eat. If you have late guests, you may need to start without them! Be absolutely sure not to set your table in a sunny window or somewhere too warm, like next to a radiator, or else your food could go off.

If your table is big enough, you may wish to display the desserts at the end of the table, but if not, clear off the remaining platters and replace with your desserts when it's time to serve them. Either way, be sure to clear away the picked-at platters before it's time to serve your lovely desserts.

RACHEL'S TIPS

* When you are preparing your dishes, have plenty of fresh herbs or edible flowers to decorate the food or the plates, like flat (not curly) parsley, sage with flowers, rosemary (with or without flowers), coriander, nasturtiums and wild garlic flowers.

* If you are serving cold roast meats and want to carve them at the table, enlist a friend to help you while you or someone else helps serve salads or replenishes empty platters or bowls. For parties over 20, try to have two people carving (assuming you're serving more than one cold meat).

* If you don't have enough platters or large bowls, borrow some! Unless you're planning to host large buffets on a regular basis, there may not be much point in owning many large serving dishes (nor much room to store them). And be sure to have enough serving spoons for each and every dish. If you want perfectly matching serving platters, you can easily hire them, along with plates, dishes, glassware and cutlery.

* Ask a friend or neighbour to help replenish platters and collect empty plates and glasses that your guests will inevitably leave around the house as they chat and relax.

* For larger parties have some pre-prepared platters ready for replenishing.

* For dessert, make sure to serve something that will sit happily for about half an hour (in other words, not ice cream!).

* Before you set the table, it's a great help to have already prepared a large tray with coffee/tea cups, bowls of sugar, tea spoons and jugs for milk. Make sure to have enough milk and sugar.

* Have it all ready for when your first guests arrive.

Index

....

RACHEL ALLEN INDEX

ACKNOWLEDGEMENTS

Huge heartfelt thanks to each and every person who helped make
this book what it is. I really enjoyed working with all of you:

Jenny Heller, Lizzy Gray and everyone at Collins – thanks again
for being such astoundingly wonderful publishers. Emma Callery,
Kate Parker and Kathy Steer for going through the book with very
fine toothcombs.

Kate Whitaker and Jan Baldwin for your beautiful photographs,
and Linda Tubby, Penny Markham, Emma Thomas and Jonni
Fitzgerald for being such stylish stylists; Smith & Gilmour and
Lee Motley for the stunning design work; and Liz McCarthy for
sprinkling me with your magic make-up wand.

Simon and Amanda Ross and everyone at Cactus TV, Brian Walsh
at RTÉ and Jane Rogerson and the whole team at UKTV.

On the home front, my gorgeous husband Isaac, my food-mad and
patient right-hand man Josh Heller, Diarmaid Falvey, Conor Pyne,
Simone and Dodo Michel, Hallfridur and Brian O'Neill (thanks
Mum and Dad!), Sam Head, Donal McGrath and all my fantastic
co-teachers at the Ballymaloe Cookery School.

Last but not least Fiona Lindsay and her team at Limelight
Management: Alison and Maclean Lindsay and Mary Bekhait.

I dedicate this book to my fantastic parents-in-law, Tim and
Darina Allen, who continue to inspire me with their never-
ending passion for food and their love of sharing it with others.

The publishers would like to thank Brickett Davda
(www.brickettdavda.com), Summerill and Bishop
(www.summerillandbishop.com) and Fired Earth
(www.firedearth.co.uk).